Richard Wright's Hero:
The Faces of a Rebel-Victim

by

KATHERINE FISHBURN

The Scarecrow Press, Inc.
Metuchen, N.J.   1977

78-08843

Library of Congress Cataloging in Publication Data

Fishburn, Katherine, 1944-
    Richard Wright's hero.

    Includes index.
    1. Wright, Richard, 1908-1960--Characters--Heroes.
I. Title.
PS3545.R815Z66   813'.5'2   76-51787
ISBN 0-8108-1013-1

To

Linda Wagner

CONTENTS

ACKNOWLEDGMENTS

The author expresses appreciation to the following for permission to quote or reprint:

W. W. Norton & Company, Inc. for quotations from Neurosis and Human Growth by Karen Horney (© 1950 by W. W. Norton & Company, Inc.).

The University of Pittsburgh Press for quotations from Richard Wright: An Introduction to the Man and His Works by Russell C. Brignano (© 1970 by the University of Pittsburgh Press).

The Princeton University Press for quotations from Radical Innocence: The Contemporary American Novel by Ihab Hassan (© 1961 by Princeton University Press); and for quotations from Anatomy of Criticism: Four Essays by Northrop Frye (© 1957 by Princeton University Press).

Alfred A. Knopf, Inc. and Hamish Hamilton Ltd. for quotations from The Rebel by Albert Camus (© 1956 by Alfred A. Knopf, Inc.).

Harper & Row Publishers and Paul R. Reynolds, Inc. for quotations from The Outsider by Richard Wright (© 1953 by Richard Wright).

Harper & Row Publishers and Jonathan Cape Ltd. for quotations from Native Son by Richard Wright (© 1940 by Richard Wright; renewed 1968 by Ellen Wright); and from Black Boy by Richard Wright (© 1945 by Richard Wright; renewed 1973 by Ellen Wright).

The World Publishing Company/Thomas Y. Crowell Company, Inc. and Paul R. Reynolds, Inc. for excerpts from "The Man Who Lived Underground" (© 1944 by L. B. Fischer Publishing Corp.), from Eight Men (© 1960, 1961 by Richard Wright).

Doubleday & Co. , Inc. and Paul R. Reynolds, Inc. for quotations from the Long Dream (© 1958 by Richard Wright).

The University of Chicago Press and Wayne Booth for quotations from The Rhetoric of Fiction by Wayne Booth (© 1961 by The University of Chicago Press).

CHAPTER I

INTRODUCTION

In studying a man's fiction, it is possible to take many critical routes, especially when that man has been as controversial a figure as Richard Wright. Thus, Edward Margolies (The Art of Richard Wright, 1969), after first discussing Wright's non-fiction, studies Wright's fiction more or less chronologically. Keneth Kinnamon, in his recently published book (The Emergence of Richard Wright: A Study in Literature and Society, 1972), primarily examines Wright's environment and literary achievements through the publication of Native Son in 1940. In contrast, Dan McCall (The Example of Richard Wright, 1969) and Russell C. Brignano (Richard Wright: An Introduction to the Man and His Works, 1970) have preferred not to divide their analyses into separate discussions of each work, but have attempted instead to bring Wright's thinking together under various topics.

Wright's fiction certainly lends itself to this latter kind of analysis since several recurring themes and topics help to unify his work. For example, his interest in and use of Marxism (especially in his condemnation of the white capitalistic society); the theme of the black man's essential alienation and invisibility in this white country; the concomitant theme of living in an unreal or nightmare world as a black man; the plea for brotherhood and the bitter protest against a society determined to make slaves of other men; the refusal of black men to accept the identities fixed for them by whites--the tacit acknowledgment, therefore, that all men are ontologically free to create themselves (the rumblings of existentialism appear in Wright's early works even before he knew of its existence as a philosophical school; The Outsider is Wright's attempt to write a consciously existential novel). And, of course, the frustrations, fears, and dangers involved in being a black man in America are always part of the fabric of Wright's fiction.

1

Because of the thematic unity of Wright's work one can discover a definite pattern in his fiction, specifically in the development of his hero--the method I take in this study. But rather than tracing its development in real time, which takes us in a circle (back to The Long Dream, Wright's fictional account of Southern childhood), I will study the hero in fictional time. That is, by rearranging the order in which Wright's books were written, it is possible to use Wright's last completed novel to help explain his first one. This journey takes us roughly from the story of an innocent victim to that of a metaphysical rebel. In this discussion, then, each book prepares us for the next by filling in the background information only hinted at in its successor. Thus Black Boy (1945) and The Long Dream (1958) help to explain the truncated lives of the heroes in Lawd Today (published in 1963 but written sometime before 1940) and Native Son (1940); these two books of latent and open rebellion, in turn, shed light on the existentialism of The Outsider (1953) and "The Man Who Lived Underground" (1944).

Thus for our purposes we begin with Wright's fictionalized autobiography, Black Boy, whose hero, the young Richard Wright, suffers the same frustrations and fears as the men he will later create in his novels and short stories. Black Boy reveals how paternalism works: through public coercion and vicious brutality, the whites struggle to maintain their racial and social superiority. And, as Wright tells it, the blacks help them by fatalistically accepting their inferior status in the community. But in the young Wright we see the seeds of his heroes' rebellions, for he absolutely will not allow either blacks or whites to form a preconceived identity for him. His story is a violent one with few sympathetic characters other than Wright himself; it is man against society.

Wright's last novel, the Long Dream, recapitulates Black Boy, since its hero, Fishbelly Tucker, is a child living in the Deep South of Mississippi. In this book Wright again presents the constant, insidious dangers of growing up black in America. Fish's initiation ritual constitutes the bulk of the novel as he is continually confronted with his special status as a black male (the book illustrates Southern sexual mores in scenes of dread and stark reality). By the end of the book, its hero, only eighteen years old, has experienced enough terror to drive him out of the country to save his life and his soul. Fish is the initiate rejected by society, the innocent victimized by a racist society.

Whereas Black Boy and The Long Dream offer Wright's conceptions of the initiation of black men in America, Lawd Today and Native Son illuminate the consequences of this dreadful ritual.

Born in the South, Jake Jackson (Lawd Today) has emigrated north and is living in a large industrial city (Chicago), employed as a postal worker. Heir to the victimization experienced by his younger counterpart, Fish Tucker, Jake exemplifies the dissatisfied but helpless black man, technically free but in reality slave to American prejudice and the American economic system. Jake has fled the South of overt bigotry to a more subtle and equally dangerous covert paternalism. In this atmosphere he leads a truncated, albeit colorful, life, separated from the Great American Dream by virtue of his race. Although Jake is unhappy, he is too busy compensating for his emasculation to really rebel. He confines his rebellion to self-pity and brawls.

Another young man, just as frozen in place and restless, is the fourth hero, Bigger Thomas (Native Son), also a transplanted Southerner. Living in Chicago with his mother and two siblings, Bigger adds another dimension to Wright's hero: outright rebellion. Victimized and despised like the men preceding him, Bigger Thomas takes a more significant step than fleeing or fighting--he murders, using the deed to win his metaphysical freedom. Alienated from the rest of the world, Bigger is also alienated from himself throughout most of the book. By the story's end, however, Bigger has resolved his self-alienation by existentially creating a new identity for himself.

The existentialism evident here is just a preview of that in The Outsider, whose hero, Cross Damon (probably the most complicated of Wright's heroes) takes up the burden of complete freedom. Taking advantage of a fluke accident to create a new personality for himself, Cross Damon becomes the epitome of the metaphysical rebel gone bad. Enchanted by nihilism, Cross comes to believe that in his protest against the world's injustices he can do as he pleases--even replace God. As a result, he thoroughly isolates himself from other men, in whose name he had supposedly been rebelling.

The final hero, Fred Daniels ("The Man Who Lived Underground"), draws all the others together under his mantle of love and brotherhood. A black outcast, victimized like the rest because of his color, Fred becomes representative

of all men. Forced to discover himself and the meaning of
life in a city's sewers, Fred concludes that all men are
alone, trapped in a meaningless world, and that they must
therefore stick together if they are to find any meaning in
life at all.

What we see in these six heroes, then, is the development of a metaphysical rebel turned prophet. None of the
men accepts his condition; all in one form or another, with
varying degrees of success, attempt to create a self for
themselves in an otherwise fluid society which is perversely
determined to fix their identities for them. Because they are
black they have a tougher time of it than other men, but they
are undoubtedly representative of modern man in search of
himself. These men may be victims, but they are not passive. The young Wright struggles valiantly to preserve his
integrity. Fish fights a losing battle, taking on the entire
Southern social structure. Jake madly compensates, falling
victim to the same vanity as Fish, but always, always complaining. Bigger thrashes out through bloodshed. Cross
murders repeatedly to protect his dearest possession, his
complete freedom. And Fred, seeing all this pointless violence and cruelty that men wreak upon themselves, emerges
from the heart of the world to plea for brotherhood. Wright's
archetypal hero is the rebel-victim who cries out for immediate universal justice, much like Ivan Karamazov.

end of intro

Many sources are helpful in a study of Wright's hero.
Not the least are his own experiences, expressed not only in
Black Boy but also in his speeches and essays, since much
of what he fictionalized he had earlier suffered himself.
Other sources, useful in understanding Wright's thinking, are
the works of such people as Charles C. Walcutt, Walter B.
Rideout, Albert Camus, Jean-Paul Sartre, Ihab Hassan,
Karen Horney, Northrup Frye, and Wayne C. Booth.

Because of Wright's early association with the Communist Party during the time when he was learning his craft,
his fiction was always marked by the influence of the proletarian school of writing. These authors (like Jack Conroy and
Henry Roth) drew extensively on the techniques used by such
literary naturalists as Stephen Crane and Frank Norris.
Charles Walcutt's American Literary Naturalism: A Divided
Stream clarifies the philosophy and the method of these men.
Walter B. Rideout's The Radical Novel in the United States,
1900-1954 helps define just what proletarian writing is.

Wright was also strongly affected by his association with existentialism. For the best explanations of his thinking along these lines, we can turn to Albert Camus' The Myth of Sisyphus, The Rebel, and Caligula. Jean-Paul Sartre's fiction and philosophy--works such as Being and Nothingness, The Age of Reason, Nausea, and The Flies-- further elucidate Wright's existential background. For a critical approach to Wright's philosophical premises, Ihab Hassan's Radical Innocence: The Contemporary American Novel is probably the best source, especially his first two chapters in which he discusses the rebel-victim in fiction. Although Hassan does not discuss Wright, his insights into the characteristics of contemporary fiction have done much to reveal the qualities of Wright's heroes as radical innocents.

As a study of human behavior, Karen Horney's Neurosis and Human Growth: The Struggle Toward Self-Realization offers the probable psychological motivations of Wright's heroes.

For general critical approaches, Northrup Frye's Anatomy of Criticism and Wayne Booth's The Rhetoric of Fiction are most useful. Frye's influence permeates the entire discussion with his definitions of ironic tragedy, myth, ritual, and archetypal criticism. Wayne Booth's astute observations about narrative technique help explain Wright's methods of effecting an emotional impact on the reader.

CHAPTER II

THE INITIATE AND THE VICTIM

Richard Wright knew from personal experience what
it was like to be both poor and black at the turn of the century. Born in 1908 in Natchez, Mississippi,[1] of destitute
parents, Wright had an unhappy childhood. His mother, Ella
Wright, was a schoolteacher who had trouble finding work;
his father, Nathaniel Wright, was a sharecropper who deserted his young family, leaving behind an embittered son.
Wright never forgot nor forgave his father. Nor did he show
more charity toward the whites, whose despotic caste system
nearly destroyed him. Furthermore, Wright had little pa-
tience for those blacks who kowtowed to the whites; as a result of his early experiences, he remained critical all his
life of those blacks who participated in their own degradation.

Wright's account of his youth and adolescence appears
in his fictionalized autobiography, Black Boy. In this book
Wright blends his own personal history with the universal experiences of his race in a conscious attempt to portray himself as a symbol of the black lower class (in doing this, according to Constance Webb, he omitted many details that
would have shown his situation as actually much more tolerable than that of the poverty-stricken blacks he was trying to
represent).[2] When Wright borrows from the legends handed
down by generations of slaves, he tells the stories as though
they truly happened to him personally. The best known example is the traditional folktale of the preacher who comes
to dinner and eats all the fried chicken; according to Black
Boy it happened to the young Wright--it wasn't just a favorite
story. Another event that Wright heard about and told as
though it were part of his own history is the anecdote of his
uncle driving him into the middle of the Mississippi River.
According to Webb, this was told to Wright by Ralph Ellison.[3]

On the other hand, Wright often deplores the traditions

of his race in Black Boy, ignoring its positive values, and making a concerted effort to remove himself from its confines. These ambivalent feelings toward blacks haunt him in all his fiction. While he perhaps subconsciously continued to exploit black folklore, he intentionally attacked and rejected the blacks' way of surviving, condemning them for aiding the white man in his emasculation of the black man. Ironically, Wright was employing the fruits of the black man's oppression--his folklore and traditions--as he was chastising the very behavior that invented these marvelous tales. Wright obviously was a complex man, struggling to come to terms with his heritage, his environment, and himself. These conflicts created fascinating fiction, chronicles of the twentieth-century black man seeking identity and a place in the world. What Wright reveals is often frightening, but it is never dull. For whenever we study an abreactive author, as Wright seems to have been, we are exploring the recesses of the human mind. Many inconsistencies appear there, but they challenge us to read more in hopes of grasping the real man.

Many of the themes that Wright would return to time and again appear in Black Boy. His fiction and nonfiction seem to have supported each other. Whereas Black Boy is autobiography laced with fiction, Wright's novels and short stories are primarily fiction with obvious borrowings from his own experiences. All his work, therefore, has a certain unity about it that discloses a sensitive and serious man living in an uncertain age. Like his fiction, Black Boy contains the themes of social- and self-alienation; it is the poignant tale of a young boy searching for his identity. In Wright's later fiction, the boy will become a criminal, but the metamorphosis illustrates Wright's expanded vision when an innocent boy and a killer share the same agony of not knowing who they are. The young Richard Wright, like all his later heroes, must wrench his identity from a hostile environment; neither Wright nor his heroes have the comfort of being accepted by their own race. All are aliens among both the whites and the blacks. A major difference between Black Boy and the fiction is that, although several stories are Bildungsromans, none are Kunstlerromans except the autobiography since it alone focuses on a budding artist. The other heroes are either lower class or petty bourgeois failures. Wright's proletarian vision prevented him, one supposes, from choosing artists as protagonists in anything other than his autobiography.[4]

Although Black Boy's story is one of fear and cruelty, Wright infuses these memories with a certain nostalgia by his

almost poetic descriptions of his yearnings for identification
with the rest of the world. It is through the magic and
beauty of words that Wright grows to love the world and becomes enchanted with its possibilities. His first experience
with the magic of words was the tale of "Bluebeard and His
Seven Wives," whispered to him by the young schoolteacher
boarding with his family. His fascination with words is
amplified when he is punished for an obscene remark he in-
nocently makes to his devil-fearing grandmother. Granny's
extreme reaction and her accusation that Ella's novels have
corrupted him mystify Richard, who vows to conquer the
power of words. From this moment, the elder Wright recalls, his perception of men and nature becomes drastically
altered. To express this change in himself Wright lists the
wonders of nature, using Whitman to help him illustrate his
urge to absorb the world and all its marvelous offerings.
The feelings seem nearly to overwhelm him as he remembers
that

> There was the drenching hospitality in the per-
> vading smell of sweet magnolias.
> There was the aura of limitless freedom dis-
> tilled from the rolling sweep of tall green grass
> swaying and glinting in the wind and sun.
> There was the feeling of impersonal plenty
> when I saw a boll of cotton whose cup had spilt
> over and straggled its white fleece toward the
> earth. 5

The young Wright's next experience with literary urg-
ings is the excitement he gleans from reading stories in the
magazine supplement of a paper he sells, specifically Zane
Grey's Riders of the Purple Sage, whose very title entrances
the imaginative child. But this particular paper, Wright discovers to his shame, is a mouthpiece of the Ku Klux Klan.
And so he is forced to give up yet another source of reading
material; Granny had already driven out the schoolteacher and
her novels. Resourcefully, he turns to second-hand maga-
zines to feed his growing desire for life outside the rural
south.

At length he tries to write a story himself. He calls
it "The Voodoo of Hell's Half-Acre," saying of it years later
in his autobiography,

> It was crudely atmospheric, emotional, intuitively
> psychological, and stemmed from pure feeling (144).

A local paper, The Southern Register, printed it; however, no extant copies have ever been found.

Later, in Memphis, Wright awakens to the ideas of H. L. Mencken and Theodore Dreiser. Through their influence he recognizes that he must leave the South in order to realize his potential. Since his environment has not given him any reason to believe in himself, he later concludes that books have been his mainstay. Although he leaves Memphis with little hope and no plans, he is convinced that staying would be suicidal, "either because of possible violence of others against me, or because of my possible violence against them" (226). After moving to Chicago, Wright learned to fight with words instead of guns and fists.

Whereas Wright emerged successfully from his initiation rituals, his heroes do not. For initiation does not necessarily guarantee social acceptance, especially in America. Here it has a peculiar outcome--that of victimization and renunciation--as Ihab Hassan has discovered:

> Our concern is the encounter between the self and the world in fiction, that confrontation of the 'hero' with experience which may assume the form of initiation or victimization. Now initiation may be understood as a process leading through right action and consecrated knowledge to a viable mode of life in the world. Its end is confirmation. The result of victimization, however, is renunciation. Its characteristic mode is estrangement from the world, and its values are chiefly inward and transcendental. [6]

Hassan also remarks that in anti-utopia there is only victimization; and that the Naturalistic mode of initiation (relevant to Native Son) is one where the hero submits to the forces of society and nature. [7]

Out of victimization, the dark side of initiation, arises the rebel-victim, the outraged hero "on trial for nothing less than his being," as Hassan sees him. [8] The paradigm of the innocent hero victimized by a guilty society is the black man in America. For, traditionally, a black youth's initiation has ended in renunciation: the white majority society rejects him and he in turn isolates himself from the rest of the world, for all practical purposes recognizing and accepting his inferiority. Deep within, however, stirs the wrath of a violated man.

The estrangement mentioned by Hassan is evident in
Black Boy. Wright is not only alienated from the dominant
white society but also from his own race since he abhors the
concept of accommodation which they embrace--albeit unwill-
ingly. Afraid of disturbing the delicate equilibrium between
the two races, the blacks complicate each other's socializa-
tion and individuation processes by pressuring their own to
maintain the status quo, to play the role demanded of them
by whites. Edward Bland calls blacks in this predicament
pre-individualistic. And Ralph Ellison, basing his statements
on Bland's theory, argues that this pre-individual state is induced artificially by blacks in order to

> impress the Negro child with the omniscience and
> omnipotence of the whites to the point that whites
> appear as ahuman as Jehovah, and as relentless as
> a Mississippi flood. Socially it is effected through
> an elaborate scheme of taboos supported by a ruth-
> less physical violence, which strikes not only the
> offender but the entire black community. To wander
> from the paths of behavior laid down for the group
> is to become the agent of communal disaster.[9]

As a result of living in constant fear and tension, the blacks
themselves enforce obedience to the code of behavior drawn
up by the whites. A black rebel lives briefly, often bringing
disaster down upon his own community before his death can
be consummated by irate whites. Therefore, as a measure
of self-defense, the blacks teach their children "The Ethics
of Living Jim Crow." In an abbreviated version of his autobiography given this name, and in Black Boy, Wright recalls
the advice other blacks offered him as helpful suggestions for
staying alive in a hostile environment. Knowing that the only
way to stay alive was to stay in line, Wright's friends warn
him to think before he speaks to whites, a lesson that comes
hard to the independently-minded young man. George Kent
has said that Wright's major strategy in Black Boy was to
portray the tension springing from the conflict between a black
outsider and his group's protective reactionary tactics, for
even as a child Wright rebelled against having his individuality
suppressed in order "to protect the group from white assault."[10] This resoluteness on the part of the self to exist
in the face of almost insurmountable destructive forces creates
in Wright's and the reader's mind some fragile hope for the
disinherited man.

All his life, Richard Wright refused to comply with the

whites' expectations of him; he rebelled intellectually and
managed, after moving to France, to lead a fairly normal,
rewarding life. Black Boy recounts Wright's early initiation,
his struggles with himself, his black neighbors, his frightened, highly religious family, and--most importantly--his
struggle with the white world. The "harrowing perspective"
of his black viewpoint reveals to Robert Bone what he calls
Wright's major literary theme, that is,

> that the entire society is mobilized to keep the Ne-
> gro in his place: to restrict his freedom of move-
> ment, discourage his ambition, and banish him for-
> ever to the nether regions of subordination and in-
> feriority. This attempt to mark off in advance the
> boundaries of human life is Wright's essential
> theme. 11

In Wright's case, the whites' attempt fails; he transcends his
situation and environment to become a prominent international
literary figure. But Wright remained obsessed with the number of victories chalked up by the white community, and,
therefore, spent the rest of his life renouncing a society that
left individuals unfulfilled and isolated from human compassion
and companionship.

Early in his life Wright himself had experienced a desire for brotherhood, a "yearning for identification" which was
loosed in him "by the sight of a solitary ant carrying a burden upon a mysterious journey" (7). But because of constant
hunger and loneliness, Wright says, he eventually grew to
"distrust everything and everybody" (26). His father deserted
the family, and his mother was forced to leave Richard temporarily with a woman whose ugly face and foul breath repelled the young boy. Wright is shuttled from one relative
to the next because the family is so poor. And, thus, he
slowly but inevitably becomes alienated from his own people,
remarking later in his autobiography, to the shock of many
blacks, that he used to ponder

> the strange absence of real kindness in Negroes,
> how unstable was our tenderness, how lacking in
> genuine passion we were, how void of great hope,
> how timid our joy, how bare our traditions, how
> hollow our memories, how lacking we were in those
> intangible sentiments that bind man to man, and how
> shallow was even our despair (33).

This bleak outlook is reflected fictionally in Native Son where
Wright paints a depressing picture of impoverished blacks.
There is no affection in Bigger's family, only bitterness and
quarreling. But Wright, speaking through Bigger, clings to
his belief that these hardened outcasts still long for a chance
to belong, to feel at home with other men and the world.

In addition to his feeling of loneliness among other
blacks, Wright had also experienced dread of whites by the
time he was ten years old; as he recalls,

> I had already grown to feel that there existed men
> against whom I was powerless, men who could vio-
> late my life at will (65).

Although he had never been personally abused by whites at
this age, he nonetheless knew their capacity for hateful acts.
And when the brother of a friend of his is murdered, it affects him deeply.

> The things that influenced my conduct as a Negro
> did not have to happen to me directly; I needed but
> to hear of them to feel their full effects in the deep-
> est layers of my consciousness ... creating a sense
> of distance between me and the world in which I
> lived (150f).

Whereas Wright says he condemns the blacks for lacking traditions and kindness, he nevertheless empathizes thoroughly
with the experiences of his race, blaming the whites for the
Negroes' shortcomings since they have refused his people the
full benefits of Western culture. Wright identifies with the
most debased of blacks; his novels give them strong voices
to protest against their condition. Thus Native Son is told
entirely from the viewpoint of Bigger Thomas, the narrator;
we never know what is in the minds of the other characters.
In limiting himself to Bigger's perspective, Wright is asking
the reader to identify with his hero and to try to understand
his motives and actions. This talent for making the reader
identify with his heroes is one of Wright's most impressive
accomplishments as a novelist. [12]

In order for us to understand more thoroughly the reasons for Bigger's attitude, however, it is helpful to first study
the last novel that Wright wrote, The Long Dream (1958).
Based to a great extent on Wright's own childhood, this book
fictionally presents the initiation rituals of a black boy in

Mississippi. It is the story of the estrangement of Fishbelly
Tucker from his own black race and from the majority white
society of Clintonville, Mississippi. In this regard, The Long
Dream has many points of intersection with Black Boy; both,
for example, illustrate the victimization of black men in
America. Moreover, because Bigger Thomas was a product
of the South before the slums of Chicago had their chance to
destroy him, his background must have been comparable both
to Wright's and to Fish's, for repression in the South has
been not only a matter of class but also a matter of race.

   Although The Long Dream has been available for study
for more than a decade, it has received very little critical
attention. Moreover, those critics who have discussed it tend
to linger overlong on its flaws, virtually ignoring any strengths
or significance it might have.[13] Probably the most devastating comment appears as a footnote in The Negro Novel in
America in which Robert Bone calls it "a still more disas-
trous performance" than The Outsider.[14] Granville Hicks'
1958 review is also quite caustic as he scorns Wright's craft,
especially his ability in characterization. Strangely enough,
Hicks entitled his article "The Power of Richard Wright"
(italics mine), mentioning this "power" only as an afterthought
as he concludes his piece. There he claims that Wright,
"alienated from reality" as he is, still has the capacity "to
touch both the emotions and the consciences of his readers."[15]
Saunders Redding is also content to attack, counterpointing
every compliment with a condition. Conceding in praise that
Wright's tone is ironic, he complains that its effect is "flat-
tened by too much iteration." Acknowledging that Wright's
theme is valid, he insists that Wright doesn't know when to
stop and that he fails to convince readers that this "lamen-
table, tragic manhood ... is the only kind of manhood possible for a Negro in the South."[16] Such critical arrogance
seems uncalled for, especially when one considers what Wright
was trying to do in The Long Dream. It seems apparent to
one who has read all of Wright's fiction that he was tracing
the sources of isolation and alienation in black men in this,
his last finished novel. For the book is unquestionably a
thorough account of what it was like to grow up in the Deep
South as a Negro male. It is therefore an invaluable prelude
to a study of Native Son and The Outsider. It is, like many
of Wright's other stories, a tragedy in the ironic mode, and
it has the further advantages of being very carefully laid in
archetypal patterns. As irony in its late phase where it

returns to myth, it presents "the world of the nightmare and
the scapegoat, of bondage and pain and confusion. "[17]

And so perhaps it is up to the more recent critics,
less emotionally involved, to more accurately assess the qualities of Wright's final work. For it is a book, like most,
comprised of strengths and weaknesses. It is a protest novel:
strong in its condemnation of racism and yet strangely weak
in its effect. For example, because the plot is episodic, its
amplitude of details tends to crush the reader into apathy instead of exciting him to anger. Wright's protest seems to
feed on the wealth of horrors that surround Fish's life, but
the reader is more stunned than outraged. Furthermore, the
book's ending is certainly too hastily handled after such ex-
haustive searchings into Fish's psyche; ultimately, the novel
resolves nothing.

On the positive side, however, Wright has finally given
us the story that helps explain the conditions and motivations
of his earlier heroes. With this fuller perspective we can
study Bigger Thomas, Cross Damon, and Fred Daniels with
greater reward. For it is in The Long Dream that Wright
gives us the whole sordid story of a young black growing into
manhood, and he spares us no details. In this respect he is
much more thorough than in his autobiography--there he omitted references to sexual maturation. [18] Here he dwells frequently on the sexual problems implicit in a racist society.
In fact, Wright seems to propose in The Long Dream that sex
is the primary cause of racial tension, for Fish's agony and
alienation are both intimately related to sex. His ritual of
initiation is always sexually oriented. Finally, we are left
with the disturbing knowledge of what it is like to be young
and black in America.

Several contemporary scholars have begun to recognize
Wright's accomplishment in The Long Dream. Russell Brignano, for one, admires the "ironies in dialogue and action and
the inclusion of mirrored episodes" in this novel. [19] And most
critics agree with Edward Margolies that Wright has created
a "remarkable portrait" in Fish's father, Tyree Tucker. [20]
Margolies further maintains that the book is more authentic
than Wright's other work, since it does not suffer from metaphysical or political debates. [21] Instead of using philosophy
to give intellectual depth to his book, Wright uses symbolism.

Carefully documented from Wright's own experiences, [22]
The Long Dream is a ritualized account of a black boy's initi-

ation into the two conflicting worlds of the blacks and the whites, a ceremony that members of both races participate in. Indeed, a major portion of character development, or more accurately character malformation, is effected by the blacks on their own kind. To insure their youths' safety, the black community abets the emasculative process begun by whites when slavery began here centuries ago. But just as surely as black parents act to destroy, they act to save. As John Williams points out in his introduction to Sissie, blacks "love their children as much as any others.... But because they are black the parental burden is greater."[23] When Wright censures his own people he is only too aware, as he points out in Black Boy, that they have been excluded from the benefits of Western culture and its traditions. How black parents react may be deplorable, but it is certainly understandable, at times even necessary for the survival of their children.

Divided into three parts, the novel covers the life of Rex (Fishbelly) Tucker from pre-school years to his eighteenth birthday, a span of time sufficient for a southern black man's complete maturation, i.e., time to wake into the world's nightmare of reality.

In order to appreciate fully the scope of Wright's accomplishment in The Long Dream, it is necessary to examine the book from an archetypal perspective. As Northrup Frye says in his essay on symbols, "From such a point of view, the narrative aspect of literature is a recurrent act of symbolic communication: in other words a ritual.... Similarly, in archetypal criticism the significant context is the conflict of desire and reality which has for its basis the work of the dream."[24] Because both the form and the content contain aspects of recurrence and the "dialectic of desire and repugnance," they reinforce one another. Their union in literature Frye calls "myth": "the identification of ritual and dream, in which the former is seen to be the latter in movement."[25] Thus ritual is mythos or plot, and dream is dianoia or thought. The Long Dream is a paradigm of this happy symbiosis where the form and content complement one another almost to perfection. Although the book is not terribly exciting to read, it does seem to be technically a minor tour de force.

The controlling image of the book is the dream, as expressed not only in its title but also in its epigraphs, Fish's dreams themselves, comments made by his father, and in its section headings: "Daydreams and Nightdreams," "Days and Nights," and "Waking Dream." These section titles illustrate another aspect of the book's theme, the tension between desire and reality. Complementing the dream motif are the ritualistic implications of Fish's initiation and his eventual expulsion from society.

In his chapter in Radical Innocence called "The Dialectic of Initiation," Hassan defines the ideal purpose of initiation, saying that

> Initiation can be understood ... as the first existential ordeal, crisis, or encounter with experience in the life of a youth. Its ideal aim is knowledge, recognition, and confirmation in the world, to which the actions of the initiate, however painful, must tend. It is, quite simply, the viable mode of confronting adult realities. [26]

Recognizing its basically dialectic nature, he observes that "Initiation takes the classic pattern of withdrawal and return; its context is the conflict between social and instinctive behavior, ideal choice and biological necessity." [27] But after studying nineteenth- and twentieth-century American fiction, Hassan concludes that initiation has backfired for American heroes. Although the end of initiation should be confirmation, this has seldom been the case for the American adolescent. Instead, rejection has been the pattern:

> Sacrifice, regression, defeat--these summed up the recurrent expense of initiation. The face of the initiate in modern America began early to shade into the face of the victim ... still rebellious and still outraged. Initiation did not end with communion; it led to estrangement. [28]

The dialectic of initiation as expressed in the conflict between desire and reality in The Long Dream is the same dialectic that Camus has identified as the condition of the absurd. Since Fish is forced to encounter and live with this tension he becomes, like the other Wright heroes, an absurd hero, a man in quest of meaning and identity. Where this search takes him is the content of The Long Dream. Its narrative pattern is the ritual of initiation: Fish is undergoing the same rituals that generations of black youth before him have experienced.

And so, as Frye suggests they should, two patterns emerge from an archetypal study of The Long Dream: one is cyclical, the other dialectic. Through his presentation of Fish's maturation, Wright continually signifies that a ritual is taking place; to support the larger ritual of growing up, he has included several minor ones, such as Chris' ritual murder, the ritual of sexual initiation, and the ritual of death as exemplified in Tyree Tucker, the undertaker. As Frye further notes, "We have rituals of social integration, and we have rituals of expulsion, execution, and punishment." Thus even the ritual whose main feature is its recurrence has aspects of conflict in it. Moreover, the dream, whose major feature is "a parallel dialectic, as there is both the wish-fulfillment dream and the anxiety or nightmare dream of repugnance," also contains the element of recurrence, the daily cycle of waking and sleeping--the reappearance of the day's activities in dream form. 29

Perhaps the single most impressive ritual that Fish witnesses is that in which Chris Sims is murdered and castrated for having a white mistress. Although this ritual of punishment and execution is indigenous to black American culture, it is often ignored or denied by the whites--its very perpetrators. It appears, moreover, in such "white" literature as William Faulkner's Light in August and Harper Lee's To Kill a Mockingbird. The general pattern is this: a white woman is attracted sexually to a black man who either: 1) denies her advances and is accused of rape by the outraged rejected woman, or 2) succumbs to her attraction and is accused of rape either by the woman when she tires of him, or by the general public who refuse to believe that a white woman could actually desire a black man. In the end, the black man is killed and often castrated.

In The Long Dream Chris Sims, a black bellhop at a local hotel, is more or less seduced by a white prostitute who lives there. When she becomes bored by him she turns him in, not only to get rid of him but to rid herself of guilt. The townspeople, enraged that one of their lily-white women has been violated by this black beast, set out on a man-hunt to track down and destroy this dangerous creature. Once they have captured Chris they torture and mutilate him until no semblance of the human remains.

At the height of the man-hunt, Tyree rushes frantically to school to pick up his son, whose safety he fears for. Al-

though Chris had been a well-liked young man, Tyree overcomes any emotional involvement he might have had with the
youth in order to convert his experience into an object lesson
for Fish. He shouts at his puzzled son, "'NEVER LOOK AT
A WHITE WOMAN! YOU HEAR?'"30 Fish, completely baffled by his father's bizarre behavior, is nevertheless convinced that he is witnessing an important event since his intuition tells him that he is watching his own initiation drama
unfold. Fish is warned to avoid white women for his own
safety. And so, to save his son's life, the father reinforces
the whites' teaching that black men have no right to white women. But, because the information is couched in less than
frank language, Fish is more perplexed than educated by the
shouted admonitions not to look at white women. "The notion
of 'looking' at a white woman seemed so farfetched as to be
funny, but he feared the fear that was now showing on his
father's shadowy face" (65). His mother symbolically hugs
him in a gesture "taking leave of his childhood, of his innocence" (65). While Chris is being beaten to death across
town, Fish is learning the cold facts of black adult life.

Not only is Fish being instructed in how to act toward
white women, but he is discovering for himself the other side
of his parents' self-assured manner; that is, their absolute
fear of whites. When he sees his mother's face "bloated with
fear" he is repelled, unwilling to accept her as the mother
he has known:

> Were these scared and trembling people his parents?
> He was more afraid of them than he was of the white
> people. Suddenly he saw his parents as he felt and
> thought that the white people saw them and he felt
> toward them some of the contempt that the white
> people felt for them (63).

After his father has screamed at him, "'They outnumber us
ten to one! ... TEN TO ONE! YOU HEAR?'" (65), he hears
his father say, "'Be a man, son, no matter what happens'"
(66). But Fish cannot swallow this advice that so obviously
conflicts with how his father is behaving; furthermore, his
father's abject fear shames him.

Having never before been confronted with "this business
of white people" (67), Fish is filled with anxiety. He cannot
understand why no one has ever discussed the problem before,
either at school or in church. He feels betrayed, isolated,
lost. And once again, in a pattern that will remain with him

all his life, he sees blacks through white eyes and "what he saw evoked in him a sense of distance between him and his people that baffled and worried him" (67). From this vantage point he deduces that the white world is the real one, that the blacks lead non-lives. How blacks arrived at this negative state he cannot determine, but Fish realizes that cringing in fear is not a solution to the problem. Thus, even before the ritual is complete, Fish has recognized his own alienation from the rest of the blacks.

Secluded in the bathroom to mull over Tyree's strange advice not to "look white," Fish discovers in an old paper a photo of a scantily clad white woman, which he tears out and places in his pocket for further reference. Unable to come to grips with this new outlook on life, he hopes the picture will help him solve the mystery of white women. He is intrigued by the fact that black men die because of white women--especially because the woman in the picture doesn't look at all dangerous. And Tyree's warning, "'When you in the presence of a white woman, remember she means death'" (64), has only increased Fish's fascinated preoccupation with the type. So far, the lesson is backfiring on Tyree.

The ritual continues when Chris' body is found in a ditch. Tyree's reaction to this discovery is a nervous relief: "'They killed im,'" he says. "'And I'm glad!'" He's glad because he sees Chris as the sacrificial animal on the whites' altar: "'We can live only if we give a little of our lives to the white folks'" (70). But this pragmatic attitude toward life takes its toll in mental anguish, and Tyree is no exception. He hates the whites for demanding victims and the blacks for yielding them--even though he knows it's necessary. Fish can appreciate the pangs his father feels in supplying the blood guaranty and so is not surprised to hear him say reverently, "'Chris died for us'" (71). Chris' (or Christ's, as Wright has made rather explicit) death buys every black man a little more time to live. Chris is innocent of the crime of rape but is brutally and incongruously murdered; he, like Christ, is the archetypal scapegoat, the pharmakos "who has to be killed to strengthen the others" and whose punishment far exceeds his crime. [31] Interestingly enough, Faulkner's sacrificial victim in Light in August also has a name closely akin to Christ, i.e., Joe Christmas. And he too, like Chris Sims, is mutilated at death by actual physical castration.

Intent on digging every possible lesson for Fish out of this horror show, Tyree takes his son with him to watch the autopsy. In a scene calculated to remind the reader of the soldiers' haggling over Christ's clothes, Tyree and Old Man White argue over the body fee; the body snatcher finally getting paid ten dollars for the mangled corpse. What follows in grisly detail is the autopsy itself, during which Fish observes that "not only had the whites taken Chris' life, but they had robbed him of the semblance of the human" (75).[32] By destroying Chris' body and castrating him, the whites have avenged the white girl; moreover, the whites have temporarily assuaged their blood thirst. And so, because Chris has died for them, the blacks will have a period of reprieve from the whites' violence. It is therefore relatively easy for the doctor and the undertaker to be calm during the autopsy, both having accepted life on the white man's terms.

But Tyree, pragmatic as he is, still grieves over the black man's condition. Echoing the book's title, he laments, "'A black man's a dream, son, a dream that can't come true. '" He expands his idea by giving Fish advice to go ahead and dream, "'But be careful what you dream. Dream only what can happen'" (79).

And that night, as on so many nights following significant days, Fish dreams. And his dream contains, as Freud has observed all dreams do, "a repetition of a recent impression of the previous day."[33] The dream's content reflects the same conflicts that the day has brought Fish: sex, race, and fear. In the dream, Fish is in his parents' bedroom. There, under his mother's chair he sees a fishbelly covered with hair; as he stoops to examine it, a white clock begins thundering, "Don't. Don't." At this point a locomotive's smokestack touches the belly and swells it to enormous proportions. Finally it bursts and blood pours out and

> he saw the naked bloody body of Chris with blood
> running to all sides of the room round his feet at
> his ankles at his knees rising higher higher he had
> to tiptoe to keep blood from reaching his mouth and
> it was too late it was engulfing his head and when
> he opened his mouth to scream he was drowning in
> blood ... (82).

It is not difficult to trace the sources of Fish's imagery and symbols in this dream:

> white clock: has a white face which can watch him; becomes the white code and the blacks who enforce it by

warning him continually against desiring white women.

fishbelly with hair: ever since the first time he saw a
fishbelly its smell has reminded him of sex; obviously
the belly with the hair on it stands for the female sex
organ.

locomotive: years ago, having caught his father un-
wares having intercourse with a customer, Fish described his father as a locomotive; the smokestack is
an obvious phallic symbol.

The immensity of the sexual mystery and problem seems to
be symbolized by the uncontrolled enlargement of the fishbelly;
furthermore, Fish and his father had originally inflated the
real fishbellies. The fact that the belly is filled with blood
seems to symbolize the violence and danger inherent in sex,
especially since Chris is revealed to be floating in this tide
of blood that threatens to drown Fish.

Although the manifest content of this dream identifies
it as an anxiety-dream, it can be seen to be latently a wish-
fulfillment dream, as Freud argues all dreams really are.
Afraid of the implications of possessing a white woman, Fish
nevertheless desires to know what it is like--apparently even
if it means his death, as his father warns him it will. Thus
the dream repeats the dialectic of the ritual he has undergone
the day before: while Fish is being initiated into the secrets
of manhood, he is also discovering his alienation from the
rest of the world.

Other incidents in his life preceding this ritual support
this interpretation. For example, when Fish is just a child
he loses his first name. Through an adventure instigated by
his father, that of blowing up fish bladders for balloons, the
child, too young to discriminate between bellies and bladders,
is forever labeled by this misnomer. Rex permanently becomes Fishbelly Tucker. An important portion of his identity
has become blemished: the king has become a lowly fishbelly.
And it "stuck to him all his life, following him to school, to
church, tagging along, like a tin can tied to a dog's tail,
across the wide oceans of the world" (13). One wonders just
how far Wright meant to go with the associations tied to these
names. The possibilities are extraordinary: for example,
Jesus Christ was called both "King of the Jews" and a "fisher
of men"; through this name Wright could be tying Fish to
Christ just as he linked Chris and Cross Damon with Him. [34]

Given an inherently noble name, the young hero is symbolically castrated by his own father--who always seems to act out
of a misguided love for his son. At the same time, "Fish
Tucker" is a name full of latent sexual overtones; i.e., fish
are symbolic of sex (besides Christianity) and Tucker certainly has aural connotations of sex. [35] Although Wright might
not have consciously intended these explicit relationships, they
do honor the book's basic premise that Fish is an innocent
victim ruined by a sick society's concept of sexual mores.
Moreover, Wright has been known to play with names before
as in Bigger (nigger) Thomas and Cross Damon (demon).
Whether or not Wright set out to create a name so fraught
with archetypal associations seems a moot point, but the fact
that it conjures them up in the reader's imagination seems in
itself to justify these sallies into the realm of conjecture.

A year after this incident with the fishbellies, Fish,
six years old, has his first encounter with whites, whom he
regards as "huge mechanical dolls," (14), completely incom-
prehensible to his limited experience. Grabbed by one of the
men to roll some dice for luck, Fishbelly is blinded by tears
and convinced that the unfamiliar term "luck" must be bad
since it sounds like a word he knows is forbidden. This fear
of the unknown is compounded by the crap players' verbal and
physical abuse--his captor's vanquished competitors throw a
brick at him when he is released--abuse only slightly miti-
gated by the dollar the winner has given him. This dollar
presents a further problem to the now thoroughly shaken little
boy, for he must account for the money to his father. Resolved to hide the truth, he cons his doting father and tells
his first lie, another response destined to reappear as a permanent feature of Fish's personality. [36]

Not only does Fish mislead his father, but he is quite
careful to keep to himself anything embarrassing or shame-
ful--losing, as a result, the comfort of sharing painful experiences. Thus his first experience with whites has taught
him to fear the race and to lie, and, in so doing, has prevented him from learning of the universality of his experiences.
Unable to find comfort in a racial heritage he remains ignorant of, Fish continues to feel different, isolated, lonely.
And so, this scene, according to Saunders Redding, "sets the
tone, which is ironic; establishes the theme, which is the
fragmentation of a personality...."[37]

In chapter three we get the first glimpse of the family's
status in the black community, when Fish, now seven years

old, is instructed not to associate with the black railroad
workers because, although they are his color, they are not
his kind (20). As a successful undertaker, Tyree Tucker has
been able to establish himself as socially superior to the rest
of the blacks in Clintonville and can therefore train his son
to scorn certain people. [38] The shame of it, however, is that
Fish is left with no body of people to call his own. Too
proud and rich to hobnob with the ordinary blacks and racially unable to fraternize with the whites of his social standing,
he is left virtually isolated. Of course, Fish, at so young
an age, cannot conceptualize the problem that he will later
face, although he intuits it vaguely, sensing "a relation between the worlds of white skins and black skins," but being
unable to "determine just what it was" (24).

A second mystery is partially unveiled to him in this
same chapter when Fish surprises his father fornicating with
a strange woman. Uncertain as to the complete significance
of what he witnesses, he is nevertheless old enough to be
impressed with his "father's ability to lie with such indignant
righteousness" (26). Having compared his father's sexual activity to a locomotive, Fish creates a symbol that will reappear in his dreams years later. Wright's imagery is particularly sensuous here:

> From that day on, thundering trains loomed in
> his dreams--hurtling, sleek, black monsters whose
> stack pipes belched gobs of serpentine smoke, whose
> seething fireboxes coughed out clouds of pink sparks,
> whose pushing pistons sprayed jets of hissing steam
> --panting trains that roared yammeringly over far-
> flung, gleaming rails only to come to limp and con-
> vulsive halts--long, fearful trains that were hauled
> brutally forward by red-eyed locomotives that you
> loved watching and they (and you trembling!) crashed
> past (and you longing to run but finding your feet
> strangely glued to the ground!) ... (27).

That night he dreams of climbing in and starting a locomotive
and becoming frightened when it starts to roar down the
tracks.

The blacks' general isolation dominates the boys' discussion of Africa in Fish's next step toward un-manhood.
Broaching a forbidden topic, race relations, Sam initiates a
flurried anger among his friends when he argues that "'A
nigger's a black who doesn't know who he is. '" Stung by the

accusation, the boys counter weakly and finally employ scorn
to save face:

> 'When you know you a nigger, then you ain't no
> nigger no more,' Sam reasoned. 'You start being
> a man! A nigger's something white folks make a
> black man believe he is--'
> 'Your Papa's done stuffed you with crazy ideas,'
> Tony said.
> 'Your old man's got Africa on the brain and he's
> made you a copycat,' Zeke pronounced (32).

Obviously influenced by Marcus Garvey's conviction that all
blacks should return to Africa, Sam's polemics attempt to
convince the boys that blacks should '"build up Africa, 'cause
tha's our true home"' (35). He attacks his friends for
straightening their hair to look like whites, which they deny
vehemently, while Fishbelly self-consciously refrains from
thinking about "why he had had it straightened" (33). Sam
announces that they are ashamed of being black and leads Fish
down an intricate series of arguments to prove the blacks'
displacement, concluding, '"You niggers ain't nowhere. You
ain't in Africa, 'cause the white man took you out. And you
ain't in America, 'cause if you was, you'd act like Ameri-
cans--"' (35). Fish, made nervous by these suggestions that
he's neither African nor the American he claims to be, decides to leave. As he goes, Sam touches his shoulder. Fish
shoves him away and they grapple with each other. Separat-
ing, they launch into verbal attacks and Fish, having the last
cruel word, returns home aware that he hadn't wanted to
fight. Unhappy with himself, he glares at his reflection in
the mirror, spits at it and hisses, '"Nigger"' (37). Although
this obviously is a key chapter in the book, the event itself
soon escapes Fishbelly's conscious thoughts, only to assist in
the accretion of subliminal self-hatred.

At a local farm fair Fish and his friends have further
experiences that teach them to hate themselves. To begin
with, they are annoyed that on Thursday, the only day for Negroes, whites can attend too if they want to: '"Hell, it's a
white folks' world,' Sam said cynically" (42). Desirous of
seeing a skin show, they are turned way because the girls are
white. So they attend a black show instead. Afterwards, they
discover a sideshow whose main attraction is

> HIT THE NIGGER HEAD
> Three baseballs for 50¢   (44)

Hypnotized, they watch while a white throws three baseballs at the bobbing head. Fishbelly's reaction is symptomatic of his by now deep-seated ambivalence toward his own race,

> Fishbelly felt that he had either to turn away from that grinning black face, or, like the white man, throw something at it. That obscene black face was his own face and, to quell the war in his heart, he had either to reject it in hate or accept it in love. It was easier to hate that degraded black face than to love it (46).

As a result, he buys three balls, as do Zeke and Tony; of the boys Tony is the only one that hits the black man in the mouth. Suddenly ashamed, the boys decide to go home.

In the last section of Part I (chapters 13-16), Fish experiences his single most significant initiation. Whereas the ritual of Chris' death had deeply affected Fish, there, at least, he was only an observer gaining knowledge vicariously through someone else's troubles. Here he comes to know firsthand the realities of black life; here he learns the nightmare side of his waking dream. Lessons include how the police treat blacks, how blacks fool whites, and what having a woman is like. The ritual begins in fairly simple rebellion against his mother's piety and ends in a commitment to rebel against all sexual codes forbidding him access to white women. It sets the pattern of his life.

During a lull in the mud fight that Fish has chosen to participate in against his mother's wishes, he and Tony are arrested by two white policemen for trespassing. And so, without warning, the world becomes very real to Fishbelly: he is a black man arrested for a crime in a white world. Since Fish's initiation into his true status must include knowledge of the sexual boundaries surrounding him, Wright chooses to illustrate his sexual limitations through the archetypal image of castration. For example, when the police stop at a drive-in restaurant, Fish, still in a daze at being arrested, stares absently at a white waitress. Annoyed with what they think is his impertinence, the police threaten to castrate Fish with a penknife. Terrified, Fish faints--to the delight and amazement of his tormentors. At the station the officers continue to torture Fish by promising to castrate him. And Fish continues to faint. But, after passing out three times, Fish is so filled with hatred that he steels himself against the sensation and manages to remain conscious, determined to die if necessary to preserve his dignity. Ironically, this threatened castration has for the moment made a man of him, although in later scenes he will be servile and slobbering.

Soon afterward Fish discovers a more subtle form of castration than physical mutilation: his father's psychic emasculation, made clear when Tyree plays the role of a humble nigger, an Uncle Tom, to the white man's vanity.[39] As on the night of Chris' death, Fish is repelled by what he sees: "This was a father whom he had never known, a father whom he loathed and did not want to know" (125-126). As soon as they are alone in the cell, however, Tyree resumes his normal mien.

> Tyree's knees lost their bent posture, his back straightened, his arms fell normally to his sides, and that distracted, foolish, noncommittal expression vanished and he reached out and crushed Fishbelly to him (126).

His astute advice to his stunned son is to obey the whites, do whatever they say, give them no opportunity to punish him further by resisting orders. Fish reacts ambivalently to his father: he is both ashamed of him and grateful for his help.

The next day, in childrens' court, the boys are paroled to their fathers. During the hearing Fish is so overcome with fear that he feels as though he is dreaming. Once freed he feels relieved, but because of his time in jail he is uncomfortably aware of himself in relation to the world. Uneasy in the white section of town, he and Tony long for the Black Belt where they know how to act. Walking home, they automatically slump into a "kind of shuffling gait" whenever they meet a white face. "Though Fishbelly was unaware of it, he too, like his father, was rapidly learning to act an 'act'" (130). Out of their humiliation, the boys vow solemnly never to reveal the weaknesses they manifested during their incarceration.

On the way home, Fish discovers a badly injured dog. In a conscious effort to prepare himself for death, he swiftly eviscerates the animal, observing ruefully, "'That's what they did to Chris'" (135). Wright's imagery is particularly effective in the beginning of this scene as he allows the act to convey the emotion; but when Fish recalls the analogous autopsy of Chris, the reader doubts Fish's ability to make the connection.[40]

Fish next arrives on the scene of the accident that had injured the dog, where a white man lies pinned under his wrecked car. Tormented by the man's suffering, Fish tries to help. As he pulls at the door wedged into the man's back, the helpless stranger commands, "'G-goddammit, q-quick, nigger!'" (137). Fish freezes. Because he has mastered himself only incompletely he leaves the white man, refusing to help someone who calls him "nigger." The white world has not yet beaten him down to complete servility. Fish climbs back up to the road, intending to flag a car for help; but the first car he sees is driven by the men who arrested him. Flashing the penknife in Fish's face, Clem peremptorily sends him home. Reality disappears. Controlled by fear, Fish, neglecting to mention the injured motorist, runs home. There, consumed by fear and shame, he shudders at his blackness, rejecting it.

The harrowing day is not yet over, however. When Fish meets his jubilant father he is disgusted and reticent, unable to reconcile his father's behavior with what a father should be. Tyree, on the other hand, brags to his son that he manipulates whites. [41] Fish interprets his father's actions in an opposite light; he "felt that Tyree was shamelessly crawling before white people and would keep on crawling as long as it paid off" (140). To him Tyree's behavior had been obscene. Consequently, when he is interrogated about his time in jail he omits the significant details: the fainting, the dog's disembowelment. By giving his father only the superficial facts, he has managed to remove his father from his life. And after his father explains how to "act," Fish feels their estrangement is complete, grievously concluding that he had lost his father on the day he had discovered the full extent of the whites' brutality. He weeps for

> the trembling he hid behind false laughter, for the self-abrogation of his manhood. He knew in a confused way that no white man would ever need to threaten Tyree with castration; Tyree was already castrated (144).

Fishbelly tries to fight this by hurting his father, yelling to him that he is a coward. Stricken by the assault, Tyree withers. Fish repents and apologizes, whereupon Tyree musters his strength and resumes the lesson, "'I got to break your goddamn spirit or you'll git killed, sure as hell!'" (145). Contrite, Fish submits to his father.

Fish's final step into manhood, that of having a woman, occurs in the section's last chapter, 16. Not one to let his son grow up unassisted, Tyree plans Fish's baptism into the world of flesh. Before taking him to the whorehouse he owns, Tyree reveals his own dream, that of Fish's becoming the educated leader of the blacks, the man the whites will respect and consult. Ironically, this earnest man's attempts to raise Fish properly end by preventing him from becoming anything other than a confused white-loving "nigger." When his father announces, "'I'm taking you to a woman tonight,'" Fish is initially startled and amazed, questioning to himself what women "have to do with courage, cowardice, and shame"; immediately, however, he relents and hero-worships his father, "marveling at his wisdom, his generosity" (148). Seeing his father as the key to life's wonderful mysteries, Fish unconsciously accepts his father's life style, including his approach toward whites. [42]

Proud of his domain, Tyree indicates that he owns the cathouse and runs it by paid arrangement with the chief of police. Fish is awed. He has been indoctrinated well. The fact that some day he will inherit this successful business humbles him and further inculcates him into his father's philosophy.

But behind Tyree's calm understatements lurks the fear of white women: he is mortally afraid that Fish, desiring a white woman, will set himself up for murder. Therefore, he explicitly states that "'The white ones feel just like the black ones. There ain't a bit of difference '" (150).

Once inside the brothel, Fish mirrors his father's behavior. He is so insouciant that Tyree later asks if it really was his first time. It had been, but Fish simply had played his father; feigning nonchalance, he had soon learned how easy it was to dominate the madam's daughter:

> 'You Tyree's son and you even talk like 'im. '
> Vera's eyes hung upon his face.
> 'Aw, I know how to handle these white folks. '
> He stepped into his father's shoes (153).

Embarrassingly obvious to some critics, this scene nonetheless indicates Fish's acceptance of his father's dogma. Afterwards the two men walk home, smoking cigarets--more evidence of Fish's emergence from childhood. During the walk Tyree casually inquires if Fish has forgotten "them. " Fish

is confused, especially to hear that Tyree had expected sex
to "wash away any appeal that the white world had made to
him" (156). Instinctively he lies to his father, assuring him
that he has forgotten the whites. Tyree triumphantly croons
on, deprecating white women and praising black ones. It suddenly dawns in Fish's mind that whites could participate in
his sexual experiences. He recaptures the memory of the
white waitress who had served the cops and

> he knew deep in his heart that there would be no
> peace in his blood until he had defiantly violated the
> line that the white world had dared him to cross
> under the threat of death (157).

Fish is unknowingly in love with the white world that says he
is so brutally dangerous that he must be killed for violating
its sacred altar, the white woman. This desire lodges within
him, becoming his reason for living.

That night Fish dreams of being on a runaway locomotive with a white engineer who keeps yelling at him to stoke
the engine with "'MORE COAL!'" Eventually Fish's labors
uncover a white woman hidden in the coal who tantalizes him
by seizing hold of his shovel. To escape the danger, Fish
leaps off the roaring train and when he looks up, Maud Williams (the madam) is saying to him: "'Honey, you know better'n to try to hide a white woman in a coal pile like that!
They was sure to find her...'" (158-159). Once more Wright
couches a wish-fulfillment dream in an anxiety or nightmare
dream. This dream not only illustrates Fish's fascination
with white women and his desire to know one, but it also shows
his fears, his realization of the dangers inherent in such an
act. Again Fish's dream parallels Fish's life: it is, as
Frye would say, a dialectic of desire and repugnance.

A fascinating explanation of the uncontrollable yearning
for white women by black men is found in Eldridge Cleaver's
Soul on Ice, in which he attributes it to the caste system we
have in this country. The lower-class men, according to
Cleaver, are attracted to the symbols of beauty and purity established by the dominant society, in this case, the white fe-
males.[43] And so it is with Fishbelly Tucker. Tantalized by
glimpses into the white world, he lusts after the apotheosis
of beauty that means his death. Unable to release himself
from the temptations and bittersweet offerings of the white
world, he has become a man possessed. But always complicating his problem and providing the dialectic tension is the

memory of Chris, who yielded to the call of the senses.
Fish's immediate solution is to take a white Negro as a mistress; although the situation dissatisfies him, it temporarily
quells the pain in his heart.

Edward Margolies expands on Cleaver's theory as he
argues that the death of Chris supplies both Wright and Fishbelly with

> central insights into the connection between sex and
> caste. The Negro, they discover, who submits to
> white oppression is as much castrated psychologi-
> cally as the bellhop is physically. Thus, for them
> the lynchings become symbolic of the roles they are
> expected to play in life. [44]

The penalty for simply desiring white women is no less real
than for actually consummating this passion. Both lead to
emasculation and a kind of death, an alienation from self.
Fish and his kind develop a certain neurotic condition in which
the real self is separated from and scorned by the idealized
self. The real self is actually victimized by the idealized
self. [45] As Horney says of the neurotic,

> Although he may be successful, may function fairly
> well, or even be carried away by grandiose fantasies
> of unique achievement, he will nevertheless feel in-
> ferior or insecure. [46]

Against the realities of the white world that agrees with his
feelings of inferiority, Fish has no recourse other than continually to fight down his real self. He begins to hate himself. Soon, like other neurotics, alienated from themselves,
he loses "the feeling of being an active determining force in
his own life." [47] But Fish continues to function as Horney and
Kierkegaard have observed other neurotics do, for it is a quiet
despair, this alienation from self:

> The loss of self, says Kierkegaard, is 'sickness
> unto death'; it is despair--despair at not being con-
> scious of having a self, or despair at not being wil-
> ling to be ourselves. But it is a despair (still fol-
> lowing Kierkegaard) which does not clamor or
> scream. People go on living as if they were still
> in immediate contact with this alive center. [48]

Throughout the rest of the book we witness Fish's

transformation into a neurotic, as he moves from "rebellion to acceptance," as he grows up.[49] As a rebel, he has a chance to retain his real self in the face of the demands from his father and the whites. But as one who accommodates himself to their injunctions and injustices, he loses contact with his real self, preferring to live instead with his idealized self. The fierce neurotic pride engendered reassures him of his superiority and godlike stature. He need not be a black among blacks, he can be a white among whites. This arrogance will be his downfall.

But at the same time that Fish is proud and self-assured in relation to other blacks, he is humble and afraid in his dealings with whites. A neurotic conflict of this sort, according to Horney, "produces a fundamental uncertainty about the feeling of identity. Who am I? Am I the proud super-human being--or am I the subdued, guilty and rather despicable creature?"[50] Although a neurotic may not be consciously aware of the existence of both of his contrasting selves, his dreams often reveal this intrapsychic conflict. Thus, in

> his conscious mind he may be the master mind, the savior of mankind, the one for whom no achievement is impossible; while at the same time in his dreams he may be a freak, a sputtering idiot, or a derelict lying in the gutter. Finally, even in his conscious way of experiencing himself, a neurotic may shuttle between a feeling of arrogant omnipotence and of being the scum of the earth.[51]

As Horney points out, a conflict arises "because the neurotic identifies himself in toto with his superior proud self and with his despised self." Therefore, if he

> experiences himself as a superior being, he tends to be expansive in his strivings and his belief about what he can achieve; he tends to be more or less openly arrogant, ambitious, aggressive and demanding; he feels self-sufficient; he is disdainful of others; he requires admiration or blind obedience. Conversely, if in his mind he is his subdued self he tends to feel helpless, is compliant and appeasing, depends upon others and craves their affection .... If these two ways of experiencing himself operate at the same time he must feel like two people pulling in opposite directions.[52]

The neurotic solutions to these stresses run roughly into three
general categories: 1) compartmentalizing--the two selves are
experienced at different times and thus no conscious conflict
arises; 2) streamlining--one self permanently overcomes the
other; and 3) resigning--the neurotic takes no interest at all
in his psychic life. [53]

Since Horney admits that these characteristic solutions
might better be labeled trends than exact categories, I think
it is safe to suggest that at one time or another Fish--uncon-
sciously, of course--tries out each solution in his attempt to
avoid anxiety. Thus, when he is with whites he tends to
compartmentalize his two selves, automatically becoming the
self-effacing, abject and cringing Negro they expect him to
be. On the other hand, when he is with blacks he is his arrogant-vindictive self. Although at times he is almost mor-
bidly dependent on his father, by Part II he has begun to use
him too, to control him in order to have his own way, mani-
festing signs of having streamlined his problem by becoming
his arrogant-vindictive self exclusively. Because he was

> Fundamentally more intelligent than Tyree, he
> quickly found that he could manipulate Tyree's mo-
> tives for ends beyond Tyree's ken. His respect for
> Tyree's money checked his tendency toward overt
> hostility and shunted his behavior into postures of
> pretended respect.... He unconsciously reasoned
> in this manner: 'Papa, you are black and you
> brought me into a world of hostile whites with whom
> you have made a shamefully dishonorable peace.
> I shall use you, therefore, as a protective shield
> to fend off that world, and I'm right in doing so'
> (163-164).

This is the same attitude that Fish takes towards the poor
blacks whose rents pay his allowance. Since he feels superi-
or to them, he is convinced that it is his absolute right to
abuse them. He is a black man cursed with a white point of
view. And the psychic conflict caused by this mental state
nearly destroys him. For when Fish's father and mistress
die he has no one to fall back on--he recognizes his own helplessness, his vulnerability, his aloneness. And yet he must
act strong and self-sufficient. Suddenly both the expansive and
self-effacing solutions fail him: he is powerless against the
whites and left without help or love. While he is in jail,
therefore, and later on the plane to Paris, he resigns himself
to his fate, taking no active interest in his psychic life.

Part II, "Days and Nights," continues the ritual of
Fish's initiation and rejection as it illustrates the book's major themes: Fish's love-hatred of the white world and its
misuse of him; his isolation from his own people and alienation from himself; and, the transference of an inheritance from
Tyree to Fish. Because Wright focuses on Tyree as he fights
for his life against a world determined to cripple and, if necessary, kill all black men, many critics have declared that
it is Tyree who runs away with this section, leaving Fish in
the wings. [54] But Fish has his own time in the limelight when
he is forced to recapitulate the ritual after his father's death.
Throughout the book Wright suggests the symbolic nature of
Fish's actions by having him often mirror his father; the ritual of castration continues indefatigably.

For example, in his choice of a near-white mistress
Fish mirrors his father, who himself has shown desire for
white flesh in the very pale Mrs. Gloria Mason. Both men
apparently try to compensate for feelings of inadequacy by
keeping mistresses who tickle their vanity. [55] Gloria even
acts like a white woman, and her self-assured aplomb im-
presses Fish. On the other hand, his own lover, Gladys,
who has accommodated herself to her low social position, irritates him. The bastard daughter of a black woman and a
white man, Gladys is an isolate admitted into neither world
and misused by both: she too has had an illegitimate daughter by her former black English teacher. But she fails to
resent her treatment. This acceptance appalls Fish who ag-
onizes over his own feelings toward the white world.

> He had never had any intimate contact with that
> world, yet he hated it. Or did he? When he
> thought of that white world he hated it; but when he
> daydreamed of it he loved it (177).

Since Gladys is mentally unable to comprehend Fish's problem,
their conversations about whites only frustrate him. And so,
as he tries to drown his dreams in Gladys, he finds that he
is being pulled further and further toward the white world that
so attracts and intimidates him. The dialectic of dread and
desire that appeared in his dreams as a child begins to haunt
him while he is awake.

As a result of being torn between conflicting attitudes
toward the whites and because of his sexual hungers and feelings of dissatisfaction, Fish finally stops attending school.
When Tyree confronts him with his flunking, Fish boldly an-

nounces that he was about to quit school anyway. Tyree, angry and disappointed at seeing his dream of an educated son disappear, nonetheless gives Fish a job as a rent-collector. Then, to impress Fish, he brags of his invisible power in the black community and his influence with whites. But Fish is so elated to be "at last on his own, a part of the black community," that he doesn't hear Tyree's cautionary statement that his power over the blacks must be kept secret, since he uses and abuses his own people to gain status with the white crooks who run Clintonville (190).[56] Moreover, Fish sees no conflict between using blacks and being a part of their community, delighted as he is to be stepping into his father's shoes: "'And I'll keep Gladys like Papa keeps Gloria,' he whispered ... " (191).

Just how removed he really is from the rest of the black community is evident during the rent-collecting scenes. The tenants, labeled "grotesque" by Edward Margolies,[57] resent him and let him know it.

> 'Tyree got goddam nerve sending a little Lead-Kindly-Light nigger like you for my rent!' Mr. Bentley would bellow. 'Shoo, you little fly-nigger, 'fore I swat you and mash your guts out!' (192).

Fishbelly is embarrassed and nervous as he listens to these tirades, patiently awaiting the ten dollars rent. Collecting from Sam's father, he must suffer the lectures on black pride and Africa; and his reaction to this is pragmatic, "'Baby Jesus ... I don't want to read nothing about Africa. I want to make some goddamn money'" (195). He seems to be convinced that money can buy him whiteness.

Fish remarks to his father that the blacks are "sick" because they complain about their oppression but do not act to end it (198). Tyree tells him to forget them. But Fish cannot, as he continues to discover the blacks' hidden hopes and obvious failures. Ultimately, however, his arrogant-vindictive self takes over and he regards them as parasites, feeling superior to them, unaware that his white outlook has scarred his own black life; he has no place in the black community because he is enticed by the white power structure. Fish is "fatally in love with the white world, because the white world could offer him the chance to develop his personality and his wealth without fear of reprisal."[58]

To survive the anguish of rent-collecting, Fish hardens

himself, becoming, like his father, a facade of a man. He
wears a fixed smile to cover the cynicism he feels. He submerges his inner self; and, although he is by now aware of
his isolation, he "acts" like a member of the community.
He has learned to play the role of nigger--even to other blacks
if it is to his advantage. (Bigger Thomas plays the role well
with the Daltons and when he is questioned about Mary's murder. Cross Damon plays the role perfectly when he applies
for Lionel Lane's birth certificate.)

Fish is trapped between two worlds. Neither wants
him. His neurotic pride ironically forces him to identify with
the elite white world, his oppressor. Furthermore, because
he has idealized himself as master of his fate, he is horrified to learn that Gladys calmly accepts her inferior status.
And when Gladys pragmatically reminds him of his money in
order to comfort his injured pride, Fish attacks its source:
"'My Papa's got money and he acts and lives like a nigger'"
(209). Although Gladys cannot understand his restlessness,
Fish, moved by love, offers to take her out of the brothel
she works in.

That same evening Gladys dies in a fire, and the ritual of death and isolation begins with shattering implications
for Fish. For soon after claiming the corpses of the victims, Fish discovers the extent of his father's complicity in
illegal activities: as half-owner of the club that burned, Tyree is morally and legally responsible for the deaths caused
by violations of safety measures. From this point until Tyree's death at the end of the section, Wright shifts the focus
of his attention from Fish to Tyree as the father struggles
for his life.

Tyree immediately calls upon his young son as his one
and only ally, who, like other Wright heroes, loses his manhood at the same time he becomes an adult; that is, although
his father treats him like a man, he has already been emas-
culated by the whites, since whenever he is in public he is
forced to play a role. As a result, he is continually confronted with the question, "Who am I? Am I independent and
self-assertive or am I dependent and self-effacing?" Since
his value as a person is based on how others perceive him,
he reminds one of Faulkner's Joe Christmas, a man treated
with respect until others learn he is black. And so, like Joe,
Fish is a man forever in search of himself, "which is to say
Long Dream [sic] is in the tradition of American novels which
deal with search for identity and rebirth. "59

The most significant scenes in Part II are those where
Tyree plays his role as "nigger," since the acting is witnessed
by Fish who is amazed at Tyree's versatility in exploiting the
white man's preconceived notions of blacks. Tyree gives his
star performance for Chief Cantley, a scene aptly described
by Edward Margolies as "one of the best ... in the novel."[60]
Secretly determined to take Cantley to court with him, Tyree
must convince the chief that the cancelled kickback checks
Cantley foolishly endorsed have been destroyed, whereas in
reality they have not been. Playing on the white man's emotions and prejudices, Tyree transfixes Fish with the show:

> Was that his father? ... There were two Tyrees:
> one was a Tyree resolved unto death to save him-
> self and yet daring not to act out of his resolve;
> the other was a make-believe Tyree, begging, weep-
> ing--a Tyree who was a weapon in the hands of the
> determined Tyree. The nigger with moans and wail-
> ing had sunk the harpoon of his emotional claim in-
> to the white man's heart (250).

Although Tyree seems to betray his race by being an Uncle
Tom, his nigger-acting temporarily saves his life by reassuring Cantley of his innocence. Tyree is following the deathbed
advice of the Invisible Man's grandfather who instructed his
son to "'overcome 'em with yeses, undermine 'em with grins,
agree 'em to death and destruction, let 'em swoller you till
they vomit or bust wide open.'"[61]

In this same scene Fishbelly himself reveals his dis-
loyalty to blacks by offering the Grove's black proprietor as
a scapegoat. But the man dies before the conspirators can
pin the negligence charge on him. Faced then with the realization that he "had acted toward his people like the whites
acted," Fish feels remorseful (253). But Fish is too im-
mersed in the white world's point of view to feel guilty for
very long; using other blacks for his own advancement seems
natural to him. Later, in fact, while his father struggles
desperately for his skin, Fish observes him, detached,
through white eyes as he acts before Mayor Wakefield. As
has been the pattern before, whenever Tyree is under stress
Fish is disgusted with his weakness; his arrogant self has
little sympathy for a self-effacing father (Fish is actively externalizing his own self-hate).

Fish does, however, learn some basic truths about
black life when Tyree consults with a white lawyer, Harvey

McWilliams, as he attempts to indict Cantley with himself. During the drive across town, Fish realizes that their lives-- all black lives--are amoral, since blacks are in the impossible situation of being at the mercy of whites. And once inside McWilliams' home, Tyree voices Fish's unspoken observations when he says,

> 'There ain't no law but white law ... I ain't corrupt. I'm a nigger. Niggers ain't corrupt. Niggers ain't got no rights but them they buy. You say I'm wrong to buy me some rights? How you think we niggers live? ... I took the white man's law and lived under it. It was bad law, but I made it work for me and my family, for my son there.... Now, just don't tell me to go and give it all up. I won't! I'll never give up what I made out of my blood!' (272-274). [62]

At last Fish can understand his father. He finally knows the "shame and glory ... the pride, the desperation and the hope" that was theirs (274). Filled with this knowledge, he can forgive his father but he still cannot accept their situation as easily as Tyree has.

That night Fish goes through his Gethsemane, fighting off the role of innocent victim--of servile nigger. It is a struggle he has known before and in the future will encounter again, since according to John Williams, "to be black is to be forever embattled not only with the world of the whites, but with one's self."[63] Fish's own identity crisis revolves around his intuition that whites are correct when they argue that his people are inferior. And because he is too rebellious to accept his second-rate status, he feels he is different from other blacks--including his father who seems to have accommodated himself to his subordinate position. During his emotional struggle to free himself from victimization, Fish is repelled again by the Black Belt and all it stands for when he remembers that the allowance he had so casually spent came partially from Gladys' earnings at the whorehouse his father had owned. To him the Belt was "tainted, useless, repugnant" (277). Because his association with the Black Belt would contradict his superior image of himself, he wants no part of it.

That night, as on so many significant nights, Fish dreams. And what he dreams reveals his true fears. As Karen Horney says of the neurotic, "His inside knowledge of

himself shows unmistakably in his dreams, when he is close
to the reality of himself. "[64] Since Fish is a compulsive neurotic, driven by his own self-hate and self-contempt, he has
the continual "feeling of being isolated and helpless in a world
conceived as potentially hostile. "[65] This "basic anxiety," as
Horney labels it, is revealed in Fish's dream. In it Gloria
and Gladys--symbols of the white world--stuff Fish's pockets
with money (guilty, unclean money earned in his father's
whorehouse). And as soon as Fish has it in his possession,
Chief Cantley rushes in to arrest him for stealing. To escape arrest, Fish climbs in a coffin and pretends to be dead;
but the chief is not fooled. By using the white-black girls
Wright seems to be suggesting that Fish fears both worlds,
that blacks will eventually betray him and whites punish him.
(And this is indeed exactly what happens to his own father.)
Although Fish is obviously suffering psychologically, he cannot consciously admit his fears, since he, like "every neurotic at bottom is loath to recognize limitations to what he
expects of himself and believes it possible to attain. His need
to actualize his idealized image is so imperative that he must
shove aside the checks as irrelevant or non-existent. "[66]
When Fish awakes, therefore, he will have forgotten his
dream--as he has forgotten all the other nightmares that have
revealed his basic anxiety.

The next day (Chapter 31) the news breaks that Tyree's
evidence has been stolen and that Harvey McWilliams is
charging high officials with fraud. Naturally Tyree is in
grave danger. Refusing police protection for obvious reasons,
he stubbornly intends to stay and fight rather than run and
admit guilt. Tyree then presents Fish with his last will and
testament, a gesture Fish interprets as uniting the living with
the dead. Fish's intuition once more proves itself as Tyree
is shot.

Brutally coercing Tyree's friends into betraying him,
the police chief arranges Tyree's murder. Tyree is shot
point-blank by the chief's men when he is called to Maud's
brothel. The story is then circulated that Tyree charged into
the house, firing pistols, and was then mortally wounded by
the police in self-defense. Nobody believes the story but nobody will deny it either, since they fear for their own lives.

In the meantime, Fish, left at the undertaker's, muses
over the blacks' constant, self-sacrificing worship of whites:

Black people paid a greater tribute to the white

enemy than they did to God, whom they could sometimes forget; but the white enemy could never be forgotten. God meted out rewards and punishments only after death; you felt the white man's judgment every hour (289).

When Fish learns that his own father has been sacrificed to this harsh enemy, he goes wild, throwing things, smashing them, screaming for blood.

Arriving at Maud's, Fish learns of her involuntary participation in Tyree's immolation. Incapable of surrendering their own lives to a higher loyalty--that of rebellion and freedom--these blacks have given fealty to a lesser one, and once more have assisted the white man in his rape of their souls. Fish, already angered, is further infuriated when Tyree is refused a doctor. His dying father reasons with him, advising him to play along with the police, swearing that he will fight from his grave to convict Cantley. Soon he dies.

At once Chief Cantley approaches Fish, ready to talk business. He has an officer relate the police version of the incident, and Fish does not argue. Maud and the girls obliquely declare "him their new boss" (301). Fish, realizing that he is being measured by his father's assistant, the whites, the whores, and his mother, feels inadequate, incapable of replacing Tyree. But, confronted by the mutual hostilities of the two worlds, Fish abruptly announces that he's heading for the office--his office now--vowing, "'Papa left me in charge, and, goddammit, I'm going to take charge and all hell ain't going to stop me!'" (304). The mantle of responsibility has been passed on to a new generation; the ritual of castration continues.

The final section, "Waking Dream," reveals the father reincarnated in the son. Its title seems to be from Keats' "Ode to a Nightingale" (1. 79) and its epigraph is from Cymbeline (Act IV, ii, ll. 306, 307); the heroine Imogen speaks, having just awakened from a death-like stupor caused by a drug she had taken as a restorative. Her dream had been a reflection of the reality surrounding her in sleep and so she says,

The dream's here still: even when I wake it is
Without me, as within me: not imagined ... (305).

Similarly, life for Fish from now on will be a mirror of his

dreams, a nightmare. All the anxiety and fear that his
dreams have illustrated will be brought to the surface as he
too fights for his life as his father had. As the first section
was Fish's initiation, the second his probation, the third is
his total victimization. He is society's neurotic child, playing the role society dictates but forbidden entrance into its
coveted demesne. And society demands that he, a Negro in
Mississippi, must be a victim. Therefore, in order to survive, Fish plays his role just as Tyree for years had played
his.

The first thing that Fish does is deliver a packet of
papers to Gloria, obeying one of the mandates of Tyree's
will. At her house he discovers her and Dr. Bruce in the
process of running away to escape the hostile white law. Although their leaving increases Fish's sense of loneliness, he
generously abets their escape by letting them use his hearse.
Before going, Gloria chastises Fish for speaking in a nigger
dialect; in reply Fish argues, "'Hell, I just want to talk like
everybody else,'" and slips back into his drawl (312). Cognizant of the effect of his language on other blacks, Fish has
learned to talk like them so that they will trust him. He
feels superior to other blacks but is canny enough to pretend
he isn't; another manifestation of his role playing. Not only
does Fish disguise his real self from whites and blacks but
he hides it from himself. Deep down he knows that someday
he will be forced to run too; for the troubled truce he has
made with himself will drive him to seek his soul elsewhere,

The first step he takes in his struggle against the white
world that has killed his father is to break all ties with his
mother. She and Tyree's assistant, Jim, attempt to force
him back into childhood and school, but he resists, knowing
that to fight the enemy he must remain an independent man.
And yet he "was with the enemy against his own people" while
hating "that enemy because he saw himself and his people as
the enemy saw them" (315). Cursed with ambivalence, he is
forever stranded between the two worlds, an isolate. He
leaves home to take his stand.

Having the same double vision about his father as he
had when Tyree was alive, Fish is incapable of truly mourn-
ing for him or of truly hating his murderers. He had seen
him through white eyes but he also knew the problems that
the man had faced as a black,

for, in a sense, Tyree was that shadow of himself

cast by a white world he loved because of its power
and hated because of its condemnation of him.
Thus, though he could not grieve for Tyree, his
living had to become a kind of grieving monument
to his memory and a reluctant tribute to his slay-
ers (317).

Just as Ahab's and the Parsee's shadows merge in the final
chapters of Moby Dick, Tyree has become Fish's shadow, his
darkened alter ego. And Fish takes up where Tyree left off,
playing the game with Cantley, working with but not respecting Maud, and arranging the enormous funeral--which now includes his father's coffin.

This funeral consummates the ritual of death and destruction which began with the freak fire at the nightclub.
Ironically, the man who arranged for and organized the mass
funeral was himself responsible for the deaths; furthermore,
he is among the corpses waiting to be buried. Tyree Tucker,
the undertaker who made his money burying black dreams,
has not been invulnerable to death, has met the end of his
own dream.

The funeral of the forty-three is attended by a huge
crowd, packed in the sweltering church to mourn their black
brothers and sisters. But the comfort of the ritual sermon
is lost on a musing Fishbelly, since the only source of interest to him is the fact that his liaison with the white world
lies dead before him. During the Reverend's thundering, Fish
receives a mysterious letter. Writing from Detroit, Gloria
sends Fish her love and the other half of the cancelled
checks. Cantley has no certain knowledge of their existence,
as Fish had not until this moment. He is astounded again at
Tyree's cunning and also aware of the danger those checks
hold for him, since Tyree had been killed because of them.

As he leaves the church Maud stops him. He is immediately suspicious of her. His doubts are confirmed when
she mentions that Cantley has visited her and asked about
some checks. Fish lapses into his act to convince his spying
business partner that he's innocent. There is, he realizes,
no one he can trust.

Back in his tiny apartment, he hides the checks in the
chimney hearth. No sooner has he done this than Harvey
McWilliams arrives to apologize for having failed Tyree, explaining that they have common enemies. Fish, however,

is wary and cannot trust the white man. McWilliams leaves and Fish rushes after him to repeat his father's words verbatim, "'There's ten of 'em for every one of us'" (336). He cannot trust whites, he says, even McWilliams, because there is no way for him "'to know which one's honest and which one's crooked. They ain't got signs on 'em and they all look alike ... '" (336). Out of respect for Fish's candor, McWilliams shakes his hand. Fish wants to return the trust but cannot; all he can do is sob.

The next day his acting talents are put on the line when Cantley visits him at the office. Fish is uneasy since "he could not determine what kind of reality he reflected in the white man's mind" (338). Cantley confronts him with McWilliams' visit and Fish knows instinctively that he will have to lie convincingly if Cantley is to believe him. Making his voice quiver, he vehemently denies the checks' existence. Shame drives him to sobbing as he recognizes that he is acting as his father had, "symbolizing the continuing fate of the Southern Negro."[67] He is filled with bitter hatred of himself and of Cantley, who has driven him to such means.

Fish lies, cries, and acts confused. Finally Cantley asks if he knows how Tyree was killed. Clever enough to speak the lies spread by the police, he mutters, "'Resisting arrest.'" When the chief asks if he believes it, Fish must assert that he does. Cantley then tells him the truth that he already knows, that Tyree had worked for a syndicate and was killed for breaking the code of silence; what follows is a classic interrogation, indicative of how the whites regard blacks as a subhuman species:

> 'Now, Fish, you're mad about what happened to Tyree--'
> 'Nawsir!' he shouted, his lower lip quivering.
> 'It'd be natural. Niggers can get mad--'
> 'I ain't mad at nobody, Chief!' he screamed, seeking refuge in the folds of prejudice in the white man's mind (341).

Cantley counters with the statement that he doesn't really know Fish as he had known his father. This scares Fish since Cantley is attempting to enter his secret soul that so hates this particular white man. But instead of lashing out with the truth and signing his death warrant, Fish merely sobs. Cantley is driven to distraction, claiming that he can't rust Fish because he's one of the new breed of niggers who can't speak what they feel. In his frustration he pinpoints the crux of the matter, "'We make you scared of us, and then we ask you to tell us the truth. And you <u>can't</u>! Goddamit you <u>can't!</u>'" (343). He leaves angrily. [68]

Later Emma and Jim try to reason with Fish, Jim explaining that "'you say the right words, but they don't believe you'" (344). Fish feels that they have sided with the whites against him and resolves to flee, bemoaning his cursed state in Cain's terms,

> 'Papa ... you left something that's <u>marked</u> me! It's like it's in my <u>blood</u>! ... My papa, my papa's papa, and my papa's papa papa, look what you done to me' (345-346).

What black fathers have done throughout the generations, according to Wright, is teach their offspring to kowtow to whites until they have no pride left, in themselves or their heritage.

Before Fish can act on his resolution to run, he is arrested. That night, sometime after he is asleep, a young blonde girl knocks on his door. Fish thinks that he is experiencing a waking dream for this is unmistakably a white girl offering herself to him. She insists that Maud has sent her, but Fish is afraid, a feeling born of inchoate and forbidden desires and dreams. He tumbles out of the room while the girl continues her friendly prattle. Fish's thought is to find Cantley immediately in order to explain the situation. Suddenly he encounters the Chief who has been waiting for him, having planted the white girl in Fish's room himself. As Fish is arrested for attempted rape, his black neighbors hurriedly slam their doors in his face, symbolically and actually disowning him. Fish is alone.

The procedure at the station is farcical. The woman shows no signs of having been raped, or even molested. And soon Cantley comes to the point, demanding the checks. Fish realizes that he will either have to give them up or stay indefinitely in jail. Although he is totally isolated from former friends and the rest of the black community, he determines to keep his mouth shut--even if it means his death. In this manner he seems to be asserting his manhood, but in reality he is instinctively fighting for his life: to save it he must remain silent, for if the checks materialize his death would be certain.

The next day he experiences the pangs of introspection,

finding a lack in himself:

> There was some quality of character that the con-
> ditions under which he had lived had failed to give
> him. Just beyond the tip of his grasp was the re-
> alization that he had somehow collaborated with
> those who had brought this disaster upon him (356).

In his own people he finds no golden history to emulate, no
heritage to be proud of, no ideal to strive to attain, no future
to plan boldly for. All he is left with is a drab present.
He has no life except that in a poor imitation of whites; he
has no traditions or mores he can call his own. He is truly
an outsider, bereft of a personal coherent self.

Held illegally in jail, Fish is kept isolated from all
other prisoners, although his only crime had been "that he
did not know how to act in a reassuring manner toward the
white enemy" (362). Wright thus indicates his hero's basic
innocence. Fish has been incapable of coping with the harsh
white world because he ingenuously believed that he could retain his self-hood while pretending not to. The whites are
too experienced to allow this sham to pass, seeing in Fish
the desire to be his own man. Unlike Tyree, who was beaten
down, Fish at least always attempted to fend off the defeat of
his self-esteem. He wanted whites' respect, not just their
collusion in crime. And the pathetic irony of his situation is
deepened when Fish recalls Tyree's warnings about white wo-
men--Fish has never so much as even touched a white woman
and yet he has been imprisoned for having one in his room
against his will.

The final six chapters of the book conclude the story
rapidly. Fish's sentence is extended for eighteen months after
he beats up a black stoolpigeon. Zeke's second letter from
Paris confirms Fish's plans to flee to France. When he is
released near his eighteenth birthday he assures Cantley that
he "'ain't mad at nobody'" (373). This scene almost ruins
Fish who "acts" desperately in his eagerness to escape the
clutches of white Clintonville. He gets the checks, some
money from the office safe, tells the dead Tyree, "'Papa, I'm
leaving.... I can't make it here'" (377), and sets out for the
old world. Commenting on Wright's resolution of The Long
Dream, Donald Gibson finds it "retrogressive" insofar as here
"he returns to his starting point, to 'Big Boy Leaves Home,'
to the most basic and least conscious response to fear pre-
cipitated by confrontation with convention, flight."[69] But for

Fish, flight is the only alternative; powerless to survive continuous clashes with the Omnipotent Administrators because
of a lack of inner and communal resources to sustain him,
he must leave the field of battle, hoping for freedom elsewhere.

On the plane, in rather obvious irony, a white second-
generation Italian reminisces over his father's statement that
"America was His Wonderful Romance" (379). When he discovers that Fish is from the south he sympathetically asks
what life for blacks is like there. Fish lies, unwilling to open
his secret wounds to this stranger for he "was not yet emotionally strong enough to admit what he had lived" (380). So
he assures the man that blacks live just like anybody else,
while brooding over the nightmare that America had been for
him. Noticing the contrast between the man's white hand and
his own black one, he surreptitiously tries to cover his right
black hand with his left black hand to hide his "shameful
blackness" (380).

In the final scene Fishbelly ponders the dream images
of his life. Realizing that he and the whites share the same
world, he knows nonetheless that his is a different world because of his past:

> He had fled a world that he had known and that had
> emotionally crucified him.... Could he ever make
> the white faces around him understand how they had
> charged his world with images of beckoning desire
> and dread? Naw, naw.... No one could believe
> the kind of life he had lived and was living (383).

He therefore, as an act of faith, not as an act of de-
ception, decides to deny his world. He will thus be better
able to acclimate himself to a new world, and eventually perhaps be accepted, be at home among people. This is his
sweetest dream, after all, that of becoming a person, one
welcomed by other human beings. Wright in The Long Dream
is protesting "against the injustice that destroys his spirit,
crushes his dignity."[70]

The tragedy in Fishbelly Tucker is his ruined potential. Fairly intelligent, endowed with his father's native cunning, and overly sensitive, Fish is at the mercy of his environment, especially because of this latter quality. Through
his perspicacity he was able as an adolescent to see the significance of incidents surrounding his maturation, grasping
almost instinctively the implications of Tyree's acting, Chris'

death, his own identity crisis. He consequently has the capacity to become a person, aware of people's feelings and his effect on them. But this sensitivity is also Fish's weakness, the Achilles' heel that the whites irritate. His high-strung, easily hurt psyche can tolerate neither the whites' brutalities nor their subtleties. Instead of reaching out to others Fish has learned to focus on himself, thus aiding his own victimization. Becoming so sensitive of his own needs and desires that he lives solely for himself, he develops a neurotic personality: fearful and envious of the whites, scornful and exploitative of the blacks. Simultaneously, he abhors his situation, hating himself, craving friends and understanding. He tries against the odds to retain his self-esteem and manhood but is forced to surrender them to survive. Complicating this capitulation is his sensitivity: he continually resents his inferior status and the necessity for role-playing, realizing that no man should have to buy his life with his emasculation. Fish is an unwilling victim, a man on the prowl to regain selfhood.

In summary, The Long Dream is a parody of romance, a tragedy in the ironic mode, characterized by such demonic imagery as the nightmare, the mob, the sacrificial victims, the whores, and the fire that destroys. Because the novel parodies romance, its movement is analogous to and its content often in conflict with this other mode. That is to say, the ironic hero goes forth into the world in quest of an identity but instead of being successful, as he would be in romance, he fails and is rejected by society. Furthermore, according to Frye, conflict is the archetypal theme of romance and The Long Dream operates on the same dialectic of desire and reality found in both ritual and dream.

> Translated into dream terms, the quest-romance is the search for a fulfillment that will deliver it from the anxieties of reality but will still contain that reality.... Translated into ritual terms, the quest-romance is the victory of fertility over the waste land. Fertility means ... the union of male and female. [71]

Fish does not realize his dream, for the novel ultimately is tragic irony, giving the reader "the sense that heroism and effective action are absent, disorganized or foredoomed to defeat, and that confusion and anarchy reign.... "[72]

As a result, at the end of the book, Fishbelly Tucker,

isolate, victim, and castrated man, is left with the responsibility of continuing his existential search for self. Because of the conditions in the United States, Fish's initiation has resulted in alienation; the initiate has become a victim through the rituals of sacrifice, regression, and defeat. The dream ends in flight.

Other, poorer, blacks fled the nightmare of their lives by migrating north, to the large industrial cities. What happened to their dreams is illustrated by Wright in Lawd Today and Native Son. The Long Dream and Black Boy, in their detailed accounts of black male childhood in Southern America, are the perfect preludes to these two novels, since they help explain the behavior of men like Jake Jackson and Bigger Thomas. Although Wright gives the reader ample reasons for Jake's frustrations, he does not dwell on his background (a Southern one); moreover, Wright gives the reader very few specifics on Bigger's early life, concentrating instead on the results of unremitting mistreatment. And so, it is with a better understanding of both their suppressed and expressed attitudes that we turn to Jake and Bigger, men born and raised in the Deep South.

Notes

1. George E. Kent calls it "the racially most repressive state in the union" in his essay "Richard Wright: Blackness and the Adventure of Western Culture," CLA Journal, XII (June, 1969), 323.

2. Constance Webb, Richard Wright: A Biography (New York: G. P. Putnam's Sons, 1968), pp. 205-206. See also Ralph Ellison, "Richard Wright's Blues," Shadow and Act (New York: New American Library, 1966), pp. 89-104.

3. Webb, Biography, p. 409, n. 8.

4. Although it is true that Eva Blount in The Outsider is an artist, she is not the central character and serves often only to illustrate Wright's later contempt for the way the communists treated him.

5. Richard Wright, Black Boy: A Record of Childhood and Youth (New York: Harper & Brothers Publishers, 1945), p. 40. (All subsequent page references to this

work will appear in parentheses in the text.)

6. Ihab Hassan, Radical Innocence: The Contemporary American Novel (Princeton: Princeton University Press, 1961).

7. Ibid., p. 47.

8. Ibid., p. 60.

9. Ralph Ellison, Shadow and Act (New York: New American Library, 1966), p. 95.

10. Kent, "Adventure of Western Culture," 324.

11. Robert Bone, "Richard Wright," University of Minnesota Pamphlets on American Writers, No. 74 (1969), p. 14. (Hereafter referred to as Pamphlet.)

12. See Chapter V for a discussion of this.

13. In contrast, see Guy de Bosschere's "Fishbelly [the French title], de Richard Wright," Syntheses, No. 174 (Nov., 1960), pp. 63-66, in which he states "Par la magie du style, par la suggestion verbale--violente et efficace chez Wright--l'oeuvre accède à un haut degré d'art" (p. 66).

14. Robert Bone, The Negro Novel in America (New Haven: Yale University Press, 1958), p. 142, n. 1.

15. Granville Hicks, "The Power of Richard Wright," rev. of The Long Dream by Richard Wright, Saturday Review, XLI (Oct. 18, 1958), 13, 65.

16. Saunders Redding, "The Way It Was," New York Times Book Review (Oct. 26, 1958), p. 4.

17. Northrup Frye, Anatomy of Criticism (Princeton: Princeton University Press, 1957), p. 147.

18. Except for the incident in which Wright spies on their landlady who is a prostitute.

19. Russell Carl Brignano, Richard Wright: An Introduction to the Man and His Works (Pittsburgh: University of Pittsburgh Press, 1970), p. 43.

20. Edward Margolies, The Art of Richard Wright (Carbon-
    dale: Southern Illinois University Press, 1969),
    p. 158.

21. Ibid., p. 154.

22. Ibid., p. 149.

23. John A. Williams, Sissie (Garden City, N.Y.: Double-
    day Anchor Books, 1969), pp. ix-x.

24. Frye, Anatomy of Criticism, pp. 104-105.

25. Ibid., pp. 106-107.

26. Hassan, Radical Innocence: The Contemporary American
    Novel, p. 41.

27. Ibid., p. 43.

28. Ibid., p. 59.

29. Frye, p. 106.

30. Richard Wright, The Long Dream (New York: Ace Pub-
    lishing Corporation, 1958), p. 64. (All subsequent
    page references to this work will appear in parenthe-
    ses in the text.) Reprinted (Chatham, N.J.: Chatham
    Bookseller, 1969.)

31. Frye, Anatomy of Criticism, p. 148.

32. Ibid., p. 148. This is the demonic imagery of canniba-
    lism found in the late phase of the ironic mode as it
    returns to myth, "technically known as sparagmos or
    the tearing apart of the sacrificial body, an image
    found in the myths of Osiris, Orpheus, and Pentheus."

33. Sigmund Freud, The Interpretation of Dreams, trans.
    James Strachey (New York: Avon Books, 1972), p. 213.

34. Is it possible that Fish is also the Fisher-King, the
    wounded hero who must be healed if the wasteland is
    to flourish again?

35. For an interesting discussion of the significance of the
    name "Fish" as symbolic of the child's fear of cas-

tration, see Margolies, The Art of Richard Wright, pp. 152-153, in which he argues that Fishbelly is sexually confused, connecting the fish with his father and mother; and that Fishbelly's nightmares of white bellies are symbolic of his fear of and desire for white women.

36. Like the pattern of seeing his parents through "white eyes" and therefore despising them (see Chapter II, p. 18.

37. Redding, "The Way It Was," p. 4.

38. "What were the ways by which other Negroes confronted their destiny? In the South of Wright's childhood there were three general ways: they could accept the role created for them by the whites and perpetually resolve the resulting conflicts through the hope and emotional catharsis of Negro religion [Fish's mother]; they could repress their dislike of Jim Crow social relations while striving for a middle way of respect-ability, becoming--consciously or unconsciously--the accomplices of the whites in oppressing their brothers [Tyree]; or they could reject the situation, adopt a criminal attitude, and carry on an unceasing psycho-logical scrimmage with the whites, which often flared forth into physical violence [Fish's potential situation]." Ralph Ellison, "Richard Wright's Blues," Shadow and Act, p. 94.

39. According to Herbert Hill, an Uncle Tom is a black man who behaves "without self-respect and dignity and with-out racial pride in relation to white persons and white-controlled institutions" ("'Uncle Tom,' An Enduring Myth," The Crisis, LXXII [May 1965], 289).

40. See Chapter V, pp. 176-177.

41. Tryee regards himself as a "second-degree Uncle Tom." I refer to William H. Pipes' Dream of an "Uncle Tom" (New York: Carlton Press, 1967), in which he states, "I accept Wyatt T. Walker's definition of an 'Uncle Tom'--an American Negro who survives (and even sometimes thrives) by accommodation: playing the role of something less than a man, as expected of him by the white man. But two types of the 'Uncle Tom' emerge: the accommodating Negro who really

feels innately inferior ('Uncle Tom' in the first degree), and the Negro who knows he is not innately inferior, but accommodates out of expediency ('Uncle Tom' in the second degree)" (p. 6).

42. Wright, it has been suggested, has developed the strong and strangely admirable Tyree in an attempt to create a father image for himself in his fiction that he lacked in his life (see, for example, Margolies, Art of Richard Wright, p. 158).

43. According to Cleaver's interpretation, in a class society the differentiation of roles is followed by a sexual differentiation between members of the same sex. When the societal roles are complicated by a racial caste system, the results are simply more obvious. Thus the thinkers, the powerful male members of the elite class, are designated the Omnipotent Administrators--in America, the whites. The blacks take on the role of Supermasculine Menial. The white woman, to compensate for the effeminate characteristics of the Omnipotent Administrators, becomes Ultrafeminine, relinquishing her own strength to the black woman, the Strong Self-Reliant Amazon. The Supermasculine Menial is attracted to the Ultrafeminine, the symbol of beauty established by the elite for the whole society (Eldridge Cleaver, Soul on Ice [New York: A Delta Book, 1968], pp. 178-190).

44. Margolies, Art of Richard Wright, p. 150.

45. According to Horney, the "idealized self" is the product of our imagination, what our neurotic pride says we ought to be; the "real self" is the potential for growth that we can return to after conquering neurosis (Karen Horney, Neurosis and Human Growth: The Struggle Toward Self-Realization [New York: W. W. Norton and Company, Inc., 1950], p. 158 et passim). See also Chapter III, pp. 78-79, 81.

46. Ibid., p. 111.

47. Ibid., p. 157.

48. Ibid., p. 158, quoting from Søren Kierkegaard, Sickness Unto Death (Princeton: Princeton University Press, 1941).

49. Brignano, Richard Wright: An Introduction to the Man and His Works, p. 45.

50. Horney, Neurosis and Human Growth: The Struggle Toward Self-Realization, p. 188.

51. Ibid., p. 188.

52. Ibid., p. 189.

53. Ibid., p. 190.

54. See Margolies, Art of Richard Wright, p. 158.

55. Wright has given us a clue to explain this behavior in his epigraph to Part II which states in part: "The men are less fortunate ... it is they who display the celebrated racial inferiority complex in its purest form, with its fantastic compensations in the form of vanity. " Taken from O. Mannoni's Prospero and Caliban: The Psychology of Colonization, the quote actually refers to the girls and men of Madagascar--to the girls who can "With a little coquetry ... make a place for themselves in the European community" and the men who "tend nowadays to engage in the black market and other more or less parasitic economic activities" (Trans. Pamela Powesland [New York: Frederick A. Praeger, 1964], p. 119). It is certainly significant that a colonized people would manifest the same behavior as a supposedly free people in a free country. Fish's vanity is further illustrated, like Jake Jackson's in Lawd Today, in his love of flashy clothes.

56. Because Tyree has been a successful confidence man, he has attained stature among the black people; but because he is to them an Uncle Tom, he is still, in the words of W. E. B. DuBois, a "'White folks' nigger,' to be despised and feared" (quoted by Nancy M. Tischler, Black Masks: Negro Characters in Modern Southern Fiction [University Park, Pa.: Pennsylvania State University Press, 1969], pp. 41-42). Tyree is admired for his money and power but unloved.

57. Margolies, Art of Richard Wright, p. 162.

58. Brignano, Richard Wright: An Introduction to the Man and His Works, p. 44.

59. Margolies, Art of Richard Wright, p. 154.

60. Ibid., p. 161.

61. Ralph Ellison, Invisible Man (New York: New American Library, 1952), pp. 19-20.

62. From France, Marcel Lemaire observes that according to Wright's world in The Long Dream, "if the black man wants to make for himself a place in the sun he has to adjust to an unjust situation; ... if he wants to survive, he must be mendacious, hypocrit [sic], smooth-faced, knavish, cunning" ("Fiction in U.S.A. from the South," Revue des Langues Vivantes, XXVII, 3 [1961], 247-248).

63. Williams, Sissie, p. x.

64. Horney, Neurosis and Human Growth: The Struggle Toward Self-Realization, p. 111.

65. Ibid., p. 18.

66. Ibid., p. 36.

67. Brignano, Richard Wright: An Introduction to the Man and His Works, p. 47.

68. "After all, the problem is for the white Southern people, who cannot reconcile themselves with their own image as it is reflected in the fate they have designed for the colored people, to get rid of their fear and hate, to learn how to live with themselves. It is one of this novel's virtues that it brings this moral problem fully to light" (Lemaire, p. 248).

69. Donald B. Gibson, "Richard Wright and the Tyranny of Convention," CLA Journal, XII (June, 1969), 356-357.

70. Margolies, Art of Richard Wright, p. 151.

71. Frye, Anatomy of Criticism, p. 193.

72. Ibid., p. 192.

CHAPTER III

THE VICTIM AND THE REBEL

Lawd Today is Richard Wright's dialect novel,[1] written from the perspective of a black man in Chicago in the thirties. In this stylistically most experimental of his novels, Wright attempts to encompass all the details of a single day in the life of one man, Jake Jackson. Using Dos Passos and Joyce as his models, Wright includes newspaper clippings, junk mail, movie posters, and a radio program to give the flavor of Jake Jackson's day. Unfortunately, however, the book is very unevenly written, ranging from strong tight scenes (such as his bitter quarrel with his wife, Lil) to long boring ones (such as the bridge game which even includes diagrams of the hands). And where Joyce used mythology to add depth to his modern Odyssey, Wright is limited to the irony arising from juxtaposition: he portrays his modern postal workers as latter-day slaves to the U. S. Government, with a constant chorus in the background celebrating Lincoln's birthday and the emancipation of blacks. There is no doubt that the contrast makes for bitter irony, but the technique fails to carry the book.[2]

As a result of its many weaknesses, the critics have not been particularly kind to Lawd Today--nor have they necessarily been in agreement as to its flaws and strengths. A sampling: Nick Aaron Ford in his review remarks that "Lawd Today is important only because it reveals another chapter in the apparent decline of the once magnificent talent of the late Richard Wright ... Lawd Today is a dull, unimaginative novel."[3] Dan McCall, although impressed with the book as an admirable beginning for a young writer, condemns Wright's obtrusive irony and the "long, tedious stretches of dialogue and detail that seem less like fiction and more like sections of a tape recorder which Wright turned on and forgot to turn off...."[4] Edward Margolies calls the book "an interesting, ambitious, and lively novel."[5] Russell Brignano says that "As a work of art, <u>Lawd Today</u> is beset by numerous short-comings. The amount of sheer dialogue is overburdening; the meager, often-monosyllabic vocabulary is shallow and poorly descriptive; and the unrelenting stress upon the smallest of details, even to the extent of picturing the card distributions in bridge games, is tedious."[6] Yet contemporary critics agree that the book is a valuable document in the study of Wright since "it defines," according to George Kent, "at least an essential part of black life, points up the importance of the inscriptions from other writings as aids to understanding his intentions, and enables us to see Wright examining a slice of black life practically on its own terms."[7] This finally, after all critical arguments are weighed, is the book's single undebatable achievement: it is a vivid record of black life.

For its strengths, therefore, we can look to the in-credible detail of black life so painstakingly recorded by a newly emerging black author. Without a doubt it is a graphic account of the anguish and latent violence of the black man trapped in an America that doesn't want him. Moreover, al-though the blacks presented may be despicable, the novel's implied author asks us to sympathize with them, asks us often to join in the moments of laughter and extravagant humor that bring a feeling of relief from the general tedium of these men's lives. And how can the reader truly despise someone he is laughing with?

Subconsciously aware of their displacement, Jake and his friends compensate for their empty lives by sporting flashy clothes, drinking long and hard, laughing too loud and too often, and spending their salaries on whores.[8] As Dan McCall says, "The book is a side show. It is a hopeless, helpless carnival of brutalization...."[9] It is a montage of colorful grotes-queries with Jake Jackson spinning in the center of each scene. And although he laughs, it is to forget, for his entire day is one of disappointments and put-downs.

His first frustration is that of not being able to finish an erotic dream (although this is a slightly amusing problem, it is nonetheless tragic to him). The rest of the day takes its cue from this disappointment. Jake quarrels with his wife about another man and about her health (he himself had forced her to have an abortion years ago and she still suffers from the hack job the incompetent doctor did on her). He is forced to pay his barber an exorbitant amount of money to smooth out his relations with the Postal Board. At work he is disci-

plined for his sloppy work. At the whorehouse he visits to
unwind, he is robbed, losing all the money he had borrowed
earlier in the day.

Jake Jackson is a man who never quite makes it--al-
though he likes to think of himself as a big spender and man-
about-town. His marriage belies his success with women;
he and his wife quarrel bitterly and seem to get satisfaction
only from hurting one another. Moreover, although he has
an opportunity of bettering himself by getting work as a railroad conductor, he is unable to apply himself to memorizing
the train schedules. He is simply too easily distracted by
the pleasures of the body. A young man, he is already a
failure, having no real ambition that can be translated into
positive action.

And so, Jake Jackson smolders. He is sensitive
enough to feel a nagging dissatisfaction with himself and his
life. He has his pride too--mostly in his appearance: he owns
ten suits and spends agonizing moments slicking down his recalcitrant hair. A nobody in the outside world, he constantly
strives to be the boss of his own apartment, aching to be a
force in his wife's life. "Again he searched for something to
say that would rouse her to a sharp sense of his presence."[10]
Proud of his own job as a postal employee, he scorns his
wife's report that people are starving in America. And yet
he too wishes for a better life; for example, always hopeful
of making it big, he regularly plays the numbers--never win-
ning, of course.[11] Jake also refuses to identify himself with
the poor blacks; he sides with the successful ones as part of
his delusion over his self-image:

> 'Niggers is just like a bunch of crawfish in a bucket.
> When one of 'em gets smart and tries to climb out
> out of the bucket, the others'll grab hold on 'im and
> pull 'im back ... ' (55).

To keep himself from having to think about the poverty of his
life, Jake throws himself into the colorful, noisy world of the
streets:

> The clang of traffic, the array of color, and
> the riot of flickering lights infected Jake with a
> nervous and rebellious eagerness. He did not want
> to leave all this life in the streets; he had a feeling
> that he was missing something, but what it was he
> did not know (101).

To forget about his nagging wife, his deadly job, and chronic debts, Jake wastes his day playing bridge and drinking, occasionally lazily complaining about his fate as a black--"a nigger just stays a nigger" (103).

In a footnote in The Rhetoric of Fiction Wayne Booth notes "how much more importance titles and epigraphs take on in modern works, where they are often the only explicit commentary the reader is given."[12] Written entirely without authorial intrusion (except for the two scenes noted where Wright gives factual information), Lawd Today instead offers the reader several of these textual clues as to how the implied author feels about his characters and their lives. Each of the titles of the book's three sections acts as a summary of the implied author's attitude toward the life that Jake Jackson exhibits therein. Additionally, the epigraph appearing at the beginning of each part elucidates the significance of the chapter headings. To illustrate,

> Part I: Commonplace
>
> ... a vast Sargasso Sea--a prodigious welter of unconscious life, swept by groundswells of half-conscious emotion. ...
>> Van Wyck Brooks' America's Coming-of-Age
>
> Part II: Squirrel Cage
>
> ... Now, when you study these long, rigid rows of desiccated men and women, you feel that you are in the presence of some form of life that has hardened but not grown, and over which the world has passed. ...
>> Waldo Frank's Our America
>
> Part III: Rats' Alley
>
> .... But at my back in a cold blast I hear
> The rattle of the bones, and chuckle spread from ear to ear.
>> T. S. Eliot's Wasteland

Part I, half the book, is appropriately labeled "Commonplace." This word operates on two levels: the incidents are commonplace events in Jake's existence; and Jake's life is surely a commonplace one, void of promise and satisfaction. In this section he makes a covenant with himself to study for the new job with the railroad; but, as he vows to improve, he seems to know that his are hollow intentions. He quarrels with his sickly wife about the same things they quarrel about day in and day out: his razor blades, his stocking for his hair, her illness, her conversations with the milkman, her cooking. Jake is continually enervated by an excess of self-pity. For excitement he plays the numbers and reads the paper.

Part II, "Squirrel Cage," discloses the boredom and bodily exhaustion that emanate from working in the sorting room at the Post Office. Taking no interest in their jobs (and Wright makes it crystal clear as to why no one could take an interest: it is incredibly tedious work offering little or no sense of accomplishment), the men try to forget by telling stories of their sexual escapades. It is a regular litany of sensuality. [13] At the same time they indicate just how much they hate their white bosses, how much they hate the system that forces them to toss letters into bins for a living and, more significantly, that forces them to brag about their sexual prowess to assert their manhood. They resent the whites but have no solution for changing the power structure, for these men are socially and politically impotent.

To release their frustration at being cooped up in the Squirrel Cage, the men visit "Rats' Alley" in Part III. The whorehouse is the highlight of their day; here they eat and drink excessively while Jake throws money around to prove his manliness. Jake is so enraptured by his own success with the women that he fails to notice the theft of his wallet. When he attempts to pay the bill he realizes what has happened and, almost as a relief, starts a fight. Thrown out of the establishment with his friends, he fails to yield to depression:

> He had exactly eighty-five cents. One hundred dol-
> lars gone in one night! And I got to pay Doc. Gawd-
> damn that whore! He straightened, smiled, and
> yelled to the top of his voice:

> 'BUT WHEN I WAS FLYING I WAS A FLYING
> FOOL!' (185).

Unconsciously, Jake knows the danger of admitting his short-comings. He must maintain the fiction of himself as a daunt-less Don Juan--otherwise despair would destroy him.

Once home, Jake retaliates against the world by attack-ing his wife viciously, trying again to make an impression on

her, closing the day as he began it. Lil defends herself with
a chunk of broken glass and Jake eventually passes out. The
violence expressed in this final scene indicates the extraordinary depth of Jake's frustration. Superficially a happy-go-
lucky, laughing black man, Jake Jackson is in reality an embittered, defeated slave, unable to find a viable mode of rebellion. He is caught in a web of debt and unhappiness--the
forgotten failure in a land of opportunity.

But Jake and his friends have something to recommend
them: their zest and outrageous determination to have a good
time regardless of the consequences. The book lives through
their colorful language and bawdy behavior. Beaten at the
better things, they still know how to have a good time. Although their finer impulses may have died and, seen at the
end of a debauch, their faces must express the utter emptiness of desiccation and despair, these men daily give it a go,
trying their best to wrench some happiness out of a dreadful-
ly disappointing life. [14] These are the black proletariat, the
dispossessed who found freedom to be as confining as slavery.
Written from the viewpoint of the masses, Lawd Today nonetheless lacks the commitment to Marxism that Native Son contains. Moreover, the latent violence of these postal workers
is translated into action in Native Son: there the slave learns
how to rebel. As George E. Kent observes,

> Lawd Today enlarges our perspective on Native Son,
> for it creates the universe of Bigger Thomas in
> terms more dense than the carefully chosen symbo-
> lic reference points of Native Son. The continuity
> of Wright's concerns stand [sic] out with great clar-
> ity and depth. Running through all Wright's works
> and thoroughly pervading his personality is his iden-
> tification with and rejection of the West, and his
> identification with and rejection of the conditions of
> black life. Lawd Today is primarily concerned with
> the latter. [15]

With the scenes set in Black Boy, The Long Dream, and Lawd
Today we are now ready to witness the terrible ordeal of a
black rebel in Native Son.

Native Son is Richard Wright's novel of outrage. It is
his bitter condemnation of the American mores and laws that
have ravished the Negroes' spirits since slavery. It is also

Wright's tribute to the Biggers he knew who refused to knuckle
under, who declared their frustration with the world by engag-
ing in crime and murder.   With his anger never far beneath
the surface, Wright warns the world to expect universal rebellion and violence from all its Biggers--its downtrodden masses.
Here is a man writing out of a personal passion for justice, a
man who knew victimization intimately--as a child in Mississippi and as a young man in Chicago during the Depression.
Although Wright would later receive international acclaim and
prestige, he never forgot his people.   His work is evidence of
this.

> Native Son is the emotional autobiography of a man
> who refused to be either a thing or a criminal.
> Bigger Thomas forced recognition by an act of mur-
> der, Wright by an act of art. [16]

     In his essay, "How 'Bigger' Was Born" (1940), Wright
discusses at length the bond between himself and Bigger.   Re-
calling no fewer than five Biggers that he has known, Wright
says of one, "he left a marked impression on me; maybe it
was because I longed secretly to be like him and was afraid.
I don't know."[17]   The Biggers that Wright remembers stand
out in his mind because they stubbornly challenged the system
that sought to "keep them in their place."   In their own desperate and often pitiful ways they fought the status quo.   This
Wright admired.

     Besides being based on autobiographical material,[18]
Native Son, like much of Wright's other work, contains a mixture of two seemingly opposed philosophies, naturalism and
existentialism, and is permeated with a third, Marxism--to
its detriment, many critics feel.   Whatever its flaws, the
book stands as an anguished cry of pain, a work of art as
expressive of its time as Picasso's Guernica.   Although no
hint of the impending war appears in the novel, the darker
philosophical questions of what it means to be human, of the
origin of man's terrible loneliness, and his willingness to in-
flict suffering on others are exposed in Native Son.   Man's
eternal search for a way out of his human dilemma appears
here also in the guise of the Communist Party.   The only solution, however, as Bigger discovers in the tormented hours
before his execution, is for each man to accept himself for
what he is, transcending the world's horrors and contradic-
tions.   Camus says in The Myth of Sisyphus that "There is
no fate that cannot be surmounted by scorn" and that "One
must imagine Sisyphus happy."[19]   Native Son is the quest of

Bigger Thomas for this transcendence, for this state of being
able to assert life in the face of an irrational world that
seeks his soul; it is his journey into selfhood. As he goes
to his execution, one must imagine Bigger Thomas happy.

Bigger's totally modern search for self is analogous
to the ancient allegorical quest-romances that appear in Chris-
tian and vulgar literature, whose "essential element of plot"
is adventure. And the "major adventure" in a romance Frye
labels its "quest," explaining that

> The complete form of the romance is clearly
> the successful quest, and such a completed form
> has three main stages: the stage of the perilous
> journey and the preliminary minor adventures; the
> crucial struggle, usually some kind of battle in
> which either the hero or his foe, or both, must
> die; and the exaltation of the hero. [20]

I am not suggesting that Native Son is a quest-romance; it
is more precisely an inverted romance, an ironic tragedy. [21]

Bigger's preliminary minor adventures prepare us for
his confrontation with his naked self. He skirmishes with the
rat and overcomes it. He quarrels with his family and his
friends, asserting his right to be himself. He kills a white
woman in her own bedroom--his most significant act since he
frees himself from bondage by breaking a potent taboo. He
flees into the heart of darkness, the Black Belt, to escape
the police and is captured there. From this point on in the
book, Bigger flees back into himself. The most crucial encounter occurs in Bigger's mind as he struggles to accept
himself while he is locked up in jail. There, in isolation and
anguish, he ponders his deeds and motivation. Before dying
he triumphantly declares himself a murderer.

Although Bigger is victorious, he remains an ironic
hero since the evil he struggles against is identified with society itself and his exaltation is purely a personal one. As
he seeks an identity he is, like the modern absurd hero, "in
spirit ... Ishmael still, searching for a strayed, runaway, or
uncreated self. He becomes an alien in his familiar land."[22]
Bigger engages in the Quest Absurd, a situation in which

> It is this real world which has become irrational
> (unreal, a nightmare) ... as exemplified in such
> modern writers as William Faulkner, Wright Morris,

or J. D. Salinger. And as the world of these recent novelists has become more irrational, their
visions--the dreams of their searchers and seek-
ers--have become more rational, humble, and human. [23]

All Bigger wants is to be accepted as a human being, wishing
once and for all to shed his cloak of invisibility and to be re-
spected as a man among men. He succeeds in forcing the
world to admit his existence, but he comes into being only as
a criminal.

Native Son is a tragedy written in the ironic mode.
And as a proper tragic hero, Bigger is isolated from society.
But he might be more accurately called an anti-hero since the
term "hero" carries with it an aura of superiority that an
ironic hero does not have; instead, the ironic hero is inferior
to us in power or intelligence, and thus, to paraphrase Frye,
when we watch an ironic tragedy, we look down on a scene of
bondage and frustration. [24] This is the proper setting for absurdity. And Bigger Thomas is an existential or absurd hero
whose "adventures" constitute a metaphysical quest for the
meaning of existence--his and, by implication, ours.

According to Frye, the archetypal theme of irony is
"the sense that heroism and effective action are absent, disorganized or foredoomed to defeat, and that confusion and anarchy reign over the world." [25] Archetypally, then, Native
Son could be categorized under Frye's fourth phase of satire,
the ironic aspect of tragedy, [26] since the "central principle of
ironic myth," according to Frye, "is best approached as a
parody of romance: the application of romantic mythical forms
to a more realistic content which fits them in unexpected
ways." [27]

As a phase of irony in its own right, the fourth
phase looks at tragedy from below, from the moral
and realistic perspective of the state of experience.
It stresses the humanity of its heroes, minimizes
the sense of ritual inevitability in tragedy, supplies
social and psychological explanations for catastrophe,
and makes as much as possible of human misery
seem, in Thoreau's phrase, 'superfluous and evit-
able.' This is the phase of most sincere, explicit
realism.... [28]

Throughout most of the book, Wright explains Bigger's down-

fall in proletarian terms: the white capitalistic power structure has alienated Bigger, forced him into criminal activities.
Society, therefore, is directly responsible for creating this
"monster." Bigger has been trapped in an absurd environment, much like Cass Kingsolving in William Styron's Set This
House on Fire, which requires him to destroy life in order
to reaffirm its value.

In writing Native Son Wright began his examination of
Bigger Thomas from the outside, exploring Bigger's family,
his friends, and surroundings. And they were certainly instrumental in forming him. But as he got deeper into the
character, he must have found that social and psychological
explanations were inadequate. There was more to Bigger than
the naturalists, communists, or psychologists could explain.
For Bigger, as Wright must have discovered, was not satisfied to be labeled and forgotten. He was rebellious enough
to want to forge an identity out of his black experiences, in
spite of--or to spite--society. Wright, although he most
likely did not know it at the time, had created an existential
hero, a metaphysical rebel.

Later, when asked to identify the source of Bigger's
alienation, Wright replied with a political explanation that has
overtones of Miller's absurd world in it. In this 1940 essay
Wright said that as far as he was concerned Bigger "is a
product of a dislocated society; he is a dispossessed and disinherited man.... " Wright goes on to identify himself with
his creation.

> He was an American because he was a native son;
> but he was also a Negro nationalist in a vague sense
> because he was not allowed to live as an American.
> Such was his way of life and mine; neither Bigger
> nor I resided fully in either camp. [29]

As outsiders, living in no-man's land, both Bigger and Wright
had unique perspectives on the American way of life--a vantage point later put into words by another Wright character,
Ely Houston, in The Outsider. [30]

Since Wright's own view of life during the thirties was
strongly influenced by the Communist Party--as was the thinking of many writers and intellectuals at that time--his style
of writing shows the mark of its spokesmen, the proletarian
novelists, who themselves drew on the realistic and naturalistic traditions in literature to express party dogma. Using

detailed physical descriptions and concentrating on the common
man as their subject, the communists protested shrilly against
the injustices inherent in a capitalistic country. Meeting with
these writers at the Chicago John Reed Club, Wright became
excited by their ideas and their passionate commitment to a
new order. As a black man, Wright says he "began to feel
far-flung kinships, and sense[d], with fright and abashment,
the possibilities of alliances between the American Negro and
other people possessing a kindred consciousness."[31]

Although Wright would eventually dissolve his affiliation
with the Communist Party in a public statement, he never
truly renounced his Marxist viewpoint. Even when he broke
with the Party in 1944 he still managed to convey how strongly he had been attracted to its call to the world's disinherited:

> It was not the economics of Communism, nor the
> great power of trade unions, nor the excitement of
> underground politics that claimed me; my attention
> was caught by the similarity of the experiences of
> workers in other lands, by the possibility of uniting
> scattered but kindred peoples into a whole.... It
> urged life to believe in life.[32]

The bonds ran deep. And Wright never lost faith in his vision of brotherhood. Later critics would see this attachment
to the ideals of communism as a watermark of his work,
arguing that Wright

> in spite of the shifts in his formal political affilia-
> tions, was always essentially a Marxist thinker....
> He used Freud, for example, primarily to score
> Marxian points, and even his later involvement with
> existentialism seemed to have political revolution
> as its basic motive.[33]

Wright was encouraged to submit articles and poetry
to The Masses (later The New Masses), an organ of the Communist Party. The fruit of this enthusiasm for his work appears in the first collection of his short stories, Uncle Tom's
Children, printed in 1938, which shows Wright's strong attachment to the Party. "Fire and Cloud" reveals Wright's dream
of unity between the lower classes of both races. In this
story the people, starving during the Depression, show such
strength of will in their togetherness that the town's officials
are forced to release supplies of surplus food to them. The
story closes with their assertion that "'Freedom belongs t'
the strong!'"[34]

In the book's last story, "Bright and Morning Star," Wright tries to illustrate his conviction that even the most ignorant and poor black woman can become a vital force in the cause of freedom. Although Aunt Sue is not a communist, her son Johnny-Boy and his white girl friend Reva are. When Johnny-Boy's life is endangered by the presence of an anti-communist informer, it is Aunt Sue's down-home intuition that tells her who the Judas is. Before the man can report to his friends, Aunt Sue, winding sheet in hand, shoots him dead. She and her son die slow and torturous deaths at the hands of these people, but the comrades' identities are kept secret because an old black woman has seen the bright and morning star.

Ironically, Wright's most successful and famous proletarian work was not acceptable to the Communist Party. Although Native Son fits the definition of a proletarian novel as posited by Walter B. Rideout in his study The Radical Novel in the United States, that is to say, a novel written from the Marxist viewpoint,[35] it was nevertheless criticized by the communists for not following the party line on the Negro question. With its publication, then, Wright's love affair with communism began to pale. Nonetheless, the book stands today as one of the better proletarian novels to come out of the thirties. It suffers, like the others, from its author's not so subtle proselytizing, but its strength evolves from the sheer horror it can evoke in the reader's imagination. After Little Rock, Detroit, and Watts, it can still kindle a flame of outrage. And much of its effect is directly attributable to the narrative techniques that Wright learned from other proletarian writers, such as his use of realism, ironical juxtaposition, and a proletarian point of view--that is, the novel is told from the perspective of a member of the masses.

Wright identified with these inarticulate masses, who are like the people in Winesburg, Ohio and Paterson in that "the language fails them." Determined to speak for these people who are struck dumb with poverty and hopelessness, he intentionally wrote Native Son "so hard and deep that [people] would have to face it without the consolation of tears."[36] To do this Wright employed the harsh style of the realists and coupled it with the devastating attitude of environmental determinism so prevalent in the naturalistic novels of this century. Continually, Wright protests against the dehumanizing effects of the white American capitalistic system by illustrating the life of one of its victims, Bigger Thomas. Unlike so many of the proletarian novels that today seem to be nothing more than period pieces, Native Son increases in relevance, owing in part, interestingly enough, to the same techniques that have tended to date the other radical novels.

Even Wright's use of realism seems only fitting. For he is portraying the bleakness of Bigger's soul by exposing the poverty of his outer life. In the book's opening scenes, for example, Wright is at his dramatic best as he vividly illustrates the impoverished lives of lower class blacks who are forced to live on Chicago's South Side. As a realist, Wright carefully delineates the details of slum life, reminding the reader of Henry Roth's style in his proletarian novel of an immigrant boy in New York, Call It Sleep.

In Chicago, as in all cities, ghetto life revolves around the ubiquitous rats. And so, Wright begins his novel with these uninvited guests. While his family watches in fear, Bigger stalks a huge yellow-fanged black rat. Although the rat is vicious and bold--attacking Bigger on the leg--it is nevertheless finally cornered and killed. This sordid little drama effectively summarizes Native Son's entire action, for Bigger, like the rat, is black and daring, striking out against a stronger foe. But he is no match for the enemy. R. C. Brignano finds Bigger's action in this scene "ironically symbolic [since later] Bigger will assume the role of a hunted animal, and the rat will be interchanged in the minds of the whites with Negroes in general."[37] Even Bigger unconsciously identifies himself with the rat when he is running from the police. Looking for a place to hide in the Black Belt, he sees a rat slipping into a nearby building and gazes "wistfully at that gaping black hole through which the rat had darted to safety."[38] He is jealous of the rat since he can find no hole to lose himself in. Quickly, he is trapped and captured--no better than an animal at bay.

It is this feeling of being treated like an animal, of being kicked and beaten like an unwanted dog, that so infuriates Bigger that he cannot function as an ordinary human being. He is tormented by the vast distances between his dreams and the world's reality; he is ripe for rebellion. In 1951, Albert Camus seemed to speak for Bigger as he studied the characteristics of the metaphysical rebel, finding that

> The first and only evidence that is supplied me, within the terms of the absurdist experience, is rebellion. Deprived of all knowledge, incited to murder or to consent to murder, all I have at my disposal is this single piece of evidence, which is only

> reaffirmed by the anguish I suffer. Rebellion is
> born of the spectacle of irrationality, confronted
> with an unjust and incomprehensible condition. But
> its blind impulse is to demand order in the midst
> of chaos.... It protests, it demands, it insists
> that the outrage be brought to an end.... [39]

Where other men might have the comfort of family and
friends, Bigger is alone with his fear. Like most modern
heroes Bigger is an outsider, exemplifying with his life the
harsh philosophical truth that man is alone and that the death
of God goes without saying.

America has stolen Bigger's family from him--just as
she did to the blacks two hundred years ago to keep those
slaves from building strong family ties. Bigger's father is
dead, having been killed in a race riot when his son was a
young child. Bigger's mother is on welfare and constantly
troubled by a lack of money. Transplanted from his native
Mississippi, Bigger himself is unable to stay out of trouble
or find a decent job in the north. In Chicago, he lives in
one room with his mother and two siblings, Buddy and Vera.
The dreadful tension in this family is evident from the conversation in the first scene. As R. C. Brignano notes:
"Quickly Wright sets Bigger apart from the sharing of any
warm and strong associations with members of his own family and of his young gang companions."[40] When Bigger teases
Vera by swinging the dead rat in her face, their mother re-
sponds bitterly, "'Bigger, sometimes I wonder why I birthed
you!'" (17). Although she claims to have sacrificed her life
for her son she shows him little love or understanding. She
has had a hard life. Obviously bitter about her son's lack
of ambition, she challenges his manhood and sanity:

> 'We wouldn't have to live in this garbage dump
> if you had any manhood in you.... ' (7)

> 'He's just crazy.... Just plain dumb black
> crazy.' (8)

> 'Bigger, honest, you the most no-countest man
> I ever seen in all my life!' (12).

This lack of affection in Bigger's family is quasi-autobiograph-
ical: Wright's own strongly matriarchal and highly religious
family failed to give him a sense of love or belonging. According to Wright's memories, his family seems almost to

have taken pleasure in squelching his poetic nature.

And yet Bigger's family is not entirely to blame for his bizarre behavior. After all, they too are victims--victims of white capitalism and traditions. Through a steady accretion of facts Wright compiles a brief that indicts the white power structure for ravaging blacks--for destroying their lives, their families, their heritage.

By confining himself to presenting only Bigger's point of view, Wright forces the reader to identify with his hero. We see only what Bigger sees, hear only what he hears.[41] And it is shattering: the loveless home; the friendless gang; the matter-of-fact murders and disposal of bodies; the painful and frightening flight. Through it all, Wright's careful, almost reportorial account even of the most terrifying moments tends to understate the horror of what is happening. This is a technique used often by naturalistic writers, according to Walcutt: "where the subject matter is sensational, the style is likely to be restrained and objective."[42]

Another of Wright's trademarks as a craftman, his heavy use of irony, was probably learned from the proletarian school since it is also an outstanding characteristic of their work. In Native Son these ironic contrasts serve to point out the polarities of American life, the differences between the elite and the poor, and the discrepancy between what things should be and what they really are.[43] Several ironies, for example, surround Mr. Dalton, real estate broker and philanthropist. This man charitably hires Bigger as his chauffeur to give him a new start in life. But this man also owns the squalid tenement building that Bigger lives in. During Bigger's trial two interesting facts emerge about Dalton: one, that he won't fight an old custom that keeps blacks locked in the ghetto; and, two, that he won't lower the rents in the ghetto because he thinks it would be unethical to undersell his competitors (277-278). Although he puts on a good show of respectability and tranquility, he obviously feels guilty: to salve his uneasy conscience, he regularly donates money to Negro education and has provided pingpong tables for the South Side Boys' Club.[44] Completing this rather obviously ironical situation is the information that Bigger and his gang used the club as a meeting place to plan their robberies.

Further ironic contrasts surround the descriptions of the Thomases' apartment and the Daltons' home. Whereas everything at Bigger's is loud, crowded, and collapsing, at

the Daltons' it is subdued, expansive, and expensive. Naturally Bigger is ill at ease among such surroundings, especially
when Mary Dalton impetuously confronts him. Bursting with
tolerance and radical ideas, Mary threatens Bigger with her
impertinence toward her father and what he stands for. Bigger
immediately fears and hates her. Ironically, she is one person who makes a sincere attempt to understand him. But she
is tactless. Not only do she and Jan Erlone touch him frequently, but they make him sit in the front seat of the car
between them and take them to a black restaurant where they
all eat together--to Bigger's shame.

In a somewhat heavy-handed ironic scene, Mary unconsciously reveals the enormous chasm between the races
when she wistfully wonders aloud how blacks live:

> She placed her hand on his arm.
> 'You know, Bigger, I've long wanted to go into
> those houses ... and just see how your people live
> ... I want to know these people. Never in my life
> have I been inside of a Negro home. Yet they must
> live like we live. They're human.... (60).

Indicative of their separation is her constant use of
"you," "your," and "they"; Wright obviously had concluded
that Mary and her kind feel no emotional bond with blacks.
In fact, these intellectual liberals are twice removed from
Bigger, by race and by class. Wright seems to be trying
to destroy once and for all the myth that America is a class-
less society.

When Wright begins his narrative of Bigger's trial he
slips into the pitfall of preaching to the reader--a flaw seen
in much proletarian writing. Up until this point in the book
Wright had allowed Bigger and the facts of his existence to
speak for themselves. But here Wright apparently felt he
could not rely on his reader's perceptive abilities, so he steps
in to tell him what the book has been about. In his essay,
"How 'Bigger' Was Born," Wright mentions this impulse of
his to explain but does not apologize for it, feeling in his own
mind that it was necessary to make his thesis obvious. This
major stylistic flaw weakens an otherwise devastating story. [45]

Through the mask of Boris Max, Wright protests the
oppressive conditions that prevent blacks from achieving self-
realization. According to Max, the communist spokesman,
society is responsible for Bigger's becoming a murderer.

Therefore, as a product of a criminally negligent capitalistic society, Bigger is blameless. Hugh Gloster identifies this theme of oppression as the "all-pervading thought of Native Son," the idea

> that a prejudiced and capitalistic social order, rather than any intrinsic human deficiency, is the cause of the frustration and rebellion of underprivileged Negro youth of America. [46]

To state it another way, Wright is illustrating Hassan's concept of the rebel-victim, the innocent man victimized by a guilty society. Amazingly enough, Wright has couched a very modern idea in a proletarian novel.

While Wright was working on Native Son during the thirties, the communists were rallying around the Negro cause. Thus it is not surprising that Wright--himself caught up in the communist struggle for civil liberties--would paint the communists in a sympathetic light. In Native Son the communists are more than eager to help Bigger as a further excuse to blast the white power structure, the bourgeois class. Although Wright tempers his admiration of the communists by portraying them as rather insensitive do-gooders, he does characterize them as loyal, determined fighters of injustice. They don't really know or understand Bigger but they fight diligently for his rights. By 1940 Wright had already become disenchanted with the Party, but he still seems to have had some sort of faith in the integrity of its motives. After all, Max's speech is an impassioned call for justice, and it is the only time in the book that a man--black or white--defends Bigger publicly. Wright had to have some bond with this Party to portray such emotional force in his communist spokesman--to choose a communist as his spokesman.

In his discussion of Native Son as a proletarian novel, Walter B. Rideout praises this intensity and forgives the book's weaknesses, saying that

> The end of the book comes close to being a tract, but it is saved by the emotional force of its terrible warning ... [T]he imaginative expansion of the book ... comes from the relating of the truncated lives of Negroes in the United States to those of all the other 'have-not's,' the humiliated and despised, who are goaded on by the American Dream and whose American Tragedy it is to be blocked from the dream's fulfillment. [47]

It is this discrepancy between man's inner desires and the world's realities that forces men into states of alienation --and Bigger to murder. Native Son is clearly an ironic title, for Bigger Thomas has no place in the sun in America. He is an alien in his own land. He thinks like the young Richard Wright in Chicago, who resented being yelled at by a Jewish shopkeeper and so instictively saw his boss' yelling as a symptom of the woman's feeling of racial superiority:

> I reasoned thus: though English was my native tongue and America my native land, she, an alien, could operate a store and earn a living in a neigh- borhood where I could not even live. [48]

Although Wright later realized that he had misinterpreted Mrs. Hoffman's motives, he knew that his reaction was typical of oppressed blacks and an appropriate one in many other in- stances in America. He vowed to battle the world's genuine injustices with words:

> I would hurl words into this darkness and wait for an echo; and if an echo sounded, no matter how faintly, I would send other words to tell, to march, to fight, to create a sense of the hunger for life that gnaws in us all, to keep alive in our hearts a sense of the inexpressively human. [49]

Although Native Son is, without question, a proletarian novel, it remains something more. In this powerful novel Wright straddles the opposing forces of naturalism and exis- tentialism, wearing the boots of a Marxist. At first Bigger Thomas seems to be at the mercy of his environment, deter- mined by nature and society to become a killer. But Bigger, using sheer will, manages to transcend his world, to accept himself for what he is and to accept the consequences of what he has done. Underlying and somehow strangely supporting this amazing transformation is Wright's Marxist conviction that the revolution of the masses is inevitable, imminent, and justified. This movement or change in ideology has been ob- served by Robert Bone in an essay on Wright, in which he says that

> The novel moves, in its dénouement, toward values that we have learned to recognize as existentialist. Having rejected Christianity and Communism Bigger finds the strength to die in the courageous acceptance of his existential self: 'What I killed for, I am!' In embracing his own murderous instincts, however,

> Wright's hero is compelled to sacrifice other and
> perhaps more basic values. He has established an
> identity through murder, but that identity, by vir-
> tue of its horror, has cut him off from the human
> community of which he longs to be a part. That is
> the meaning of Max's profound revulsion in the final
> scene. [50]

This interpretation of Bigger as an existential hero is further
corroborated by Donald B. Gibson in his essay, "Wright's Invisible Native Son." [51] For as Wright matured, his work
more and more invited comparisons to the French existentialists instead of the proletarian novelists. Native Son, therefore, stands as a watershed between these two dominant philosophical influences on Wright's thinking. Given little credit
by certain of his peers for being comfortable with the abstruse
and varied tenets of existentialism, Wright nonetheless was
able to draw on the horrors of his own life and his extensive
readings to create a number of existential heroes. [52]

As I read it, then, the theme of Native Son is the
quest for identity, the self-realization of a personality, the
growth from neurosis to joyful self-actualization. With skill,
Wright moves his character out of a deterministic situation
into an existential one, simultaneously protesting against a society that forces men to crime in order to express themselves.
To appreciate the unity of Native Son it is necessary, therefore, to establish the relationships in it between naturalism
and existentialism, two such opposing philosophies.

Since both philosophies revolve around a concept of
determinism, this is a good place to start. As the major
theme in naturalism, determinism carries, according to Walcutt, "the idea that natural law and socioeconomic influences
are more powerful than the human will." [53] Conversely, in
existentialism, it is precisely the human element that is the
stronger. Man alone must create himself; in fact, he has to,
he has no choice. As Sartre describes Mathieu in The Age
of Reason, he was, like all men, "condemned forever to be
free." [54] Naturalism, then, can be seen as the obverse side
of existentialism.

On the naturalistic side of the coin are such books as
Studs Lonigan and An American Tragedy. Because of environmental factors he can neither control nor avoid, Studs Lonigan, a sensitive and rather poetic young man, is doomed to
failure and an inglorious death. Similarly, Clyde Griffiths,

attempting to improve his impoverished life, is predestined by circumstance to social ostracism and death row. On the existential side are works like Caligula and The Age of Reason, where both Camus' and Sartre's protagonists recognize their total freedom and the necessity of creating their own values. For Caligula the rest of the world is simply his instrument for carrying out his plan to live by absolute logic. For Mathieu, freedom is so dear that he cannot make commitments to anyone but himself:

> He had never been able to engage himself completely in any love-affair; or any pleasure, he had never been really unhappy; he always felt as though he were somewhere else, that he was not yet wholly born. He waited. [55]

Between the two extremes of absolute determinism and absolute freedom stands Native Son. Bigger is born poor and black in a country that puts a premium on being wealthy and white. Naturalistically, this means that Bigger is predestined to become a pariah, a ne'er-do-well, and, climactically, a murderer. But Hugh Gloster thinks, as I do, that "the book seeks to show that the individual's delinquency is produced by a distorting environment rather than by innate criminality."[56] Therefore, if Bigger can transcend his environment, rise above the pressures of the slum, he can create himself anew. Naturalistically, this is inconceivable--existentially, it is not only possible but unavoidable for a man to continually create himself. [57] But in order for Bigger to become aware of his own potential for growth and self-determination, he must first rebel. He must reject his slavery and affirm himself. As Camus says in The Rebel,

> ... the movement of rebellion is founded simultaneously on the categorical rejection of an intrusion that is considered intolerable and on the confused conviction of an absolute right which, in the rebel's mind, is more precisely the impression that he 'has the right to.... '[58]

At the same moment the rebel affirms a yes and a no, he begins to think, to consider, to become aware of himself:

> Awareness, no matter how confused it may be, develops from every act of rebellion: the sudden, dazzling perception that there is something in man with which he can identify himself, even if only for a moment. [59]

In his Narrative Frederick Douglass records the epiphany he experienced having actually resisted a beating by his
overseer; he recalls that

> This battle with Mr. Covey was the turning
> point in my career as a slave. It rekindled the
> few expiring embers of freedom, and revived with-
> in me a sense of my own manhood. It ... inspired
> me again with a determination to be free ... I felt
> as I never felt before. It was a glorious resurrec-
> tion, from the tomb of slavery, to the heaven of
> freedom. My long-crushed spirit rose, cowardice
> departed, bold defiance took its place; ... the day
> had passed forever when I could be a slave in
> fact. [60]

Once Bigger rebels, he unleashes, in Camus' words, "a
raging torrent"[61] since he is no longer a slave but a free
man in search of his soul. He has broken the spell of determinism.

The same tension between intention and reality that
existentialists after Camus have called "the absurd" occurs
also in naturalism. According to Walcutt's interpretation of
literary naturalism, this conflict occurs because man is torn
between defying nature through biological competition, and
submitting to nature, dissolving into apathy, failure, or death.
Naturalism faces the unresolvable "tension between the ideal
of perfect unity and the brutal facts of experience."[62] (Compare Camus' statement that "The absurd is born of this confrontation between the human need and the unreasonable silence of the world."[63]) Man desires to be at peace with nature (intention) but the harsh world precludes this (reality).
To survive in this state of tension, Bigger is forced to rebel.
In rebelling he moves from determinism to freedom.

As Wright guides his hero through the rites of passage
from determinism to existentialism, he transforms his proletarian novel into a very modern existential novel. Donald B.
Gibson summarizes this transition in Native Son in a key para-
graph in his essay, "Wright's Invisible Native Son":

> I do not want to argue that Wright was not strongly
> influenced by American literary naturalism: cer-
> tainly he was. But he was not as confined by the
> tradition as has been generally believed. If my
> thesis about Native Son is correct, then Wright is

not an author whose major novel reflects the final
phases of a dying tradition, but he is instead one
who out of the thought, techniques and general orien-
tation of the naturalistic writers developed beyond
their scope. Native Son ... looks forward rather
than backward. It is a prototype of the modern existentialist novel and a link between the fiction of
the 1930's and a good deal of more modern fiction.[64]

By the end of this extraordinary novel, Bigger is convinced of his absolute freedom. He denies that any outside
force is responsible for him. He refuses all available scapegoats, cursing neither God nor society. He goes to his death
proud of his accomplishments. Although he does not know it,
he has realized Camus' assertion that "'man, without the help
of the Eternal or of rationalistic thought, can create, all by
himself, his own values.'"[65]

Bigger's success derives from an act of pure violence,
another intersection of naturalism and existentialism in Native
Son. Violence rages in many forms through most naturalistic
literature; sheer animal survival is the key activity. To quote
Walcutt:

> Animal survival is a matter of violence, of force
> against force; and with this theme there emerge
> various motifs having to do with the expression of
> force and violence and with the exploration of man's
> capacities for such violence.[66]

Existentialism also explores man's capacities for violence.
For violence is, indeed, as Hassan observes, the "ultimate
form of introspection," where the hero has recoiled utterly
against himself, bidding permanent adieu to society.[67]
Metaphysical rebellion begins with protest against man's situation. It leads to the deification of man; God's order is re-
placed by man's, often through violence and crime.[68]

Although superficially the murders Bigger commits
seem to stem from an animal instinct to survive, a naturalistic reaction, they are in truth caused by more complex
impulses. Since each woman irritates him, and each manages
to put him in a vulnerable position, Bigger is himself convinced that he has killed to protect himself. It isn't until
much later that he realizes that other factors were involved:

> 'For a little while I was free; I was doing some-

> thing.... I killed 'em 'cause I was scared and
> mad. But I been scared and mad all my life and
> after I killed that first woman, I wasn't scared no
> more for a little while' (300).

Bigger's lawyer, Boris Max, also interprets his first murder
as a positive act, calling it "'the most meaningful, exciting
and stirring thing that had ever happened to him'" (333). He
concludes that Bigger has accepted these violent acts because
they made him free, made him feel that his decisions and
actions "carried weight." For Brignano,

> The 'act of creation' that Bigger sees in his quasi-
> accidental killing of Mary is creative. It raises
> him, and with him his Negro-ness, from the level
> of obscurity to the realm of recognition. He ac-
> complishes alone something sensational. In so do-
> ing, he projects his now unavoidable presence into
> the white world. His satisfaction is, of course,
> perverse; but, Wright implies, it is legitimate--the
> logical outcome of an acknowledged release from a
> consciously subservient group. [69]

One existential aspect of Bigger's personality that
Wright must have recognized very clearly is his sense of
alienation from the rest of the world. It is an alienation that
Wright himself often experienced--as a child and as a man.
Both Wright and Bigger felt alienated from their own families.
Both were rebellious, alienated by status and personality from
other people. Although Wright overcame his social alienation
and Bigger never did, they did share a lessening of self-
alienation.

Bigger's alienation identifies him with several contemporary fictional hero types. He is similar to James E. Miller's "alienated hero" who suffers a "severe sickness of the
soul--a spiritual nausea"; he is in opposition to the world. [70]
He also resembles David Galloway's "absurd hero" because
he accepts his absurd condition and "makes it his God"; his
existential leap leaves him content to be a murderer. He has
formulated his own values. [71] Further, his situation is analogous to Richard K. Barksdale's "anti-hero" who is alienated
from his culture and society. He has no purpose or power;
his fate is martyrdom and defeat. [72] Bigger, however, is
defeated only in society's eyes. He is, after all, condemned
to die as a murderer; but this so-called defeat is really a
victory for Bigger who has rejected this world's ethical code.

Closest of all the heroes is Hassan's anti-hero, the "rebel-victim." Bigger is victimized by society, but he rebels against this condition, and, thrown entirely upon his own resources, successfully creates an identity for himself.[73]

The source of the term "alienation" lies with the German philosopher, Georg Hegel, who believed the phenomenon to be an ontological fact. "Alienation, in its original connotation, was the radical dissociation of the 'self' into both actor and thing, into a subject that strives to control its own fate, and an object which is manipulated by others."[74] Alienation was the inescapable dualism of the "I" shaping itself and the "me" being shaped by others. For Hegel, the principle of action was the key to overcoming this dualism; however, his description never developed beyond abstractions. Bruno Bauer contended that the solution was to discover the real motives behind human actions and thus overcome dualism through self-consciousness. Ludwig Feuerbach felt that all alienation stemmed from religion, which taught that all good in the world was transcendent, apart from men; the solution, therefore, lay in returning the divine to the human. But Feuerbach also talked only of the abstraction Man. Finally, Karl Marx located alienation in something specific and concrete: work. Man, according to Marx, has become nothing more than a commodity in the organization of labor; he has become an object directed and used by others and therefore he has lost his sense of self.[75] To combat this capitalistically induced alienation the system itself must be overturned, bringing man back into a sense of identity and feeling of personal worth. This idea in Marx's thinking has been hidden by the historical concept of the man, but is currently being studied and revived; it is seen as one of the most basic statements about the sociological condition of man's current alienation.

Kenneth Keniston, in his landmark essay, "Alienation and the Decline of Utopia," speaks of the gap between man's aspirations and the world's actualities as the cause for alienation.[76] Richard K. Barksdale, in his discussion of alienation and the anti-hero, lists four reasons for the alienation in modern America: 1) the gap between the great "American dream and the ugly historical fact"; 2) the fact that "the power and the glory now belong to the machine"; 3) the fact that the "great society" is continually confronted by "the threat of mass annihilation through nuclear war"; 4) the existence of the "pseudo-Eden" created by what he terms "Madison-avenueism."[77] Sidney Finkelstein, in Existentialism and Alienation in American Literature, comments on the Negroes' estrangement in the United States and their portrayal as subhuman creatures in literature and journalism.

> As long as a mass of white people conceive whatever minimal security they think they have as resting on the secondary status of the Negro ... this 'monster' image will emerge as a product of their own alienation. People who have essentially the same hopes, feelings and potentialities as they, who should be seen as human kin, are seen as fearsome and alien. The alienation felt by an exploiter for the exploited can be given ideological support, like theories of the alleged inferiority of Negroes or 'strangeness' of Jews. But alienation itself is psychological and self-divisive, a projection by the hater upon others of the image of the inhuman practices to which he himself feels driven. [78]

Since each discipline has certain valuable insights to offer for a more complete understanding of this tortured man, Bigger's alienation can be viewed as a psychological, sociological, and philosophical phenomenon.

As we have seen from Karen Horney, one cause of self-alienation is the conflict in a neurotic person between the actual and the idealized self. [79] The neurotic loses the feeling of being in touch with himself, of being in control of his life. Bigger, trying to live up to the idealized self patterned after the white man's standards of beauty and success, cannot help but despise his own only too-lacking actual self. He cannot tolerate his feelings of impotence. As a result he drives himself to the extreme, the point of self-alienation.

Afraid to admit fully his truly dreadful situation, Bigger has built a protective wall around himself. Like Fishbelly, Bigger prefers to live on the surface of life. Not only is it simpler, it is safer. Both men compartmentalize their experiences, allowing only tolerable thoughts to emerge, a phenomenon directly attributable to their neuroses which, according to Horney, "lower the threshold of awareness of self." [80] Since Bigger is under the controls of his "shoulds" --the demands from his idealized image of himself--he cannot afford to recognize his shortcomings and failures. He uses this device to prevent the "upsurge of self-hate which otherwise would follow a realization of 'failure'.... "[81]

Although this repression allows people like Bigger to avoid
life's harsher realities, it really only serves to increase further the neurotic's alienation from self:

> At the core of this alienation from the actual
> self ... is the remoteness of the neurotic from his
> own feelings, wishes, beliefs, energies. It is the
> loss of the feeling of being an active determining
> force in his own life. It is the loss of feeling him-
> self as an organic whole. [82]

Faced with his own inadequacy as a black man in a white society, Bigger has suppressed the conditions of himself and his
family so he doesn't lash out and kill indiscriminately (9-10).
Besides hating himself, he hates his family because he is
"powerless to help them" (9).

Bigger's loss of self resembles Fishbelly's in that it
is a subtle process wearing him down gradually, like Blake's
"invisible worm that flies in the night. " And, according to
Horney, there are four major contributors to this alienation
of self in a neurotic. The first is the compulsive nature of
a neurosis. The person is deprived "of his full autonomy and
spontaneity. " Secondly, the person becomes entrapped by his
"shoulds. " 'In other words, the tyranny of the should drives
him to be something different from what he is or could be. "[83]
Third, neurotic pride keeps him ashamed of his real and actual selves (Kierkegaard's "despair of not wanting to be oneself," according to Horney). "Finally, there are active moves
against the real self, as expressed in self-hates. "[84]

Bigger's self-hate is evident in the scenes where he
is with Mary Dalton and her lover, Jan Erlone. These two

> made him feel his black skin by just standing there
> looking at him.... He felt he had no physical ex-
> istence at all right then; he was something he hated,
> the badge of shame which he knew was attached to
> a black skin (58).

This sudden feeling of self-hate is induced by whites--people
who have taught others to despise themselves because of skin
coloring.

A second way to approach Bigger's alienation is through
sociology, since he suffers from the five main components of
alienation as identified by Melvin Seeman: normlessness,

powerlessness, meaninglessness, social isolation, and self-estrangement. [85] Normlessness is comparable to Durkheim's concept of anomie, the state in which a man experiences uneasiness and anxiety, a feeling of pointlessness or that no goals exist. Beyond his disquietude about daily life, Bigger has forebodings about the future, fearing that eventually he will lose control and strike out at society. Recognizing that he is not in control of his fate, he feels helpless in the face of the rest of the world; for example, the welfare agency has threatened to cut off the relief checks if Bigger refuses to take the job at the Daltons':

> Yes, he could take the job at Dalton's and be miserable, or he could refuse it and starve. It maddened him to think that he did not have a wider choice of action (11).

To compensate, he and his friends turn not only to violence but to a milder form of rebellion, that of role-playing. Pretending to be white, they not only mock the whites, but, sadly, themselves.

At the book's beginning, as I have suggested, Bigger is powerless to control his own fate. Kept in check by unwritten white laws that forbid him from living outside the black belt, Bigger cannot break out of his crippling environment. Hampered by an inadequate education and lacking specific goals, Bigger is also an alumnus of reform school. Since he has no skills valued by society, he is forced to accept the position of chauffeur the welfare agency assigns him to.

Out of this feeling of powerlessness evolves a sense of meaninglessness. To compensate, Bigger indulges in activities that stimulate his senses: sex and drinking. But his sex with Bessie is without love and his drinking without joy. Ultimately his senses become deadened, a welcome relief to a man trying to forget his misery.

Further outcomes of Bigger's inadequacies are his social isolation and self-estrangement. According to Seeman and Dean, social isolation is the condition in which a man rejects society's goals and beliefs, often innovating asocial means to realize his own goals. Bigger hasn't exactly rejected society's goals; more precisely, he has been prevented by society from participating in its meaningful activities. He too would like to have money, status, and an interesting job. But he isn't allowed to. So Bigger turns to crime, an asocial activity, to obtain fleeting financial security.

Of all the types of alienation, certainly the most hor-
rifying is self-estrangement, the condition, in Fromm's terms,
in which the "'person experiences himself as an alien.'"[86]
A man suffering from self-estrangement is less than he ideal-
ly should be; he has no pride in himself; his work has no
meaning; and he is incapable of finding any self-rewarding activities to engage in. Bigger Thomas is just such a victim
of self-estrangement, alienated from himself as a result of
societal influences and pressures. He is bitterly ashamed of
himself. He has no "coherent sense of self.'"[87] He has lost
his identity, which "depends upon the awareness that one's
endeavors and one's life make sense, that they are meaningful in the context in which life is lived ... [Identity] is a
sense of wholeness, of integration, of knowing what is right
and what is wrong and of being able to choose.'"[88] As a self-
alienated person, Bigger continually endures the agonies of
what could be called an "identity crisis." Since he doesn't
know who he truly is, and the world tells him he's a nobody,
he represses disagreeable events in order to have the will to
survive. As a neurotic, he is forced to reject his real (and
actual) self in favor of his idealized self.

To cope with stressful situations, Bigger instinctively
blots them out. This blotting out or blindness becomes one
of the book's major motifs.[89] It appears in Bigger when he
does not want to perceive the truth about himself. According
to Horney this is a fairly common neurotic sympton. "As a
protection against this terror [of being oneself] the neurotic
'makes himself disappear.' He has an unconscious interest
in not having a clear perception of himself--in making himself, as it were, deaf, dumb, and blind. Not only does he
blur the truth about himself but he has a vested interest in
doing so--a process which blunts his sensitiveness to what is
true and what is false not only inside but also outside himself.'"[90] Bigger's fragile equanimity cannot tolerate a conscious recognition of his victimization; although he occasionally dips into the realities of his actual self and thinks about
his plight, confessing, for example, to Gus that he often feels
as though he's "'on the outside of the world peeping in through
a knothole in the fence'" (17). He is, after all, drawn inexorably to the sore that festers in him: the inequality between
the races that forces him to be a despised outcast. Because
of this fascination with the cancer in his soul, Bigger has pre-
monitions that "something awful's going to happen" to him (17).
It is no wonder that he tries to blot out people and events that

conflict with his inner world.

The philosophical explanation for Bigger's alienation is found in existential literature. According to Camus, man's absurd condition arises from the clash between intention and reality; in other words, between man's inner desires and the negative world forces. [91] Bigger himself is only too well aware of the absurd. For him, it is the white world in particular that collides with his blackness reminding him of the "divorce between man and his life, the actor and his setting,"[92] and causes him to feel alienated.

> 'Them white boys sure can fly,' Gus said.
> 'Yeah,' Bigger said, wistfully. 'They get a chance to do everything' (14).

Although Bigger consciously experiences alienation only when he is confronted by the absurd, he is in truth inherently alienated, for man's alienation is an ontological fact according to Camus and David Galloway. Man is not alienated because he is faced with a specific set of noxious or unbearable circumstances, but because he is human. As Galloway writes, alienation

> is the fate of any and all men who think and feel with any intensity about their relationship to the world which surrounds them. Therefore man does not become alienated (the word itself ceases to have connotations of 'process'): alienation is his birthright, the modern, psychologically colored equivalent of original sin. [93]

Bigger is a rebel because, like the other absurd heroes of the twentieth century, "he refuses to avoid either of the two components on which absurdity depends": intention and reality. [94] Instead of turning away, he challenges the absurd condition. "The theme of permanent revolution is thus carried into individual experience. Living is keeping the absurd alive. Keeping it alive is, above all, contemplating it."[95]

Of great value in understanding the philosophical make-up of Bigger Thomas is Ihab Hassan's Radical Innocence. Within this essay on contemporary literature Hassan expands on his concept of the "rebel-victim," the existential hero who rebels against society and yet is still victimized by it. He is marked by a "radical innocence." Hassan explains that the anti-hero's innocence is "radical" "because it is inherent in his character" (radical = root), and also because it is "extreme, impulsive, anarchic, troubled with vision."[96] His innocence derives from the Eternal Yea, the inner impulses of man that confront the outer realities of the world:

> It is the innocence of a Self that refuses to accept the immitigable rule of reality, including death, an aboriginal Self the radical imperative of whose freedom cannot be stifled ... [T]he innocence we speak of also has a divine element in it; has, like Dionysus, that inner energy of being, creative and sacrificial ... [97]

The concept of the existential hero's basic innocence is further supported by James E. Miller, who believes that the hero is alienated from an irrational world gone-crazy.[97] Since the irrationality lies in the world and not in the hero, it is the world itself which is the villain in the drama. But predictably it is the anti-hero who is doomed to failure and censure. He must then be admired for embracing a fight he cannot hope to win.[99]

Another critic who has entered the struggle to define the existential hero characterizes the Dionysian principles mentioned by Hassan as negative. Richard Lehan, instead of seeing the anti-hero's activity as positive and divine, sees it as destructive. He blames the demise of the Apollonian principles (civilizing, measured, sublime) on Nietzsche's vision of the darker Dionysian forces (chaotic, primordial, orgiastic). For Lehan the existential quest is demonic and the existential hero is an inverted Christ figure.[100] The hero destroys or sacrifices himself by affirming his own identity. According to Lehan's interpretation, Camus' Meursault and Dostoyevsky's Kirilov "die so that others may understand the nature of absurdity."[101]

An absurd hero, a rebel, a man in search of an identity--Bigger Thomas is an existential hero and Native Son the record of his quest. Because Bigger is searching for an identity, a very private, introspective quest, his activity removes him from the rest of the world. Once he has murdered, fled and been captured, Bigger must contemplate in isolation what he has done and discover its meaning for him. He must turn in upon himself, dwelling there until he can wrench an identity out of his spiritual anguish. No one can help him. Furthermore, as Hassan has noted,

> In its recoil the modern self has once again dis-
> covered that all truths must be bloody and person-
> al truths, that is, <u>experienced</u> in anguish and ac-
> tion. [102]

Bigger is the anti-hero, the man whose search for "freedom
and self-definition" leads him to an ultimate alienation from
the world. [103] As an outsider forced to create his own values,
Bigger simply continues the pattern of his life since he has
never really been a part of this world. He has been isolated
from whites because of his color and alienated from blacks
because of his rebellious nature--his violence is regarded as
dangerous by the black community eager to continue accommodating the whites. The "novel reflects ... the isolation of the
Negro within his own group and the resulting fury of impatient
scorn. "[104]

Although Bigger may be isolated, he has not intended
himself to be (witness his sad, strained relationships with his
friends and Bessie: unsatisfactory, but the only contact with
other people he could manage). When he said "no" to his
bondage, he was speaking for all the world's Biggers. "When
he rebels, a man identifies himself with other men and so
surpasses himself, and from this point of view human solida-
rity is metaphysical. "[105] Unable to tolerate his spiritual oppression and anonymity any longer, he lashes out in the only
way he knows. [106] He tells Max,

> 'I hurt folks 'cause I felt I had to; that's all. They
> was crowding me too close; they wouldn't give me
> no room.... I was always wanting something and
> I was feeling that nobody would let me have it. So
> I fought 'em. I thought they was hard and I acted
> hard.... But I ain't hard even a little bit' (355).

Bigger seems from this passage to be truly one of Camus'
innocent murderers who thwart violence with violence. [107]

What Bigger is unable to convey to Max is that he,
like all the rebels, speaks for the community of man:

> He had lived outside of the lives of men. Their
> modes of communication, their symbols and images,
> had been denied him. Yet Max had given him the
> faith that at bottom all men lived as he lived and
> felt as he felt (353).

As Camus concludes in The Rebel, "the freedom to kill is not
compatible with the sense of rebellion" since "I have need of
others who have need of me and of each other."[108] Therefore, Bigger himself must give up his life for those he took.
Otherwise, "From the moment you accept murder, even if
only once, you must allow it universally."[109]

And so, Bigger dies to reaffirm the value of life.
It follows that if life had no value he would not be asked to
give up his for taking the lives of others. In effect, his death
is a symbolic gesture reasserting his faith in the community
of man. Although he does not want to die, he understands
that he must now sacrifice himself as he had earlier sacrificed Mary and Bessie. "If the individual, in fact, accepts
death and happens to die as a consequence of his act of rebellion, he demonstrates by doing so that he is willing to sacrifice himself for the sake of a common good which he considers more important than his own destiny."[110]

Bigger has been driven into a corner like a trapped
animal; there society tantalizes him with its rewards but refuses to let him out to share them. To obtain what most
people take for granted, independence and self-identity, Bigger has been forced to kill. Before his murderous acts he
had been invisible; through them he asserts himself as an individual, not until later realizing the significance of his rebellion. Bigger's activities fit Sartre's description of how
men create themselves--

> man first of all exists, encounters himself, surges
> up in the world--and defines himself afterward[111]

--since he doesn't really discover who he is until the very
end of the book. Bigger hasn't set out to kill, he just has
done it--without plan or forethought (or regret). Once he has
murdered he must endure great spiritual anguish before he
can finally accept himself for what he truly is. He is a murderer and that is good--for him but not for others, so he
must die to reaffirm the value of life.

Although written in the thirties, Native Son is thema-
tically quite contemporary, having obvious similarities to many
existential novels. One particular novel that comes to mind
immediately is Paul Bowles' Let It Come Down, written in
1952. Like Bigger, Nelson Dyar is a victim who has no control over his own fate (he calls it being in a cage--like Jake

Jackson in the squirrels' cage in <u>Lawd Today</u>). A failure in
his thirties, Dyar is forced to compromise his principles and
turn to crime and chicanery in order to rustle up some self-
respect. After stealing money from a group of men engaged
in illegal money-exchanging, Dyar has a moment of lucidity
when he realizes that he is responsible for himself:

> 'I wanted to do this,' he told himself. It had been
> his choice. He was responsible for the fact that
> at the moment he was where he was and could not
> be elsewhere. There was even a savage pleasure
> to be had in reflecting that he could do nothing else
> but go on and see what would happen, and that this
> impossibility of finding any other solution was a di-
> rect result of his own decision. [112]

Later, in his hideout, Dyar again rejoices at his having "escaped becoming a victim" as he puts it. [113] That night, overcome by the narcotic effects of the majoun (hashish) he has
eaten, Dyar accidentally kills his Arab companion, Thami
Beidaoui--although <u>he</u> <u>has</u> <u>wished</u> <u>him</u> <u>dead</u>, just as Bigger
feared Mary and wished her dead before accidentally killing
her. Rising in the night to secure a banging door that has
annoyed him before, Dyar drives a nail through Thami's head.
This gruesome scene is related very quietly by Bowles, giving
it a dreamlike quality--just the effect that Wright evokes when
Bigger chops up Mary's body after smothering her.

When Dyar's acquaintance, Daisy de Valverde, comes
up the mountain to help him she discovers what he has done
and abruptly leaves him in disgust. At this moment Dyar
finally realizes that life is real, no longer a game. The book
ends with Dyar's new knowledge about himself:

> Later he would be able to look straight at this
> knowledge without the unbearable, bursting anguish,
> but now, at the beginning, sitting here beside Daisy
> in the room where the knowledge had been born, it
> was too much.... He stood there in the patio a
> moment, the cold rain wetting him. (A place in
> the world, a definite status, a precise relationship
> with the rest of men. Even if it had to be one of
> open hostility, it was his, created by him.)[114]

Richard Lehan describes this horrible murder as effectively
bolting the "door between [Dyar] and humanity." As he says,
"both Bigger and Dyar have made such extreme commitments

to themselves that they forever isolate themselves from the rest of the world unlike Bellow's Joseph and Camus' plague-stricken [who] are able to reaffirm their initial identity and to return to the original community."[115] From what we learn about both Bigger and Dyar, neither would be willing to relinquish his newly created identity, since both were without any before their crimes, suffering as they were from self-alienation. Both again seem to be examples of Camus' innocent murderers. Similarly, Cass Kingsolving in William Styron's Set This House on Fire is an innocent murderer intent on returning logic and order to an absurd environment. His rebellion "expresses a nostalgia for innocence and an appeal to the essence of being. But one day nostalgia takes up arms and assumes the responsibility of total guilt; in other words, adopts murder and violence."[116]

What Camus calls the innocent murderer, Hassan calls the rebel-victim. Whatever the term used, this modern antihero contains within himself a dual heritage, exhibiting traits of both the eternal rebel, Prometheus, and the eternal victim, Sisyphus (who also rebelled in favor of life). Through the epigraph he chose, Wright evidently was identifying his hero with another archetypal victim, Job:

> Even today is my complaint rebellious,
> My stroke is heavier than my groaning.

Notably Wright has selected a passage that illustrates Job's Promethean defiance; the verse (23:2) appears as part of the dialogue between Job and his friends in which he defends himself, proclaiming his righteousness and unjust treatment at the hand of God. In Frye's essay, Job is his example of the pharmakos or victim, and Prometheus is the archetype of the tragic hero, the figure "who is human and yet of a heroic size which often has in it the suggestion of divinity."[117] The "central principle of tragic irony is that whatever exceptional happens to the hero should be causally out of line with his character";[118] for example, the story of Job is a tragic irony since he is a pharmakos, unfairly victimized but incapable of making a tragic Promethean figure of himself. As I have pointed out, Native Son is also tragic irony since Bigger, like the heroes in Saul Bellow's novels, is a random victim unable to attain tragic stature because of the limitations of his nature.[119]

Bigger as pharmakos is neither completely innocent nor entirely guilty. As Frye defines him,

> He [the pharmakos] is innocent in the sense that
> what happens to him is far greater than anything
> he has done provokes, like the mountaineer whose
> shout brings down an avalanche. He is guilty in
> the sense that he is a member of a guilty society,
> or living in a world where such injustices are an
> inescapable part of existence. [120]

Bigger, although he is guilty of murder, is still imbued with
a certain basic innocence since what happens to him seems
out of proportion to his crime. In Frye's scheme, therefore,
Native Son is incongruously ironic, a condition "in which all
attempts to transfer guilt to a victim give that victim something of the dignity of innocence. " The archetype in this category is Christ, "the perfectly innocent victim excluded from
human society. "[121] Bigger is no paragon of virtue but he is
identified with Christ by Wright. [122] Furthermore, although
Bigger is a killer, somehow society overreacts to him, calling him a black ape, a sub-human creature, a monster. He
is treated like Yakov Bok in Bernard Malamud's The Fixer
(1966):

> A hand reached forth and plucked him in by his
> Jewish beard--Yakov Bok, a freethinking Jew in
> a brick factory in Kiev, yet any Jew, any plausible
> Jew--to be the Tsar's adversary and victim; chosen
> to murder the corpse His Majesty had furnished
> free; to be imprisoned, starved, degraded, chained
> like an animal to a wall although he was innocent.
> Why? because no Jew was innocent in a corrupt
> state, the most visible sign of its corruption its
> fear and hatred of those it persecuted. [123]

Across the world Jews have been treated as eternal victims.
In America the Negro has been the ubiquitous scapegoat.

Aware of this country's predilection for punishing innocent blacks for its own crimes, Wright symbolically presents Bigger in Messianic images, as a black Christ sacrificed for his race. For example, when Bigger is captured,
the police stretch out his arms "as though about to crucify
him" and place their feet on his wrists (229). When his family visits him in jail, Bigger feels like Christ. Seeing that
they are ashamed of him, Bigger is convinced that they should
instead be proud since he has "taken fully upon himself the
crime of being black. " He feels that they ought to "look at
him and go home contented, feeling that their shame was

washed away" (252). While wearing a cross given him by his
mother's preacher,[124] Bigger chances to see a burning cross
set up by the Ku Klux Klan. Cursing, he rips off his own
cross, shrilly asserting, "'I can die without a cross! '" (287).
In his anger, his own body "seemed a flaming cross as words
boiled hysterically out of him" (288). Not only does Bigger
assume the Christlike attributes of being a sacrificial victim,
but he becomes his own vehicle of crucifixion. Like Camus'
rebel, "he is acting in the name of certain values which are
still indeterminate but which he feels are common to himself
and to all men."[125] He has acted in behalf of his race and
its displacement; although he is an individual man he transcends his uniqueness to represent higher values of order and
reason; as Brignano suggests,

> Although Bigger is estranged from both the religion
> and folk culture of his race ... [he] can still re-
> present the Negro in abstract terms of Negro re-
> sponses to their being placed outside of many as-
> pects of the American Dream.[126]

Again he reminds the reader of Yakov Bok, who says to his
absent father-in law,

> 'Live, Shmuel. Let me die for you.'[127]

Whereas Yakov Bok waits years to come to trial, Bigger's trial is swift and merciless. Its outcome is predeter-
mined, the result of his being black and despised. Bigger's
motivation for Mary's murder had been the fear that came
from the knowledge that he could never explain his presence
in her bedroom. His sacrifice is therefore, on the one hand,
inevitable in a white society. And yet because Wright has
depicted him through frequent Messianic symbols and identified him outright with Job, his sacrifice is also incongrous.
He simply does not deserve the maltreatment he has been
given for twenty years, nor does he deserve the accusations
leveled at him during the trial, nor the vile epithets appearing in the papers.[128] Furthermore, since Bigger has acted
out of a need to express himself in human terms, those hor-
rifying murders could be regarded as innocent acts. He, for
one, does not consider himself guilty. And society, in attempting to lay all the blame on him, manages to create a
certain innocence in this frightened black youth, whose life
has been nothing more than a slow dance of death. Thus his
role as scapegoat is both inevitable and incongruous: his
blackness destines him to the role but does not justify it.

It is probably predictable that numerous arguments have been waged over the identity of Bigger Thomas. [129] One side argues that Bigger functions primarily as a symbol for his race or for all underprivileged men; thus he is Everyman. The other side contends that Bigger is more than a function of a protest novel, that he is indeed an individual with personal fears and desires, most notable his very private dread of death and his urge to be accepted into society. He is, to these critics, very simply, a man.

Because the first school of thinkers tends to regard Native Son solely as a proletarian novel, a protest novel written from a communistic perspective, they fail to see that Bigger's personality is explored. They believe Max's argument that Bigger multiplied twelve million times will yield "'the psychology of the Negro people,'" and, as a consequence, they, like Max, cannot see Bigger as a single individual (333). But an exchange between Max and Bigger has been identified by Donald B. Gibson[130] as a key scene for revealing the mistaken position of critics who favor the social or symbolic function of Bigger:

> [Max:] 'Well, this thing's bigger than you, son. In a certain sense, every Negro in America's on trial out there today. '

> [Bigger:] 'They going to kill me anyhow' (312). (italics mine)

The two men's opposing perspectives on just what Bigger is recur in the final scene when Bigger reveals to a horrified Max that he has accepted himself. Gibson allows that the tension revolving around Bigger's status is not resolved until the end of the book; but he also insists that clues to the dénouement appear throughout the first two sections.

As Gibson points out, Bigger could not be expected to understand Max's speech since it deals with him in abstract, symbolic terms. Instead he intuits its meaning from Max's tone, feeling proud because "Max had made the speech all for him, to save his life. It was not the meaning of the speech that gave him pride, but the mere act of it" (339). Since Max's attempt to save Bigger's life is doomed from the start, Gibson argues that the significant problem is whether or not Bigger will be able to save himself "by coming to terms with himself. This we see him doing as we observe him during long, solitary hours of minute introspection and self-analysis. " (131)

Bigger's final victory is that he does arrive "at a definition of self which is his own and different from that as-
signed to him by everyone else in the novel. "[132] But before
he can discover himself, he has to shed the misconceptions
about himself that the world has taught him. He must, in
other words, see himself through his own eyes and not through
someone else's.

Fittingly, Wright entitled Part I "Fear." For fear in
all its disguises controls Bigger's life. He is afraid of specifics, like whites or stealing or his gang. But he is also
haunted by a more pervasive and less directed sense of dread,
where no particular object can be identified as the cause of
his discomfort. On the superficial everyday non-cognitive
level, Bigger fears; underneath, on the ontological level, Bigger fears. Therefore, for him to live from day to day on
any sort of level at all, Bigger must repress his fear, hide
it from his conscious self:

> [H]is courage to live depended upon how success-
> fully his fear was hidden from his consciousness....
> As long as he could remember, he had never been
> responsible to anyone. The moment a situation be-
> came so that it exacted something of him, he re-
> belled. That was the way he lived; he passed his
> days trying to defeat or gratify powerful impulses
> in a world he feared (36).

Although Bigger ultimately rebels by murdering, he
first rebels against society by mentally negating its distaste-
ful elements; by blotting things out, to use Wright's phrase.
As I have suggested, this "blotting out" becomes a major motif in the novel.

When Bigger is with the Daltons he repeatedly tries
to blot them out since they make him so uncomfortable. At
their home to be interviewed by Mr. Dalton, Bigger impul-
sively blots out this well-meaning but misguided philanthropist
because he cannot tolerate the atmosphere of wealth surrounding him. Dalton ruins his composure to the extent that Bigger blots himself out. He begins to pose, to play the role
he thinks is expected of him:

> He stood with his knees slightly bent, his lips
> partly open, his shoulders stooped; and his eyes
> held a look that went only to the surface of things
> (42).

This role-playing under stress is paralleled by the heroes in both The Long Dream and The Outsider.

In these scenes with the Daltons Wright is playing with words: "Daltonism" is a form of color blindness. Wright seems to be saying that although the Daltons try to be color blind and not see Bigger's color, they really don't see him at all. And since they are totally blind to his reality, Bigger will be able to get away with murder right under their eyes. The physically blind Mrs. Dalton is the only witness to Bigger's crime, but the others do not even suspect him because he is invisible to them. Bigger has no more impact on them than Ralph Ellison's Invisible Man has on the white people he meets. [133]

Before murdering Mary, Bigger had wanted to blot out her and her communist boyfriend, Jan, as he drove them to a restaurant in the Black Belt. Their bizarre behavior--a mixture of concern and almost flippant disregard for his feelings--had driven Bigger to despair. His self-hate was so great at that moment that he had longed to blot out the entire car, himself included. Treated like a speciman rather than a man, Bigger wavered between fear and hatred of these odd people. But Jan and Mary had chatted on, oblivious to Bigger's emotional upheaval as he squirmed beside them.

It isn't until after the murder that Bigger truly sees his home and family for what they are. When he realizes that he hates the apartment and all its inhabitants, even himself, he wants to blot them out. All his life, he feels, his family has shackled him, prevented him from living his own life. Like the whites they have been instrumental in his victimization.

But then, in the middle of his despair, he realizes with a start that in killing Mary he has created a new life for himself. The murder becomes a "barrier of protection between him and a world he feared" (90). He is suddenly proud of the murder, recognizing it as a personally satisfying act, something that no one can take from him. It becomes the "hidden meaning of his life" (90). All the inchoate ideas that have disturbed him for twenty years are taking on shape and significance. He is creating a self (90).

This new awareness of himself and the world, born of rebellion, shows him the potential inherent in the circumstance that everyone is blind--has always been blind. As

Robert Bone observes, Bigger begins to use this knowledge immediately,

> Bigger learns to exploit the blindness of others, 'fooling the white folks' during his interrogation, and this is again something deep in his racial heritage, springing from a long tradition of telling whites whatever they want to hear.[134]

Bigger later plans to cash in on the world's blindness by collecting ransom money from the Daltons:

> Now, who on earth would think that he, a black timid Negro boy, would murder and burn a rich white girl and would sit and wait for his breakfast like this? Elation filled him (91).

Out of rather hideous conditions, this anti-hero has created a new life of infinite possibilities. And Bigger exults in his rebirth, eager to explore strange new lands.

But Bigger is not yet totally free. He is still in bondage to certain old ideas and relationships--especially where his own people are concerned. He feels alienated from them as he did before, angry with them for not asserting themselves as a group. And, although he does have a dim hope for their future, his immediate reaction is to blot them out. He does realize, however, that the whites have conditioned him to fear and distrust his own people (98).

Bigger regularly uses sex and liquor to blot out the world. But after sexually having his girl Bessie, he yearns to blot her out because she is too limited for him. Blind like the others, she circles continually in her narrow meaningless orbit (119). Bigger obviously does not love her: as he himself admits later, he had to have a girl so he had Bessie (298).

Suffused with a feeling of power and emboldened by his newly acquired ability to control his own fate, Bigger at least temporarily "blot[s] out the fear of death" (127). Not only is he now confident of his capabilities, but he also revels in a sense of fullness, for he is free of the invisible binding forces that have plagued him for twenty years. He asserts this new strength during his examination by Mr. Dalton and the police, momentarily leading them off the track by heading them toward Jan and the other communists.

At the same time that Bigger is acting boldly to save
his skin, his mind is covertly continually hovering over his
crime, caressing and probing it, trying to discover its meaning for him. His earliest conclusions foreshadow Max's
speech. For deep down he is convinced that Mary's murder
wasn't accidental, that he had in truth "killed many times before, only on those other times there had been no handy victim or circumstance to make visible or dramatic his will to
kill" (90). Suddenly he sees this single consummated murder
as the hidden meaning of his life; jealously he protects it,
having a "kind of terrified pride" that someday he will be able
to take credit for this crime publicly. "It was as though he
had an obscure but deep debt to fulfill to himself in accepting
the deed" (90-91). He is learning to accept the consequences
of his actions, as Sartre says all men must. Through this
sense of being responsible for himself Bigger is being reborn.
Mary's murder and its violent aftermath have struck a chord
deep within Bigger's soul that vibrates with a hitherto unknown
intensity. Its resounding music drowns out Bigger's old per-
sonality--the timid, fearful black boy conditioned by society to
feel innately inferior to whites.

In a caste system which isn't supposed even to exist,
the hatred engendered by oppression is enormous. And so,
because whites have treated him as an untouchable, Bigger
sees them as the enemy, despising them, eager to do violence
against them given the chance. Thus it is not surprising that
he feels no regrets over having murdered Mary Dalton, since
he can rationalize that his action was justified "by the fear
and shame she had made him feel" (97). Because of their
caste differences Mary had been no more real to Bigger than
he to her. As far as Bigger was concerned, whites weren't
even people--they were a "great natural force" that directed
his actions (97). Once Bigger realizes that they are vulner-
able--even mortal--he is freed from the mythology of their
omnipotence. No longer will they be able to control him by
fear and coercion. Bigger has discovered not only that he
can murder whites, but that he can get away with it. It is
truly a revelation for him. From the moment that he becomes certain that "his whole life was caught up in a supreme
and meaningful act" (99), he heads toward a new life, a new
identity forged out of blood and violence.

Although Bigger seems to be steadily progressing toward self-integration, he still has not resolved the problem
of how to get along in this world. Confident of his newly
discovered inner strengths, he is still frequently susceptible

to the whites' intimidation. And blacks continue to annoy him. Bigger knows both fear and temerity, fluctuating between a wild dream of escaping and a stubborn determination to bluff his way out of trouble. He finally decides to stay, confident that the whites' blind pride will protect him since they will continue to deny that blacks are capable of planning and executing such a bold crime (cf. pp. 125, 138, 159, 207). Recognizing his invisible power, Bigger, as we have seen, recklessly plots to collect ransom money for Mary. Although he is representative of the metaphysical rebel, he is still driven by practical and mundane desires. It isn't until the very end of the book that Bigger is released from such dross concerns.

In the meantime, Bigger's sense of security stems from his gun. Not armed with a glib tongue, Bigger instinctively reaches for a weapon whenever he feels threatened. For example, when Bessie asks him if he has harmed Mary, Bigger automatically longs for "something in his hand, something solid and heavy: his gun, a knife, a brick" (123). Eventually, Bigger is able to force down this fear that threatens to engulf him, for inside he knows that he can escape whenever he wants to; he controls his own fate now (cf. pp. 127, 140, 161-162).

Clever and cool as he has been, Bigger finally falls out of the catbird seat. Because he could not bear the thought of possibly seeing Mary's bones in the furnace, he has avoided shaking down the ashes. As the newspaper reporters wait there for further news of the crime, smoke begins to pour into the basement. Annoyed with Bigger, who is immobilized by fear, the men open the bin to clear the vent and in so doing discover Mary's bones. Bigger has trapped himself. His discovery seems inevitable and almost right since he has committed such an ugly crime and got away with it so smoothly; society must be put back in order. And yet, it is incongruous that the perfect crime should be ruined by a simple human failing; and somehow the reader doesn't want Bigger to get caught. (An analogous dramatic irony and tension surround Oedipux Rex as he unwittingly curses himself and sets out to effect his own downfall.) When Mary's body is discovered, Bigger relapses into the fear-hate-fear syndrome identified by Horace Cayton;[135] although he longs to strike back he must flee. Driven by his reappearing fear, he kills Bessie by smashing her face in with a brick and throwing her body down an air-shaft.

Once more Bigger discovers a bloody and violent truth

about himself: that he is free. Wright tells us that these
two murders have given Bigger the chance to experience the
consequences of his actions; that he is aware of the fact that
he can no longer be locked in the ghetto and forgotten. He
knows intuitively that his life up until this time has lacked
wholeness, that his will and mind have been fractured. The
only real need that he can articulate now is his desire to
merge with the rest of the world, "to lose himself in it so
he could find himself, to be allowed a chance to live like
others, even though he was black" (204). (This need is much
more profound than his earlier ones for bodily satisfaction.)
But Bigger's crime has forever sealed him off from other
people. And so, his self-integration can be reached only at
the expense of his social integration. Like Cross Damon,
he has used murder to create a new world for himself, one
which he will inhabit entirely alone. Bigger is not asking to
be God; he is simply asking to be a man. And since even
rebellion cannot brook murder, Bigger must himself die to
attain metaphysical unity with other men.

Even though he feels that he has acted in behalf of
other blacks, Bigger continues to have trouble sorting out how
he feels about them; although he hates them, he identifies with
them. And as a fugitive hiding in the Black Belt, Bigger
learns that blacks in their turn feel ambivalent about him:

> 'Jack, you mean t' stan' there 'n' say yuh'd
> give tha' nigger up t' the white folks?'
> 'Damn right Ah would! ... Ef Ah knowed where
> tha' nigger wuz ah'd turn im up 'n' git these white
> folks off me.' ...
> 'But, Jack, ... [y] uh gotta stan' up 'n' fight
> these folks' (212).

One black is tolerant, the other wants to pay the devil his
due. When Bigger hears this he clutches his gun, ready to
use it on his own people if they attempt to turn him in.

From the moment he is captured to the time of his
sentencing, Bigger alternates between defiance and depression.
On the roof, about to be captured, Bigger resolves to rely on
himself and defy the police, but once he is arrested he slips
into a physiological stupor, a blessing that allows him to be
oblivious to his torture while his mind actively seeks an answer to the meaning of his life. Bigger's struggle to find
direction and comfort is agonizing--so much so that he flirts
with the idea of suicide. Tormented by failure, he desires

to reunite with the "dark face of ancient waters" because he cannot rejoin the society of men (234). He thinks he can quell the troublesome inner desires that will not be denied--and that have driven him to a second murder--only if he dies. This is Bigger's darkest hour of despair.

The terrors of the trial add to his misery and confusion. During the trial he hears Max explain that his life style had been one composed of total guilt, that his "'entire attitude toward life is a crime!'" (335). Max blames society for Bigger's aberrant behavior. Then rather melodramatically he pleads to the court to have Bigger incarcerated rather than electrocuted, so that society can grant him an identity by giving him a number.

But Bigger wants to be more than a number. He wants what Allen Wheelis calls a "coherent sense of self," where what he does and feels makes sense, has meaning;[136] where he will experience fullness and integration; where he will have a moral code to help direct his actions. And he finds an identity and code by accepting the murder that sets him free (234). Although Bigger's conception of what is immoral deviates from society's, he has chosen what he believes is right for himself.

Finally, in a moving scene, Bigger lets down the wall that he had erected between himself and the rest of the world. He allows himself to confide in Max, speaking to him "as he had never spoken to anyone in his life; not even to himself" (305). This confession acts as a catalyst, allowing him to examine his relationship to other people. And what he envisions is so daring that it weakens him; for he sees a future clothed in a blinding light that melts away all differences among men. No longer does Bigger wish to die.

But since he has opened his soul to the dream of brotherhood, he is more than ever open to "the hot blasts of hate" (308). And because he is in limbo between an inherited unwanted identity and a self-created welcome one, he is vulnerable to all attacks on his psyche, undecided as to whether he should have hope or give way to despair. He sees two conflicting pictures of himself: one where he is isolated, ready to die; and another where he is about to begin a new life under society's protection.

When Max visits him on the eve of his execution, Bigger admits that he is vulnerable, never truly having been a

hard man (a difficult disclosure for someone who acted so
tough all his life--like Studs Lonigan permitting his poetic
nature to surface when he is with Lucy). But Bigger's faith
in himself is still uncertain until he listens to Max's impassioned raving about capitalism and the proletariat. Max
claims that the world has stopped growing because of a few
selfish doubters who own all the property; that, furthermore,
these men protect their holdings at the expense of men like
Bigger who long to share the world's wealth. Max swears
that the world itself is held together by faith, by men's beliefs. This statement strikes a fire in Bigger's imagination.
He proudly announces his new credo, belief in himself, to a
horrified Max. Having concluded, thanks to Max's political
pep talk, that it was right of him to want a part of the world,
Bigger argues that he should have fought for recognition as
a human being. Since murder was the only way for him to
rebel successfully, his crime was a morally fine act for him.
So Bigger exults, laughing and shouting,

> 'I believe in myself ... [W]hat I killed for, I am!
> It must've been pretty deep in me to make me kill!
> ... It must have been good! When a man kills,
> it's for something.... I didn't know I was really
> alive in this world until I felt things hard enough
> to kill for 'em! (358).

Bigger's jubilation in the face of death corresponds to Kirilov's and Oedipus' responses to their fate. Camus says,

> Kirilov must kill himself out of love for human-
> ity. ... Thus, it is not despair that urges him
> to death, but love of his neighbor for his own sake.
> Before terminating in blood an indescribable spiri-
> tual adventure, Kirilov makes a remark as old as
> human suffering: 'All is well!' [137]

And of Oedipus,

> Then a tremendous remark rings out: 'Despite so
> many ordeals, my advanced age and the nobility of
> my soul make me conclude that all is well.' ...
> [A]nd that remark is sacred. It echoes in the wild
> and limited universe of man. It teaches that all is
> not, has not been, exhausted.... It makes of fate
> a human matter, which must be settled among
> men. [138]

Bigger's existential self-realization terrifies Max, who had been pursuing the dialectics of communism. For Bigger launches himself onto a higher plane of existence where he alone is responsible for himself and his crimes. There, he accepts himself as a murderer, creating his own values and even his own world where he is an heroic figure. Esther M. Jackson calls Native Son

> perhaps ... the most moving and passion-filled portrait of a Negro as man in revolt against Fate ... a record of man's dramatic encounter with Fate in the climate of the absurd.[139]

Bigger has thrown himself into battle with absurdity and won.

Bigger's existential self-creation is strongly positive, analogous to what Abraham Maslow calls the "peak-experience" in self-actualized people. Like the subjects Maslow interviewed, Bigger loses his fear and anxiety at the moment of insight, feeling a unity within himself and a transcendence of his conflicts. He seems to have become himself at long last. Maslow defines this experience

> as an episode, or a spurt in which the powers of the person come together in a particularly efficient and intensely enjoyable way, and in which he is more integrated and less split, more open for experience, more idiosyncratic, more perfectly expressive or spontaneous, or fully functioning, ... more ego-transcending, more independent of his lower needs, etc. He becomes in these episodes more truly himself, more perfectly actualizing his potentialities, closer to the core of his Being, more fully human.[140]

Although Bigger does not have an opportunity to repeat this experience or even to act upon it, since he is about to die in the electric chair, he nonetheless delights in knowing himself, however fleetingly, and thus goes to his death wearing a "faint, wry, bitter smile" (359). At this stage in his life Wright was obviously attracted to existential thinking; it isn't until the end of The Outsider that he seems to reject it, finding it too nihilistic.

In summary, Native Son protests against man's inhumanity to man, specifically that of the whites' in regard to

the blacks. A proletarian novel designed to bring the plight
of the black masses to public attention, this book also illustrates the quest for identity observable in existential literature.
It is therefore possible to read the book both as an indictment of
racism and as exploration into the nature of man. It poses an
answer to the question asked in one of Langston Hughes' poems,
"What happens to a dream deferred?"[142] According to Wright,
it explodes. Futhermore, since Wright saw the black man as the
metaphor for modern man, he equates Bigger's quest for identity
with that of all men. To quote Wright: "The voice of the American Negro is rapidly becoming the most representative voice of
America and of oppressed people anywhere in the world today."[143]
But clearly it was of considerable significance to Wright that his
hero be seen first as a black and then as a man.

Native Son therefore continues the story of black oppression and estrangement begun in The Long Dream and
Lawd Today. With Native Son, however, a third element ap-
pears--that of rebellion. For Bigger is not only an unwilling
slave but--unlike Fish and Jake--he acts definitely to end his
repression, the deed which serves to free him being, of
course, his first murder. But, ironically, the key to his
freedom is also the final blow to his hopes for social acceptance. Accordingly, although he dies a free man, he also
dies a lonely man. Moreover, the environment that Bigger
has managed to transcend has in reality controlled his mode
of expression, leaving him only one way to end his servitude.
Because Bigger was not give the freedom or the means to
develop a healthy personality, he became a mean-spirited,
emotionally stunted delinquent. Poor and black and of limited
intelligence, he is unable to fight his way out of the ghetto--
physical and psychological--through conventional methods since
society has closed all its doors to him. The only way left
is for him to rebel in the most dramatic and shocking way
he can--by killing.

Although society has forced this act upon him, Bigger
executes a coup de grace by rejecting society's evaluation of
the murder as morally debilitating. By interpreting the deed
as morally sound and beneficent, Bigger is able to escape the
confines of his environment and gain an identity. Instead of
remaining a victim of naturalistic forces, Bigger, by the end
of Native Son, has become the master of his fate. Though
still a pariah, Bigger is no longer invisible.

A more extreme advocate of individual freedom is Cross
Damon, existential hero of The Outsider, whose story takes up
where Native Son ends.

Notes

1. That is, in this particular case, a novel written by a
    black man, in dialect, from the perspective of another
    black man. It is closely related to Raman K.
    Singh's concept of a "Soul Novel" which, according to him,
    "implies two basic elements: one, a rejection of the
    machine-culture of western society; and two, a recog-
    nition that the black life-style can act as a living,
    potent force capable of saving the soul of a decadent
    west." His examples are Cane and Invisible Man
    ("The Black Novel and Its Tradition," The Colorado
    Quarterly, XX [Summer, 1971], 27).

2. This technique of ironical juxtaposition, probably learned
    from the proletarian writers, also appears in Native
    Son; See Chapter III, pp. 68-69 for discussion and
    examples.

3. "Review of Lawd Today, by Richard Wright," CLA Jour-
    nal, VII (March, 1964), 269.

4. Dan McCall, The Example of Richard Wright (New York:
    Harcourt, Brace and World, 1969), p. 19.

5. Margolies, Art of Richard Wright, p. 101.

6. Brignano, Richard Wright: An Introduction to the Man
    and His Works, pp. 22-23.

7. Kent, "Adventure of Western Culture," 335.

8. See Chapter II, p. 33.

9. McCall, The Example of Richard Wright, p. 22.

10. Richard Wright, Lawd Today (New York: Walker and
    Company, 1963), p. 31. (All subsequent page refer-
    ences to this work will appear in parentheses in the text.)

11. In this scene Wright explains the details of the numbers
    racket, an unnecessary intrusion by the implied au-
    thor who also explains how the letter sorting works
    in the post office. One assumes that Wright was at-
    tempting to fill in the gaps for an audience unfamiliar
    with these common aspects of black life (see Chapter V).

12. Wayne C. Booth, The Rhetoric of Fiction (Chicago: The

University of Chicago Press, 1967), p. 198, n. 25.

13. McCall, The Example of Richard Wright, p. 20.

14. Brignano says of this: "Wright does not fancy his heroes in Lawd Today to be lovable creatures maintaining a philosophical cheerfulness in a land of plenty turned barren because of the Great Depression. Their happy moments arrive as relief from both the hardships and the drabness of the Black Belt; however all too often these moments come in the forms of liquor, narcotics, and illicit sexual indulgence.... Just as the actions of Bigger Thomas ... are socially repugnant and despicable, so are those of Jake Jackson and other Negroes in Lawd Today. Wright implies in both novels that framing the superstructure of society dominated by the white world is capitalism, which is a force that smothers and denudes the individual personality" (p. 23).

15. Kent, "Adventure of Western Culture," 339.

16. Nelson Algren, "Remembering Richard Wright," Nation, CXCII (Jan. 28, 1961), 85.

17. Black Voices, ed. by Abraham Chapman (New York: New American Library, 1968), p. 540.

18. See: Keneth Kinnamon, "Native Son: The Personal, Social, and Political Background," Phylon, XXX (Spring, 1969), 66-72; and Frederic Wertham, "An Unconscious Determinant in Native Son," Journal of Clinical Psychopathology and Psychotherapy, VI, 1 (July, 1944), 111-115.

19. Camus, The Myth of Sisyphus, trans. Justin O'Brien (New York: Vintage Books, 1955), pp. 90, 91.

20. Frye, Anatomy of Criticism, p. 187.

21. See Chapter II, p. 15 et passim.

22. James E. Miller, Quests Surd and Absurd (Chicago: University of Chicago Press, 1967), p. 14.

23. Ibid., p. viii.

24. Frye, Anatomy of Criticism, p. 34.

25. Ibid., p. 192.

26. Ibid., p. 236.

27. Ibid., p. 223.

28. Ibid., p. 237.

29. "How 'Bigger' Was Born," Black Voices, ed. by Abraham Chapman (New York: New American Library, 1968), p. 554.

30. See: Phyllis R. Klotman and Melville Yancey, "Gift of Double Vision: Possible Political Implications of Richard Wright's Self-Conscious' Thesis," CLA Journal, XVI, 1 (September, 1972), 106-116.

31. "How 'Bigger' Was Born," Black Voices, p. 546.

32. "I Tried to be a Communist," The God That Failed, ed. by Richard Crossman (New York: Harper & Row, Publishers, 1963), p. 118.

33. Albert Murray, "Something Different, Something More," Anger and Beyond, ed. by Herbert Hill (New York: Harper & Row, Publishers, 1968), p. 130.

34. Uncle Tom's Children (New York: Harper & Row, Publishers, 1965), p. 180.

35. Walter B. Rideout, The Radical Novel in the United States, 1900-1954: Some Interrelations of Literature and Society (Cambridge: Harvard University Press, 1956). Rideout recounts the arguments posed by leftwing critics attempting to define a true proletarian novel. One group, Rideout reports, contended "that subject matter, the expression of proletarian existence, was the chief characteristic distinguishing the proletarian novel from the usual 'bourgeois' one. Other critics polarized around what was, in terms of tradition in the American radical novel, a more usual definition. They maintained that the only important consideration was the conscious ideology of the author, whether he attempted, whatever his class origin, to work out in his fiction a Marxist analysis of society" (166). Rideout accepts the latter definition as most useful and appropriate.

36. "How 'Bigger' Was Born," Black Voices, p. 557.

37. Brignano, Richard Wright: An Introduction to the Man and His Works, p. 31.

38. Richard Wright, Native Son (New York: Harper & Row, Publishers, 1940), p. 211. (All subsequent page references to this work will appear in parentheses in the text.)

39. Albert Camus, The Rebel, trans. Anthony Bower (New York: Alfred A. Knopf, 1961), p. 10

40. Brignano, Richard Wright: An Introduction to the Man and His Works, p. 31.

41. See Chapter V for a more thorough discussion of this.

42. Charles Child Walcutt, American Literary Naturalism: A Divided Stream (Minneapolis: University of Minnesota Press, 1956), p. 22.

43. It is a narrative technique that allows Wright to avoid direct commentary while reminding the reader of where his sympathies lie (see Chapter V).

44. One is inevitably reminded of Dickens' Mrs. Jellyby Bleak House) who sends money to Africa while neglecting her own family.

45. See Chapter V, pp. 177-179.

46. Hugh Morris Gloster, Negro Voices in American Fiction (Chapel Hill: University of North Carolina Press, 1948), p. 34.

47. Rideout, The Radical Novel in the United States, 1900-1954: Some Interrelations of Literature and Society, p. 261.

48. Richard Wright, "The Man Who Went to Chicago," Eight Men (New York: Pyramid Books, 1969), p. 172.

49. Crossman, The God That Failed, p. 162.

50. Bone, Pamphlet, p. 22.

51. Donald B. Gibson, "Wright's Invisible Native Son," American Quarterly, XXI (Winter, 1969), 728-738. See also Chapter III, pp. 90-91.

52. For a discussion of Wright and existentialism, see "Reflections on Richard Wright," Anger and Beyond, ed. Herbert Hill (New York: Harper & Row, Publishers, 1968), pp. 196-212.

53. Walcutt, American Literary Naturalism: A Divided Stream, p. 20.

54. Jean Paul Sartre, The Age of Reason, trans. Eric Sutton (New York: Alfred A. Knopf, 1966), p. 320.

55. Sartre, Age, p. 64.

56. Gloster, Negro Voices, p. 233.

57. See Chapter IV, pp. 129-131.

58. Camus, Rebel, p. 13.

59. Ibid., p. 14.

60. Frederick Douglass, Narrative of the Life of Frederick Douglass: An American Slave: Written by Himself (Garden City: Dolphin Books, 1962), p. 74.

61. Camus, Rebel, p. 17.

62. Walcutt, American Literary Naturalism: A Divided Stream, p. 20.

63. Camus, Sisyphus, p. 21.

64. Gibson, "Wright's Invisible," 737.

65. Quoted by David Galloway, The Absurd Hero in American Fiction (Austin: The University of Texas Press, 1970), p. 15.

66. Walcutt, American Literary Naturalism: A Divided Stream, p. 20.

67. Hassan, Radical Innocence: The Contemporary American Novel, p. 27.

68. Camus, Rebel, pp. 23, 25.

69. Brignano, Richard Wright: An Introduction to the Man and His Works, p. 35.

70. Miller, Quests Surd and Absurd, pp. 11-17.

71. Galloway, The Absurd Hero in American Fiction, p. 16, et passim.

72. Richard K. Barksdale, "Alienation and The Anti-Hero in Recent American Fiction," Part I, CLA Journal, XI (Sept., 1966), 6.

73. Hassan, Part I, pp. 9-95.

74. Daniel Bell, The End of Ideology (New York: The Free Press, 1962), p. 358.

75. Ibid., p. 360, et passim.

76. Kenneth Keniston, "Alienation and the Decline of Utopia," American Scholar, XXXIX (1960), 161-200.

77. Barksdale, "Alienation and The Anti-Hero in Recent American Fiction," pp. 1-10.

78. Sidney Finkelstein, Existentialism and Alienation in American Literature (New York: International Publishers, 1965), p. 140.

79. See Chapter II, pp. 30-32. Horney defines the terms in the following manner: "actual self is an all-inclusive term for everything that a person is at a given time: body and soul, healthy and neurotic ... The idealized self is what we are in our irrational imagination, or what we should be according to the dictates of neurotic pride. The real self ... is the 'original' force toward individual growth and fulfillment, with which we may again achieve full identification when freed of the crippling shackles of neurosis" (p. 158). [Italics mine.]

80. Horney, Neurosis and Human Growth: The Struggle Toward Self-Realization, p. 122.

81. Ibid., p. 123.

82. Ibid., p. 157.

83. Ibid., p. 159.

84. Ibid., p. 160.

85. See: Dwight G. Dean, "Alienation: Its Meaning and Measurement," American Sociological Review, XXVI, 5 (Oct., 1961), 753-758; Melvin Seeman, "On the Meaning of Alienation," American Sociological Review, XXIV, 6 (Dec., 1959), 783-791.

86. Quoted by Melvin Seeman, "On the Meaning of Alienation," 790.

87. Allen Wheelis, The Quest for Identity (New York: W. W. Norton and Co., Inc., 1958), p. 19.

88. Ibid., p. 19.

89. See Chapter III, pp. 91 ff.

90. Horney, Neurosis and Human Growth: The Struggle Toward Self-Realization, p. 160.

91. Camus, Sisyphus, p. 21, et passim. The same clash is seen in naturalistic literature where man is torn between his desire for unity with nature and his need to fight it for survival; see Chapter III, pp. 74-75.

92. Ibid., p. 5.

93. Galloway, The Absurd Hero in American Fiction, p. 18.

94. Ibid., p. 18.

95. Camus, Sisyphus, p. 40.

96. Hassan, Radical Innocence: The Contemporary American Novel, p. 6.

97. Ibid., pp. 6-7.

98. See Frye, Anatomy of Criticism, p. 42, and Camus, Rebel, p. 297, for similar observations on the hero's basic innocence in a guilty society.

99. Miller, Quests Surd and Absurd, p. 5.

100. Richard Lehan, "Existentialism in Recent American Fiction: The Demonic Quest," Recent American Fiction, ed. by Joseph Waldmeir (Boston: Houghton Mifflin Co., 1963), p. 64 (originally appeared in Texas Studies in Literature and Languages, I [Summer, 1959], 181-202).

101. Ibid., p. 65.

102. Hassan, Radical Innocence: The Contemporary American Novel, p. 18.

103. Ibid., p. 31.

104. James Baldwin, Notes of a Native Son (New York: Bantam, 1968), pp. 27-28.

105. Camus, Rebel, p. 17.

106. See Camus, The Fall (trans. Justin O'Brien [New York: Vintage Books, 1956]) when Jean-Baptiste Clamence states, "Like many men, they [the criminals] had no longer been able to endure anonymity, and that impatience had contributed to leading them to unfortunate extremities" (26).

107. Camus, Rebel, p. 297.

108. Ibid., pp. 284, 297.

109. Ibid., p. 40.

110. Ibid., p. 15.

111. Jean-Paul Sartre, "Existentialism is a Humanism" (trans. Mairet), Existentialism from Dostoevsky to Sartre, ed. by Walter Kaufman (New York: The World Publishing Co., 1972), p. 290.

112. Paul Bowles, Let It Come Down (New York: Random House, Inc., 1952), p. 241.

113. Ibid., p. 266.

114. Ibid., pp. 310, 311.

115. Lehan, "Existentialism in Recent American Fiction: The Demonic Quest," p. 73.

116. Camus, Rebel, p. 105.

117. Frye, Anatomy of Criticism, p. 42.

118. Ibid., p. 41.

119. See Chapter III, pp. 62-63.

120. Frye, Anatomy of Criticism, p. 41.

121. Ibid., p. 42.

122. As are, in varying degrees, other Wright heroes, such as Chris Sims (The Long Dream), Cross Damon (The Outsider), and Fred Daniels ("The Man Who Lived Underground"). See also "Bright and Morning Star": "The wrongs and sufferings of black men had taken the place of Him nailed to the Cross ... " (Uncle Tom's Children, p. 185).

123. Bernard Malamud, The Fixer (New York: Dell Publishing Co., Inc., 1971), p. 256.

124. Ministers are portrayed in less than complimentary lights in most of Wright's fiction. The one exception is the Reverend Dan Taylor in "Fire and Cloud," who leads the poverty-stricken masses of both races in a demonstration of strength against the forces of authority during the depression.

125. Camus, Rebel, p. 16.

126. Brignano, Richard Wright: An Introduction to the Man and His Works, p. 32.

127. Malamud, The Fixer, p. 222.

128. Critics were loath to accept these accounts as valid representations of even yellow journalism, finding them far too strong; for example, Hubert Creekmore, a white reviewer, says that "The manner and content of these newspapers exceed belief" ("Social Factors in Native Son," The University of Kansas City Review, VII [1941], 140). And yet, excerpts

from the press' coverage of the Robert Nixon case in 1938, quoted by Keneth Kinnamon ("Native Son: The Personal, Social, and Political Background," Phylon, XXX [Spring, 1969], 66-72), show that Wright was not exaggerating; for example, a headline: "'Brick Slayer Is Likened to Jungle Beast'" (69).

129. See, for example: Gibson, "Wright's Invisible." James Baldwin, "Everybody's Protest Novel," Notes of a Native Son (New York: A Bantam Book, 1968), pp. 9-17. David Britt, "Native Son: Watershed of Negro Protest Literature" and John F. Bayliss, "Native Son: Protest or Psychological Study?" Negro American Literature Forum, I, 1 (Fall, 1967), pages unnumbered. James G. Kennedy, "The Content and Form of Native Son," and Annette Conn, "Comment," College English, XXXIV, 2 (Nov., 1972), 269-286.

130. Gibson, "Wright's Invisible," 729.

131. Ibid., 731.

132. Ibid., 729.

133. Michel Fabre has noted this theme of invisibility in his Les Noirs Américains (Paris: Librairie Armand Colin, 1967, 1970): "Le thème de la non-existence du Noir reveint constamment dans sa littérature: dans Dusk of Dawn, W. E. B. DuBois évoque un monde de phantasmes semblable à celui du mythe platonicien de la caverne. Richard Wright emploie l'image du souterrain dans "The Man Who Lived Underground" ou des ombres dans "The Man Who Killed a Shadow" pour montrer à la fois l'irréalité du Noir, et l'irréalité, pour lui, du monde qui l'entoure. Ralph Ellison fait de cette transparence le sujet même du roman Invisible Man. James Baldwin insiste sur l'anonymat et intitule un recueil d'essais Nobody Knows My Name" (p. 109).

134. Bone, Pamphlet, p. 146.

135. See Horace Cayton, "Ideological Forces in the Work of Negro Writers," Anger and Beyond, pp. 42-43.

136. See Chapter III, p. 81.

137. Camus, Sisyphus, p. 80.

138. Ibid., pp. 90, 91.

139. Esther Merle Jackson, "The American Negro and the Image of the Absurd," Phylon, XXIII (1962), 364.

140. Abraham H. Maslow, Toward a Psychology of Being (New York: Van Nostrand Reinhold Company, 1968), p. 97.

141. Langston Hughes, "Harlem," Black Voices, p. 430.

142. Richard Wright, "The Literature of the Negro in the United States," White Man, Listen! (Garden City, N.Y.: Anchor Books), p. 72.

143. Wright, "Literature of Negro in U.S., 'White Man, Listen!, p. 101.

CHAPTER IV

THE REBEL AND THE ISOLATE

The longer Wright remained exiled in France, the
more he was accused of neglecting his southern origins. In
this respect, reviewers were especially critical of The Outsider, written while Wright lived in Paris.   One critic, Saunders Redding, went so far as to say that "In going to live
abroad Richard Wright had cut the roots that once sustained
him.... "[1] Having resided abroad for several years before
writing this novel, Wright undoubtedly did lose touch with
some of his American heritage.   And, caught as he was in
the maelstrom of French existentialism, he couldn't help but
create a book highly influenced by this philosophy.   Furthermore, his own background had already led him independently
to many of the same conclusions the existentialists were
reaching.   As Wright said of this relationship after reading
Kierkegaard, Heidegger, Camus, and Sartre; "'They are writing of things that I have been thinking, writing and feeling
all of my life!'"[2]

What Wright developed in The Outsider is a hybrid;
a book whose main character has ancestors spanning two
centuries, not only in the American Adams of Hawthorne,
Melville, Twain, James, and Fitzgerald, but also in the dispossessed outsiders of Dostoyevsky, Mann, Sartre, Camus,
and Genet.   Cross Damon is the double helix of American
innocence and European nihilism.   He is more alienated than
his American predecessors and more influenced by his environment than his European contemporaries.   Like Bigger
Thomas before him, he is the result of a complicated battle
among the forces of naturalism, Marxism, Freudianism, and
existentialism.   He spouts existential precepts but remains
an example of man trapped by his background and surroundings.

Cross Damon can be regarded as a prototype of more

recent American heroes, the rebel-victims identified by Ihab Hassan in Radical Innocence. Instead of creating the last of the American Adams, Wright created the first of the modern American anti-heroes. Therefore, a reasonable alternative to dismay at Wright's failure to create American homespun would be frank admiration for a man who dared to meld the foreign and the near, who recognized the inherent existentialism in the black man's American experience before his critics did.

Stylistically, the book is not without flaw. For, in presenting such a thoroughly existential hero, Wright has employed some rather obviously contrived literary devices--some so contrived in fact, that they weaken the book's mimetic effect (for although the novel centers on the working out of an idea, I believe that Wright was attempting to create people rather than just philosophical positions). The first of these contrivances is the extraordinary coincidence that allows Cross to consciously create a new identity: the subway accident and the mistaken identity. (We must allow this, however, since Wright was determined to give his hero absolute freedom; and the freedom had to arise from a conscious decision on Cross' part to create himself unhampered by the past.) The second series of patent inventions is the continual name-changing that Cross undertakes. Part of becoming a person is taking a name, and Cross takes several as he attempts to discover what he is going to be. Initially he becomes Charles Webb, an immigrant from the Deep South (an identity that occurs to him as he listens to the blues in a cafe); ironically, it is under this innocent alias that he murders his friend. But he soon rejects this image of himself as a naive immigrant. On the train to New York, therefore, he establishes himself as Addison Jordon, graduate of Fisk University; under this pseudonym he meets and captures the imagination of another outsider, Ely Houston, the deformed district attorney of New York City. Cross' third identity is that of a dead man, Lionel Lane--an appropriate identity for a man who seems to have little respect for life.

A third point of weakness is that the philosophy often takes over to the detriment of the story; instead of illustrating, Wright explains.[3] Long speeches ruin the movement of the action. Yet, curiously, this style is akin to that of one of the undisputed geniuses of modern literature, Fyodor Dostoyevsky, who himself often indulged in massive unbroken passages in which one character lectures another, especially in The Brothers Karamazov, whose hero Ivan Karamazov is the

philosophical prototype of Cross Damon. Cross is reminis-
cent not only of Ivan, but also of the nihilist Kirilov in The
Possessed and the logical criminal Raskolnikov in Crime and
Punishment. Perhaps Wright had Dostoyevsky's novels and
heroes in mind as models when he wrote The Outsider, but
Wright's own existential hero, Cross Damon, is too intellectual and intellectualized to be sympathetic or even very believable. [4] In him lies no grand passion: he is not possessed. He is another victim who cannot attain tragic stature. Furthermore, as critics have noted, his actions are
seemingly often not even psychologically motivated. [5] And
yet, all in all, the book remains a fascinating conundrum.
It is, perhaps, in the final analysis, no more obscure or in-
consistent than life itself.

The roots of Cross Damon in the American Adams are
clearly defined in his sense of innocence, place, and self.
According to R. W. B. Lewis, the nineteenth-century American Adam is characterized by his loneliness and innocence and
his need to be tested by society. He is a Walt Whitman, the
solitary individual who arrogantly acknowledges that he is a
self-made man:

> He had to become the maker of his own condition--
> if he were to have any conditions or any achieved
> personality at all.... What is implicit in every
> line of Whitman is the belief that the poet projects
> a world of order and meaning and identity into
> either a chaos or a sheer vacuum; he does not dis-
> cover it. The poet may salute the chaos; but he
> creates the world. [6]

What more existential statement of the fact that man creates
his own values exists? Like the absurd heroes identified by
Camus who feel innocent, Whitman existed in a primal innocence, accepting all, rejoicing in all, and, like the original
Adam, naming all. Cross Damon also feels strangely innocent as he sets out to create a new life for himself:

> It was for much more than merely criminal reasons
> that he was fleeing to escape his identity, his old
> hateful consciousness. There was a kind of inno-
> cence that made him want to shape for himself the
> kind of life he felt he wanted, but he knew that that
> innocence was deeply forbidden. [7]

Even as he dies he clings to his innocence: "' ... I'm ... I

felt ... I'm <u>innocent</u>.... That's what made the horror.... '''
(405).

    Later American literature developed the concept of the
"fortunate fall," the need to go beyond innocence through experience to a higher innocence, a Blakean progression. According to Lewis' interpretation of the elder Henry James'
thinking, "in order to enter the ranks of manhood, the individual (however fair) had to <u>fall</u>, had to pass beyond childhood
in an encounter with 'Evil,' had to mature by virtue of the
destruction of his own egotism. "[8] The innocent must collide
with society, undergo its initiation rituals even though they
may be painful and dangerous. [9] This is the same pattern
that Hassan identifies in modern American heroes, who are
"personified by the <u>converging</u> <u>figures</u> <u>of</u> <u>the</u> <u>initiate</u> <u>and</u> <u>the</u>
<u>victim</u>. "[10]

    For Lewis, the history of American fiction involves
"the noble but illusory myth of the American as Adam"[11]
since America has known both guilt and innocence; or as Hassan tells it, the American was both "dreamer and rapist. "[12]
Thus the heroes--Natty Bumpo, Billy Budd, Captain Ahab,
Donatello, Jay Gatsby--are caught in the web of evil and somehow aid it in its conspiracy. Yet, for Lewis, these outsiders
differ in kind from the more devastatingly alienated European
heroes:

        The Adamic hero is an 'outsider,' but he is
    'outside' in a curiously staunch and artistically de-
    manding manner. He is to be distinguished from
    the kind of outsider--the dispossessed, the super-
    fluous, the alienated, the exiled--who began to enter
    European fiction in the nineteenth century and who
    crowds its almost every page in the twentieth. [13]

These American Adams are not skeptics driven to the des-
pairing shores of nihilism, but pilgrims trying to return home.
In their more contemporary counterparts, they are the absurd,
faintly ironic heroes who in a sort of bungling way attempt to
find a place for themselves in society. They are Bellow's
Augie March, Updike's Rabbit Angstrom, Malamud's Frank
Alpine.

    But Cross Damon, born of this same background, re-
mains significantly different, more akin to Faulkner's Joe
Christmas than Hawthorne's Young Goodman Brown. Although
he would deny it, not the least of these deviations from the

model American Adam is Cross' color. ("There was no racial tone to his reactions; he was just a man, any man who had had an opportunity to flee and had seized upon it" [78]. And "being a Negro was the least important thing in his life." [264].) That is to say, he is an American Adam by virtue of some of his qualities: his loneliness, his feeling of innocence, his desire for community. Moreover, he has obvious connections with Whitman, who also stood on a precipice and created himself, and to Jay Gatsby who was corrupted by the society he tried to conquer. But his alienation is more extreme than theirs.

As a result of his race Cross Damon has never been and never will be an integral part of the American fabric. And because he has always stood outside life, he has never really participated in the heritage of his own people, although he does identify with the jazz he hears in a bar, and the first of his new identities is that of a Negro from the Deep South. But at other times he tries to dissociate himself from his race, claiming that he does not act the way he does because he is black. Wright is obviously trying to go beyond the tension of black and white relations to the larger question of what is a man. To do this he creates a man presented with the unlikely opportunity of being able to create a brand new life for himself. Therefore, when Cross leaves Chicago he relinquishes his place in the world. He becomes a man without a name, without a home, without a past. Having given up on the world of Gladys, Dot, and Joe Thomas, he must invent his own.

This is where his relationship to the European heroes of the last two centuries begins to appear. This is where Wright begins to reveal, after years of fictional silence, his response to the ambiance of French and German existentialism. Unquestionably his most philosophical book, The Outsider often suffers from its author's preoccupation with resolving the two-horned dilemma of existentialism and Marxism, the same conflict that had appeared earlier in Native Son. In fact, the major conflict of the Outsider revolves around the ideological battle between Cross Damon, existentialist, and the hierarchy of the communist party--both extremists: one in favor of absolute freedom, the other advocating total repression. Obviously, after thirteen years Wright was still searching for a satisfactory answer to the meaning of existence. Both Cross and Bigger have remarkably the same problems and experiences, as Darwin Turner has observed in his article "The Outsider: Revision of an Idea."[14] Bigger is poor, alienated,

and unhappy. Cross, although educated and able to earn good
money, is in debt, alienated from the world of white and
black men, and dissatisfied with life. Bigger, because of his
inarticulateness, is more an object of our compassion as he
cries out in horror and rage. But Cross merits our attention as an example of the quandary of modern man. After
all, Cross is testing the validity of nihilism as he acts out
a ritual that measures the consequences of being an existentialist. He is our surrogate self searching for grace through
violence.

Hassan has a provocative discussion of this propensity
toward fictional violence in his chapter, "The Modern Self in
Recoil." There he quotes Mann as saying that "'certain at-
tainments of the soul and intellect are impossible without di-
sease, without insanity, without spiritual crime, and the great
invalids are crucified victims, sacrificed to humanity and its advancement, to the broadening of its feeling and knowledge.... '"[15]
But violence, Hassan goes on to say, "has no reality in the
public realm, the domain of action"; instead it "seems almost
the ultimate form of introspection ... the experience of world
negation."[16] Wright not only seems to say that black men on
any social level are outsiders in search of meaning and acceptance but that all men--black and white--are caught in this
trap whereby they must destroy to create.[17] Man, shackled
by traditions and institutions, must break out of these confines
through crime and rebellion in order to discover himself.
Once free, a man ironically yearns for companionship, but it
is denied him since he has earned his freedom through violence against society. The wound is too great to heal.

Communism tempts these disaffected men by offering
them the promise of security and individual freedom. But in
truth it means oppression and a stifling of expression. Existentialism offers a true freedom, but it is so complete that
its followers seem doomed to isolation. They learn, like
Antoine Roquentin in Sartre's Nausea, that all men are free
and alone:

> I exist because I think ... and I can't stop myself
> from thinking. At this very moment--its' fright-
> ful--if I exist it is because I am horrified at ex-
> isting. I am the one who pulls myself from the
> nothingness to which I aspire: the hatred, the dis-
> gust of existing, there are as many ways to make
> myself exist to thrust myself into existence.[18]

Wright was torn between a society that offered brotherhood but demanded absolute loyalty and a philosophy that offered freedom but required absolute isolation. Understand-
ably, neither was entirely attractive to him, so he chose the
middle ground. He opted for freedom but cried out for brotherhood. Of all the existentialists, Camus seems to come the
closest to this position as he argues for a mutual respect for
freedom and the right to live. He says,

> the first progressive step for a mind overwhelmed
> by the strangeness of things is to realize that this
> feeling of strangeness is shared with all men and
> that human reality, in its entirety, suffers from
> the distance which separates it from the rest of
> the universe. The malady experienced by a single
> man becomes a mass plague ... I rebel--therefore
> we exist.
>
> [T]he 'We are' paradoxically defines a new form of
> individualism. 'We are' in terms of history, and
> history must reckon with this 'We are' which must
> in its turn keep its place in history. I have need
> of others who have need of me and of each other.
> Every collective action, every form of society, sup-
> poses a discipline, and the individual, without this
> discipline, is only a stranger, bowed down under
> the weight of an inimical collectivity. But society
> and discipline lose their direction if they deny the
> 'We are.' I alone, in one sense, support the com-
> mon dignity that I cannot allow either myself or
> others to debase. This individualism is in no sense
> pleasure; it is perpetual struggle, and, sometimes,
> unparalleled joy when it reaches the heights of proud
> compassion. [19]

Hazel Barnes says, in an introduction to Being and
Nothingness, that Sartre has given us his only real illustra-
tion of the existentialist hero's personal ethics in his play
The Flies. Orestes, free from the will of the gods, cour-
ageously and stubbornly accepts the total burden of guilt from
his people:

> He gives up the role of spectator and voluntarily
> commits his freedom to the cause of the people
> of Argos. He is willing to give up his peace of
> mind for the sake of suffering.... In short he ac-
> cepts the tension of absolute freedom and total re-
> sponsibility. [20]

This same freedom and responsibility Bigger Thomas takes on himself at the end of <u>Native Son.</u> Orestes' reward is banishment; Bigger's is death. Since both men have chosen to express themselves through murder, both of them have to relinquish their place in society. Cross Damon encounters a similar situation. He too struggles to balance freedom and responsibility, and his reward is alienation and death at the hands of the communists. Rather ironically, the so-called institution of brotherhood destroys the individualist.

But other institutions had been slowly eroding Cross' manhood and identity all through his life. The institutions of marriage, the government in the guise of the postal officials, religion--each has had a hand in his destruction just as other institutions have ruined Bigger who

> is executed by a capitalist democracy ... Damon is murdered by Communists. In the revision, as in the original, Wright suggested that the sensitive, questioning individual, the existentialist, will be destroyed by the organized institutions which fear him because they do not understand him and fear his questions because they cannot answer them. [21]

Although the freedom for self-actualization is denied Cross and Bigger, let it not be thought that Cross is as sympathetic a character as his progenitor. Bigger's is the cry of a hunted animal. We can pity him. Cross we fear; he is too logical to be pitied. Certainly in him we recognize our own dilemma, but his crime is so great and his reasoning so pat that we watch his downfall more objectively. [22] In noting his own emotional uninvolvement with Wright's hero, Charles Glicksberg calls the novel a "magnificent failure," explaining that although it is

> A metaphysically searching novel, it is psychologically unmotivated and therefore largely unconvincing.... By resorting to murder, the protagonist effectually alienates the sympathy of the reader. [23]

Bigger, the adolescent anti-hero who discovers himself through murder, is but a mild forerunner of the truly criminal hero, Cross Damon. Identified by David Galloway as a distinct type of absurd hero in contemporary fiction, [24] the hero as criminal has its genesis in the continental fiction of Camus, Dostoyevsky and Genet.

The precursors of the desperate criminal philosopher

apotheosized in Cross Damon can also be found in the early writings of Wright himself. Before Damon, however, the heroes have a certain inherent innocence about them, often in line with the picaresque, which the reader can sympathize with. Whereas Damon, the culpable criminal, feels innocent, these boys are made to feel guilty for simply existing--their very lives are a crime. And certainly their motivations for murder, whether of a mule or a man, are more believable than Cross', who seems to murder out of cold, passionless logic. Or as Charles Glicksberg observes, "Cross ... kills out of a feeling that he has transcended all human laws and broken the bond that ties him to humanity."[25] In contrast, in an early story, "Big Boy Leaves Home" (1936),[26] four young blacks begin a lazy idyll in the sun that ends in sudden violence and death for them. By coupling this outrage with descriptions of the boys' easy grace in nature, Wright has added a certain pathos to the old story of man's inhumanity to man. Young savages at home in the fragrant honeysuckle, the boys laugh and dance with a charming insouciance,[27] although their language illustrates the poverty of their lives and dreams. Finishing their forbidden swim in a muddy creek, they startle a white woman with their nakedness. Ironically reversing the mythological archetype of Actaeon spying on Diana in her bath, Wright comments convincingly on the sickness of southern society. Forced to kill or be killed for violating the sensibilities of a white woman, Big Boy shoots the woman's male companion.

Counterpointing the bucolic atmosphere of Part I, Part IV reeks of total violence. Seeking revenge for their outraged female--their murdered friend seems to be of secondary importance--the whites of both sexes track down, mutilate, and burn Big Boy's friend, Bobo.

Obliged to hide in a damp kiln on the hillside, Big Boy continues his initiation into violence. Having killed a man, he seems destined forever to kill other creatures in order to live. Whereas he felt at home in nature at sunrise, by sunset he has seen its denizens as his enemies. In order to occupy the kiln he must beat a rattlesnake to death; to conceal his hiding place he must strangle a bloodhound. The south has forced one more black boy to leave home burdened with premature manhood.

Even Bigger Thomas, for all his cunning and killing, is but a child in search of an identity. His first murder is accidental, his second a desperate act to survive. When he

reaches the high point of self-realization, he is jubilant and
cocky--childlike. No longer fearing death, he challenges fate
and dies, we presume, triumphantly.

Cross Damon, on the other hand, is a total criminal.
He kills out of expediency and from a will to power. Through
him Wright explores the possibilities of absolute alienation
where man becomes his own company, confessor, and god.
This is Man Alone, who without help, creates his own values,
his own identity, his own world.

Albert Camus created an analogous titan in Caligula,
who commits himself to death and destruction at the expense
of others. Through his devotion to logic and truth, Caligula
insulates himself from mankind, rejecting friendship, values,
and love. As Camus says of his despot,

> But, if his truth is to rebel against fate, his error
> lies in negating what binds him to mankind. One
> cannot destroy everything without destroying himself
> ... Caligula is the story of a superior suicide ...
> Caligula accepts death because he has understood
> that no one can save himself all alone and that one
> cannot be free at the expense of others. [28]

Wright's hero also builds his freedom at the expense of
others: "Bad faith wasn't unknown to Cross; not only had he
long been guilty of it in his personal relations, but he was
convinced that bad faith of some degree was an indigenous
part of living" (173). He steals his freedom from the three
women to whom he is committed by law or deed: his mother,
his wife, and his pregnant mistress. He maintains his freedom by murdering his friend. He embellishes his sense of
freedom by wantonly murdering two men, a fascist and a communist locked in deadly combat, negating the purpose of either
murder by killing both ideological paradigms. Later, he again
retains his freedom by murdering a man who could turn him
in to the police. He camouflages his true nature, deceiving
Eva Blount, wife of one of his victims, to such an extent that
she falls in love with him and eventually kills herself when she
discovers his real identity.

The truest relationship he has with another is with Ely
Houston, the District Attorney of New York, whose humped
back has made something of an outsider of him. Bantering
with this man, Cross theoretically reveals his criminal nature
through analogies that Houston is quick to jump on as familiar

and true, admitting the cliché that he is a cop because he could so easily become a criminal. Before dying, Cross confesses to this man that his mistake had been in trying to make it alone. His cry, "'it was ... horrible'" (405), reminds one strongly of Kurtz's in The Heart of Darkness, where that dying man cries out, "'The horror.'"

Ironically Wright's heroes seem only capable of realizing themselves through destroying others. In so doing they isolate and alienate themselves, achieving the antithesis of what they desire: love and brotherhood. Even Cross Damon, hard and ruthless as he is, longs for companionship, for someone to talk to:

> Weren't there somewhere in this world rebels with whom he could feel at home, men who were outsiders not because they had been born black and poor, but because they had thought their way through the many veils of illusion? But where were they? How could one find them? (25).

But every time someone tries to get close to him, he backs off, afraid. Against his will, however, he is inexorably drawn into conversation with Ely Houston; realizing the dangers involved, he is nevertheless so hungry for talk with a kindred soul that he boldly sets forth his philosophy to this man who understands only too well what he is saying.

To anyone even marginally familiar with the writings of Richard Wright, the motifs of criminality and violence stand out as the watermarks of his work. For the source of this violence we may look to his own life, a combination of deprivation and denigration.[29] Attacked verbally and physically by his own family and the whites he worked with, Wright learned as a child the despair of the downtrodden. To compensate he turned to rebellion, rejecting the teachings of his own race and the laws of the other. As a result, his Self was in continual conflict with the rest of the world. This state is normal for blacks, according to George Kent, who says that

> The self is battered by the white racist culture, and, for the most part, by a survival-oriented black culture, that counters the impulse to rebelliousness and individuality by puritanical repressiveness, escapism, and base submission....
> And out of that strategy [of suppressing the in-

dividual] comes an overwhelming impact. Tension, raw violence and impending violence, which evoke, psychologically, a nightmare world in the light of day. [30]

In an attempt to escape the confines of the Deep South, young Richard Wright engaged in petty thievery. And once safely ensconced in Chicago, Wright lashed out against society through his activities in the Communist Party. Given a start through the WPA, Wright soon learned that people would listen to what he wrote. After the publication of his short story collection, Uncle Tom's Children, and his novel, Native Son, Wright became a national figure, the father of new black letters. All his life Wright worked cannily from this position to publicize his distaste for white American society. For him that was the source of black violence.

Chronologically (except for those in his first and last novels, Lawd Today and The Long Dream), Wright's heroes move from a sort of innocent rebellion to a more intellectualized and nihilistic violence. His early heroes, appearing in his short stories, are invariably misjudged or accused unjustly. Thus, Big Boy must leave home because of the mores of southern society. Johnny-Boy is slaughtered for his political beliefs, just as Reverend Taylor is beaten for his. In order to save his own family during a flood Mann must kill a white man; after saving the family of the man he has killed, Mann is predictably betrayed by them and shot while trying to escape. For, him as for so many of Wright's heroes, the only true escape is death; e. g. , Silas ("Long Black Song"), Fred Daniels ("The Man Who Lived Underground"), Johnny-Boy ("Bright and Morning Star"), Bigger Thomas, and Cross Damon--all die to escape the harsh realities of life.

For James Baldwin, the reason behind Wright's violence lies in his fear of sex. Unwilling to include sexuality in his work, Wright supposedly sublimates this inadequacy through his vivid scenes of violence. [31] Although Baldwin is correct in assessing the state of Wright's literary sex as impoverished, I am convinced that Wright's concentration on violence arises from areas other than the Freudian. Early in his career a proletarian novelist and always a protestor, Wright used violence as a tool to express outrage. The violence done to him and his people is compensated for fictionally. His heroes retaliate where he could not. [32] Placed in revelatory climactic situations, these cornered protagonists strike out often, maiming and murdering the aggressive whites. Bigger Thomas, for example, finding himself twice in impossible circumstances, each time murders a helpless girl, one white, one black. Unable to cope with the hostile world that has suddenly turned against him, he acts as he has been conditioned to: he murders in self-defense. Naturally this is not the classic self-defense that would hold up in court, since neither girl could do him any physical harm, but these are just as truly acts of self-preservation.

Bigger himself illustrates the tendency in Wright's heroes to progress from innocence to experience. His first murder is an accidental one that nonetheless marks him as a brutal sex killer. His second murder is purposeful but filled with a sort of pathos, as Bigger kills the only living thing that seems to have had any feelings for him. At the end of the novel, Bigger has reconciled himself to both murders, seeing in them the potential for self-realization.

Wright's next hero is more calculating and consequently more frightening, for Cross Damon's journey, long regarded as one of the finest examples of American literary existentialism,[33] is actually a peregrination through the terrors of nihilism. Existentially free to determine his life and identity, Cross Damon engages in rituals of becoming by consciously seeking situations in which he must make decisions vital to his character. "What he needed, demanded, was the hardest, the most awful responsibility, something that would test him and make him feel his worth" (131). Crouched like an animal ready to spring, Cross reminds one of Sartre's Mathieu, whose "sole care had been to hold himself in readiness. For an act. A free, considered act that should pledge his whole life and stand at the beginning of a new existence."[34] Both men are on the fringe of life, never wholly committing themselves to anyone else; both, as Mathieu's friend observes, possessed of a freedom "'based on reason.'"[35] Moreover, both men in their isolation would have cause to echo Pascal's confession, "The eternal silence of these infinite spaces terrifies me" (Pensées, Sec. III, no. 206).

For brave as the existentialist must needs be, he has his sharp moments of doubt and despair. And words such as "fear," "dread," "despair," and "anxiety" not only describe the temper of the time that brought existentialism to its head, but are key terms in the jargon of its spokesmen. These are the words that appear with disturbing regularity in the pages of Kierkegaard, Tillich, Sartre, and Heidegger. These too are the messengers of darkness that Richard Wright chose to describe the tortured soul of Cross Damon, outsider.

Because these words have special meaning in the language of the existentialists, and because Wright was cognizant of their esoteric use--employing them for the most part quite precisely--it is important to review their philosophical denotations.

Cross Damon is haunted by a pervasive sense of uneasiness and insecurity that he variously labels "fear," "dread," and "anxiety." For Kierkegaard, Tillich and Heidegger these terms are not wholly interchangeable, since "fear" is not to be confused with angst (translated as either "dread" or "anxiety").

> Tillich. Anxiety and fear have the same ontological root, but they are not the same in actuality.... Fear, as opposed to anxiety has a definite object ... which can be faced, analyzed, attacked, endured. One can act upon it, and in acting upon it participate in it--even if in the form of struggle. In this way one can take it into one's self-affirmation. Courage can meet every object of fear, because it is an object and makes participation possible. [36]

> Kierkegaard. One almost never sees the concept dread dealt with in psychology, and I must therefore call attention to the fact that it is different from fear and similar concepts which refer to something definite, whereas dread is freedom's reality as possibility for possibility. One does not therefore find dread in the beast, precisely for the reason that by nature the beast is not qualified by spirit. [37]

Although one can assume that Tillich's book appeared after Wright had completed the bulk of his thinking about The Outsider (Tillich's book appeared in 1952; Wright's 1953), both Tillich and Kierkegaard shed light on what Wright was attempting here in his exploration of modern man's soul. Thus when Wright mentions Cross' "fear" he is illustrating what Tillich calls "anxiety" and Kierkegaard "dread."

Another philosopher that Wright was familiar with at the time he was writing The Outsider, who also made a distinction, however abstruse, between "fear" and "anxiety," was Martin Heidegger:

> That in the face of which we fear, the 'fearsome,'
> is in every case something which we encounter with-
> in-the-world....
>
> Anxiety makes manifest in Dasein its Being towards
> its ownmost potentiality-for-being--that is, its Being-
> free-for the freedom of choosing itself and taking
> hold of itself. Anxiety brings Dasein face to face
> with its Being free for (propensio in ...) the au-
> thenticity of its Being, and for this authenticity as
> a possibility which it always is. That about which
> anxiety is anxious reveals itself as that in the face
> of which it is anxious--namely, Being-in-the-world.
>
> As a state of mind ... the phenomenon of anxiety*
> will be made basic for our analysis. In working
> out this basic state-of-mind and characterizing on-
> tologically what is disclosed in it as such, we shall
> take the phenomenon of falling as our point of de-
> parture, and distinguish anxiety from the kindred
> phenomenon of fear.... [38]

For Heidegger as for Tillich an Kierkegaard, "fear"
has a definite object; angst, whether translated as "dread" or
"anxiety," has no object, being instead the reaction of a man
to the possibility of his becoming himself.

Although he occasionally deviates from the existential
philosophers' definitions of "dread" and "fear," Wright in
most instances distinguished between the two. For example,
Cross is "afraid of himself" (110), afraid of getting caught for
his crime (112-113), afraid of Ely Houston (118)--all quite
identifiable and specific objects to cope with and overcome,
although his fear of himself admittedly leads to the more indefinite sense of dread. Another of his fears stems from his
dread. After Cross has escaped from the subway wreck we
learn that he is "afraid of his surroundings and he knew that
his surroundings did not know that he was afraid" (78). This

---

*Editor's footnote to Being and Time: "'Angst.' While this
word has generally been translated as 'anxiety' in the post
Freudian psychological literature, it appears as 'dread' in the
translations of Kierkegaard and in a number of discussions of
Heidegger. In some ways 'uneasiness' or 'malaise' would be
more appropriate still" (p. 227).

fear seems to originate from a more indefinite sense of anxiety in the face of his freedom; i.e., because he is creating a new life for himself by rejecting his old identity, he must isolate himself from his former environment. He thus faces his new surroundings entirely naked, without a past, without a sense of self in relation to the world. It is a frightening experience. Instead of being able to rely on the past to give himself an identity, he must depend on the future to "determine what and who he was to be" (80):

> In a way, he was a criminal, not so much because of what he was doing, but because of what he was feeling.... There was a kind of innocence that made him want to shape for himself the kind of life he felt he wanted, but he knew that that innocence was deeply forbidden (78).

Even though Cross "loves this" magnificent opportunity to explore the full implications of freedom--

> All of his life he had been hankering after his personal freedom (77).

> That all men were free was the fondest and deepest conviction of his life ... (80).

--he is still terrified by its prospects; "to map out his life entirely upon his own assumptions was a task that terrified him just to think of it ... " (82).

But as Part I's title suggests, angst is nothing new to Cross. All his life, in fact, he has been plagued by a persistent sense of dread, a legacy bequeathed him by his mother: "his dread had been his mother's first fateful gift to him" (15), a result of her grief over her husband's death. To compensate for her hurt, she turned to God, teaching Cross not only to fear Him, but to shun all aspects of physical desire. Her admonitions, however, only heighten his desire for desire and he begins to regard the God of love as the God of hate, the everlasting No. As a child he experiences existential dread, discovering that

> his sensibilities had not been repressed by God's fearful negations as represented by his mother; indeed, his sense of life had been so heightened that desire boiled in him to a degree that made him afraid. Afraid of what? Nothing exactly,

>precisely.... And this constituted his sense of
>dread (16, 17).

Having given up his old life, Cross is nearly consumed
by terror and dread brought on not only by the necessity for
inventing himself but also by the fact that he is absolutely
alone. His "appalling loneliness" haunts him, especially
after he witnesses his own funeral (110):

>He was empty, face to face with a sense of dread
>more intense than anything he had ever felt before.
>He was alone. He was not only without friends,
>their hopes, and loves to buoy him up, but he was
>a man tossed back upon himself when that self
>meant only a hope of hope ... Nothing made mean-
>ing; his life seemed to have turned into a static
>dream whose frozen images would remain unchanged
>throughout eternity (92, 93).

Like other Wright heroes, Cross' life has been a
series of dream images, a nightmare. In Part I Wright mentions this phenomenon frequently: "the nightmare that was
life " (13); "life ... had the disorganized character of a nightmare" (23); "he felt trapped in a nightmare" (36); "he felt unreal, scarcely alive" (43). As part of his dream he kills his
friend Joe Thomas when he runs into him in the brothel.

After this murder while he is on the way to New York,
Cross realizes that the source of his dread is himself:

>He was free from everything but himself.... As
>the train wheels clicked through the winter night,
>he knew where his sense of dread came from; it
>was from within himself, within the vast and mys-
>terious world that was his and his alone, and yet
>not really known to him.... (107).

Because he does not know himself well and hates himself
pretty thoroughly, he is afraid of himself. Out of this fear
and pervasive dread arises a sense of unreality. Thus Part
II is fittingly entitled "Dream." In this section Cross meets
Ely Huston, assumes the identity of Lionel Lane, and finally
meets the communist Gil Blount whose ideas awaken Cross to
a new challenge, ending his dream.

By the beginning of Part III, "Descent," Cross has
concluded that communism can become the impetus he needs

to discover himself:

> It was an emotional compulsion, religious in its
> intensity, to feel and weigh the worth of himself that
> was pushing him into the arms of the one thing on
> earth that could transform his sense of dread, shape
> it, objectify it, and make it real and rational for
> him (174).

But by the end of the section dread is still with him, and his
life has been converted to a terrifying nightmare by the double
murder he has committed:

> He had acted, had shattered the dream that sur-
> rounded him, and now the world, including himself
> in it, had turned mockingly into a concrete, waking
> nightmare from which he could see no way of es-
> caping (212).

The nightmare is a good metaphor for dread since it is an
expression of what one desires in negative images. Moreover, since Cross' all-consuming interest is to create a self
("his decisive life struggle was a personal fight for the realization of himself" [131]), and since he has complete freedom
to do so, he is continually plagued by a sense of dread. It
is understandable that his days have an aura of unreality about
them.

Like the history of modern existentialism, which is
generally conceded to have begun with Søren Kierkegaard,
Wright's history of a single existentialist begins with an epigraph from Kierkegaard:[39]

> Dread is an alien power which lays hold of an in-
> dividual, and yet one cannot tear oneself away, nor
> has a will to do so; for one fears what one desires.

It is freedom that Kierkegaard refers to, and it is a freedom
beyond our wildest imaginings that Cross Damon realizes in
Part I. For Kierkegaard, dread is a state experienced only
by humans ("the less spirit, the less dread") and it is un-
alterably tied in with man's ability to determine himself--
"dread is freedom's reality as possibility for possibility."[40]
Man, horrified with this freedom, reacts ambivalently to it,
unable to "flee from dread, for he loves it"; unable to love
it "for he flees from it."[41] Kierkegaard describes dread as
the "dizziness of freedom which occurs when the spirit would

posit the synthesis [of soul and body], and freedom then gazes
down into its own possibility, grasping at finiteness to sustain
itself. "[42] It is this "possibility of Freedom" that chills Damon when he realizes the task he has set before himself in
accepting total freedom. For he, unlike other men, can toss
out the past and begin with the present to create himself, to
answer the question, "What is a man?"

This state of not yet being what one will be, of realizing the distinctness of self from past and future, and the resulting necessity for continually choosing in order to create
this self (without external values), Sartre calls "anguish. "
As he writes in Being and Nothingness,

> First I am not that self because time separates
> me from it. Secondly, I am not that self because
> what I am is not the foundation of what I will be.
> Finally I am not that self because no actual exis-
> tent can determine strictly what I am going to be.
> Yet as I am already what I will be (otherwise I
> would not be interested in any one being more than
> another), I am the self which I will be, in the mode
> of not being it.... Anguish is precisely my con-
> sciousness of being my own future, in the mode of
> not-being. [43]

Anguish is essentially "consciousness of freedom. " And this
freedom is "characterized by a constantly renewed obligation
to remake the Self which designates the free being":[44]

> Thus the Future qua Future does not have to be.
> It is not in itself, and neither is it in the mode of
> being of the For-it-self since it is the meaning of
> the For-itself. The Future is not, it is possibi-
> lized. ... The Future is the continual possibiliza-
> tion of possibles.... [45]

Early in The Outsider Cross argues that "'A man creates
himself'" (46; see also pp. 77, 83, 114); he knows, therefore,
that by his actions he is creating himself. The tragedy is
that he becomes what he has set out to destroy: a god-like
man who pitilessly tramples and exploits other men, breaking
the bond of humanity--making promises he cannot keep:

> He knew that he had cynically scorned, wantonly
> violated, every commitment that civilized men owe,
> in terms of common honesty and sacred honor, to

those with whom they live. That, in essence, was
his crime. The rest of his brutal and bloody
thrashings about were the mere offshoots of that
one central, cardinal fact. And for the crime of
his contemptuous repudiation of all the fundamental
promises that men live by he intended to make no
legal defense, for the good and ample reason that
he knew no such defense was possible (345).[46]

Besides suffering from the anguish of not yet being
himself, Cross also exhibits signs of anxiety as defined by
Tillich; i.e., "anxiety is the state in which a being is aware
of its possible nonbeing.... It is the existential awareness
of nonbeing."[47] It is a fact of existence appearing as three
separate but related types:

Nonbeing threatens man's ontic self-affirmation, relatively in terms of fate, absolutely in terms of
death. It threatens man's spiritual self-affirmation,
relatively in terms of emptiness, absolutely in terms
of meaninglessness. It threatens man's moral self-
affirmation, relatively in terms of guilt, absolutely
in terms of condemnation.... In all three forms
anxiety is existential in the sense that it belongs to
existence as such and not to an abnormal state of
mind as in neurotic (and psychotic) anxiety.[48]

The simultaneous presence of all three types of anxiety in
man results in the ultimate state of "despair" where being is
aware of its own nonbeing--the despair within despair. The
agonies of this state are so excruciating that man longs to be
rid of his being--to escape despair. If despair were only a
quality of ontic anxiety, the solution would be suicide: negation of self. But despair is also a product of moral anxiety
(guilt and condemnation), which cannot be alleviated by suicide. As Tillich says,

Guilt and condemnation are qualitatively, not quan-
titatively, infinite. They have an infinite weight
and cannot be removed by a finite act of ontic self-
negation. This makes despair desperate, that is,
inescapable.[49]

Spiritual anxiety is also intimately involved with ontic and
moral anxiety as elements of despair. But again there is no
escape from it. Although the anxiety of emptiness and meaninglessness as an instance of finitude could be relieved by

suicide, insofar "as it is a consequence of moral disintegra-
tion it produces the same paradox as the moral element in
despair: there is no ontic exit from it. "[50] The impulse to
suicide is based on futility.

Obviously man attempts to avoid despair since once he encounters it he has great difficulty in overcoming it. And, as Tillich hastens to add, most men successfully escape this desperate
situation. But Cross Damon does not. Precipitating himself inexorably into the abyss of despair, he becomes the epitome of
modern man: lost, alone, frightened.

The anxiety of fate and death is basic to human existence; it is universal, inescapable. And, as a sensitive man
given to introspection, Cross is vividly aware of nonbeing and
its threat to his being. Anxiety of fate centers on man's
awareness that he has "no ultimate necessity. "[51] A student
of modern philosophy, Cross admits this absurdity: "'Maybe
man is nothing in particular. ' Cross said gropingly. 'Maybe
that's the terror of it'" (125). Self-individualization seems
to intensify anxiety of death: as Cross asserts himself more
and more boldly (and finds someone to love), he increasingly
abhors the idea of death (having earlier contemplated suicide,
p. 12). The anxiety of emptiness and meaninglessness--most
common in modern man--arises from the loss of Man's
"spiritual center, of an answer ... to the question of the
meaning of existence. "[52] Haunted by his own meaninglessness
and the absurdity of the human condition, Cross strives to
create meaning for himself without having to sacrifice himself. He recognizes that his mother (and Sarah eventually)
surrenders her being to the church in return for meaning
(hers is the courage to be a part). He identifies this same
impulse to avoid doubt and insecurity in the communists, especially in Menti, whom he sees as having totally sacrificed
himself in order to escape spiritual anxiety; to him

> Menti was a hireling ... who had offered his mean-
> ingless, self-despised existence to the Party to be
> used, ravaged, dominated, and filled with a purpose,
> any purpose as long as the burden of the responsi-
> bility for his own life was lifted from his shoulders
> (307).

By this stage in his life, Wright had little sympathy
left for the communists; his hero is equally disgusted by fascists and communists, branding them both societies of little
gods. Tillich views a man who joins a totalitarian movement

as one without the courage to be himself, arguing that

> He flees from his freedom of asking and answering
> for himself to a situation in which no further ques-
> tions can be asked and the answers to previous
> questions are imposed on him authoritatively....
> Meaning is saved, but the self is sacrificed....
> Fanaticism is the correlate to spiritual self-surren-
> der: it shows the anxiety which it was supposed to
> conquer, by attacking with disproportionate violence
> those who disagree and who demonstrate by their
> disagreement elements in the spiritual life of the
> fanatic which he must suppress in himself. Be-
> cause he must suppress them in himself he must
> suppress them in others. His anxiety forces him
> to persecute dissenters. [53]

For these reasons Cross could never submit to organized religion or communism: although he despairs, he never considers relinquishing his total freedom--he embraces it and
its comcomitant horrors. It is life.

The threat to moral self-affirmation, the anxiety of
self-rejection and condemnation, also plagues Cross. Man is
given certain materials to work with, but he is ultimately responsible for what he does with himself. Tillich says that

> Man is essentially 'finite freedom' ... in the sense
> of being able to determine himself through decisions
> in the center of his being. Man, as finite freedom,
> is free within the contingencies of his finitude.
> But within these limits he is asked to make of him-
> self what he is supposed to become, to fulfill his
> destiny. In every act of moral self-affirmation man
> contributes to the fulfillment of his destiny, to the
> actualization of what he potentially is ... man has
> the power of ... contradicting his essential being,
> of losing his destiny. And under the conditions of
> man's estrangement from himself this is an actuali-
> ty. [54]

Cross recognizes this burden and self-consciously attempts
to create himself. But what he creates horrifies him. He
draws himself a monster and recoils from its image.

As a result of his total submission to all three types
of anxiety, Cross plunges into despair. Having been an out-

sider all his life, when he loses faith in himself he finds the
world to be absurd, devoid of meaning. In this purposeless
existence, Cross finds direction in absolute nihilism, where
all is permitted. As a consequence of this solution he becomes a criminal.

This type of total criminal is not unknown in modern
literature. It appears in Crime and Punishment, where Raskolnikov murders an old woman because he should be able to.
It appears in the writings of Jean Genet, who apotheosized
Notre Dame des Fleurs. But it appears in greatest similar-
ity in the fiction and philosophical treatises of Albert Camus.
Caligula, for example, could be read as an exegesis of The
Outsider. And both Caligula and Cross are understood more
fully after a reading of The Rebel, in which Camus explores
the characteristics of metaphysical rebellion.

Much of Cross Damon's behavior can be explained in
terms of Camus' concept of rebellion. [55] In this famous study
Camus poses the question of paramount importance to our age:
can murder be justified? To answer satisfactorily, Camus
ranges gracefully throughout the metaphysics and politics of
the last two hundred years, concluding paradoxically that a
man can murder only if he then consents to his own death as
proof of the community of man. Likewise, Richard Wright,
through his hero Cross Damon, explores the ultimate question
of life today. Although Camus' philosophical essay is much
the more sophisticated, Wright's novel is no minor study of
the nadir of nihilism and despair.

In his introduction Camus distinguishes between the two
major types of crime: those of passion and those of logic.
He finds the latter to be the hallmark of mid-twentieth-century
life. "We are living," he says, "in the era of premeditation
and the perfect crime." And when crime appears innocent,
"it is innocence that is called upon to justify itself."[56] His
essay delves into this strange reversal of values. For Camus, crime becomes extraordinarily dangerous when it begins
to reason about itself, to justify itself through logic.

Cross Damon is an intellectual criminal. He is not
driven to murder through passion (love or hate); he is not
pathological. He kills because he believes that he has the
perfect right to. He holds himself innocent--even at death.
He is the paradigm of Camus' logical criminal--just as perfect as Caligula.

According to Camus, absurdist reasoning neither permits nor forbids murder. On the one hand, it seems to forbid it since suicide has been proven untenable as it negates one half of the absurd, thus releasing all tension. "Murder cannot be made coherent when suicide is not considered coherent. "[57] Yet nihilism, which also finds no meaning or values in life, accepts suicide and therefore murder (Ivan Karamazov's "'everything is permitted'" leads naturally to murder). But absolute negation is "not consummated by suicide. It can only be consummated by absolute destruction, of oneself and of others.... The moment that we recognize the impossibility of absolute negation--and merely to be alive is to recognize this--the very first thing that cannot be denied is the right of others to live. "[58]

Since the absurd cannot give man a set of values to live by, Camus turns to its one truth, protest, for guidance:

> Rebellion is born of the spectacle of irrationality, confronted with an unjust and incomprehensible condition. But its blind impulse is to demand order in the midst of chaos, and unity in the very heart of the ephemeral. It protests, it demands, it insists that the outrage be brought to an end, and that what has up to now been built upon shifting sands should henceforth be founded on rock. Its preoccupation is to transform. But to transform is to act, and to act will be, tomorrow, to kill, and it still does not know whether murder is legitimate. [59]

Camus concludes that since the primary feature of rebellion is its desire for unity and order, murder and rebellion are logically contradictory. And yet, in order to affirm that which is noble in man, men are often forced to kill. In these cases, the murderers must accept their own deaths in order to reaffirm the primary value, the community of man. For what a man wants for himself he cannot deny to others, unless he too is willing to make the ultimate sacrifice--his own life. [60]

A desire for order also consumes Cross Damon. For example, he kills Hilton because he is convinced that Hilton is determined to make him a slave by controlling his life, curtailing his freedom. Like Ivan Karamazov, he cannot tolerate what he calls meaningless suffering--anyone therefore who inflicts it on another must be stopped: "I might forgive you [Hilton] if you had been going to kill me. But, no; you were going to make me a slave.... I'd have suffered, night and day. You would have dominated my consciousness. No, no, Hilton, there's more here than you say. Goddammit, there is! If not, then why all this meaningless suffering? If you had killed me, that would have been a simple act ... but why turn a consciousness into a flame of suffering and let it lie, squirming ... ? No!'" (276-277). Possessed by outrage, Cross kills Hilton as a protest against coercion, ironically depriving the man of what he demands for himself-- the freedom to control his own destiny--and thus breaking the code of rebellion.

In his brief life Cross Damon stumbles into all the pitfalls available in the history of rebellion: he forgets his bond with humanity; he desires to replace God; he turns to murder to express himself. But his original rebellion is certainly justified. Although he denies that it has had an influence on his personality, the fact that he is a black man in America is of primary consequence. He is of an oppressed people in a powerful and "free" country; his heritage is slavery. As Nathan Scott said in 1964,

> Though it is only in the occasional pockets of
> Southern depravity that the Negro is still exposed
> to the nakeder forms of violence and intimidation,
> he knows that the actuality of the American experi-
> ence continues to involve for him that most un-
> hinging kind of frustration which is a result of
> the glitter and promise of life in a great country
> being near enough for the mind to be dazzled by
> the sense of their availability, and yet far enough
> away to exact a sense of defeat more exacerbating
> than anything a slave could possibly feel. [61]

Similarly, Camus reasons that the "spirit of rebellion can exist only in a society where a theoretical equality conceals great factual inequalities."[62] Therefore, when Cross accepts his freedom, turning his back on his mother, his mistress, and his wife, he is in reality saying "no" to the world of white America. At the same time he is saying "yes" to himself and the central value he feels he as a human being has a right to. He is saying, as Camus notes slaves have said before, "'up to this point yes, beyond it no.'"[63] He affirms himself and begins a journey into the interior of rebellion whose outcome he could not have foreseen at the moment he first said "no":

> But from the moment that the rebel finds his voice--
> even though he says nothing but 'no'--he begins to
> desire and to judge.... With rebellion, awareness
> is born.... The rebel himself wants to be 'all'--
> to identify himself completely with this good of
> which he has suddenly become aware and by which
> he wants to be personally recognized and acknow-
> ledged--or 'nothing'; in other words, to be complete-
> ly destroyed by the force that dominates him. As
> a last resort, he is willing to accept the final de-
> feat, which is death, rather than be deprived of the
> personal sacrament that he would call, for example,
> freedom. Better to die on one's feet than to live
> on one's knees. [64]

This determination to control one's own destiny reminds one
of Milton's Satan in Paradise Lost, who states boldly that it
is "'Better to reign in hell than serve in heaven'" (1. 263).
As Satan pays for his rebellion by being thrown out of heaven, contemporary existential heroes pay for theirs by being
condemned to a living hell and an early death. For example,
at the end of his journey into the self, after a baffling and
stultifying life, Bigger Thomas must die for his new-found
freedom. And Cross Damon, who self-consciously embarks
on his voyage of rebellion at the outset of The Outsider, is
nearly torn apart by the nightmare of nihilism; and he too
dies violently, murdered by godless tyrants.

Cross' first trial as a newly declared rebel occurs in
the shabby hotel where he stays after the train wreck. Having
decided to opt for freedom, Cross suddenly comes face to face
with his past--a post office buddy, Joe Thomas. Surprised
into an immediate decision, Cross kills him to protect his new
life. Through this brutal murder Cross has broken a cardinal rule of rebellion by destroying in another what he claims
for himself. Moreover, his value judgments become cloudier
as he progresses down the avenue of nihilism, in contrast to
this killing which was a matter of expediency since he had to
quiet the one person who could ruin his chances for a new
life. And if we regard Joe as the symbol of Cross' old life
--his servitude--he is just one more object that Cross rebels
against. After this encounter Cross is truly free. But his
further actions are not so easily understood, as he murders
two men without reason--and feels no need of having one.
Ely Houston puts his finger on Cross' attitude when he says

that this "'mythical killer'" is a man who believes "'That no ideas are necessary to justify his acts ... '" (258).

Implicit in Cross' activity is his protest against God. He does not deny God--he replaces Him. His is a thoroughly metaphysical rebellion. Not only is he a slave protesting his servitude; he is also a philosopher outraged by his status as a man, horrified at the corruption and unhappiness of the world. He thus aligns himself with other men against God-- the personal, enigmatic God who in Ivan Karamazov's scheme allows small children to be brutalized ("'all I know is that there is suffering and that there are none guilty ... '"). [65] This is a calling to account of the god of love, and as far as modern man is concerned he has been weighed in the balance and found wanting. The handwriting is on the wall. As Camus observes,

> When the throne of God is overturned, the rebel realizes that it is now his own responsibility to create the justice, order, and unity that he sought in vain within his own condition, and in this way to justify the fall of God. Then begins the desperate effort to create, at the price of crime and murder if necessary, the dominion of man. [66]

Instead of being content to rebel against God, the hero organizes a coup: he will replace God. Kirilov, in Dostoyevsky's The Possessed, believes that the secret to man's dominion is through the first truly purposeful suicide; he dies to prove that he is God, that death has no hold on him. He dies for all the world, to begin an era of man-gods (his order). Cross Damon is convinced that all men are atheists and that this means "'that I, and you too, can do what we damn well please on this earth'" (331).

The route to establishing man's dominion lies in the dark corridors of nihilism--of absolute negation. According to Camus, "the history of contemporary nihilism really begins" with Ivan Karamazov's "'everything is permitted'"; like Caligula, Ivan "compelled himself to do evil so as to be coherent."[67] (Ivan: "'I must have justice, or I will destroy myself. And not justice in some remote infinite time and space, but here on earth, and that I could see myself.'")[68] Both heroes suffer the consequences of their terrible logic: Caligula is murdered (dying happily, finally aware of the utter futility and absurdity of life), and Ivan is driven mad by the paradoxes inherent in man's replacing God, e.g., "to become

God is to accept crime. "[69] Cross also realizes the implicit
terror in becoming a god when he says,

> 'Damned is the man who must invent his own god!
> Shun that man, for he is a part of the vast cosmos;
> he is akin to it and he can no more know himself
> than he can know the world of which he is in some
> mysterious way a part ... ' (331).

Instead of taking the absurd and making it their god,
as David Galloway asserts American absurd heroes do, these
continental heroes apotheosize themselves. Logically then,
they become criminals. This is the journey of Cross Damon,
from innocent victim (slave) to disingenuous criminal (god).
Yet somehow in all his final culpability he retains his innocence. For his is the radical innocence--the anguished cry--
that drives him to murder in order to assert himself and
deny the horror of existence.

Because of his allegiance to his logic, Damon is forced
to commit an otherwise irrational or illogical crime. Discovering a fascist and a communist engaged in bloody battle,
Cross kills both, confounding the pedestrian minds of the police who cannot accept a theory of a third man, outside the
realm of morality. The only man capable of imagining such
a rarity is Ely Houston, himself an outsider. It is he whom
Cross fears because he knows this man can grapple with the
intricate twistings of a logic that would not allow but demand
that he murder both philosophical sides to protest the fact
that they would deny him his absolute freedom. After expres-
sing his outrage through murder, Cross justifies the deed to
himself as a blotting out of two "little gods" (212); ruefully,
he later admits to having played the god himself.

This propensity for acting like God has characterized
Cross for years. For example, in the book's early exposi-
tory scenes Cross' buddies reminisce jovially about the day
that Cross tossed some loose change out of an eleventh-story
window. Watching the people scramble like idiots for the
money, Cross had said that "'that was the only time he ever
felt like God'" (5). Detached throughout the anecdote, Cross
hears his friends laughingly identify him as "'a man standing
outside of the world'" (5).

Although he is an outsider, like Nietzsche he is a man
who accepts the full responsibility of nihilism. For Nietzsche
nihilism was a transitional stage to a more meaningful exis-

tence; he believed that man must move from a state of innocence through experience to a state of higher innocence. In
this venture man travels alone, with no religious baggage to
thwart his progress. Nietzsche observed that God is dead
and rejected Christianity because it posited false values for
a nonexistent world; according to him,

> The supreme values in whose service man
> should live, especially when they were very hard
> on him and exacted a high price--these social val-
> ues were erected over man to strengthen their
> voice, as if they were commands of God, as 're-
> ality,' as the 'true' world, as a hope and future
> world. Now that the shabby origin of these values
> is becoming clear, the universe seems to have
> lost value, seems 'meaningless'--but that is only
> a transitional stage.
>
> The faith in the categories of reason is the cause
> of nihilism. We have measured the value of the
> world according to categories that refer to a purely
> fictitious world. [70]

Nietzsche would have denied Christianity even if its god were
not dead. But he observed that God truly is dead and pro-
ceeded to explore the consequences of this fact in nineteenth-
century Europe.

For Nietzsche the world as it exists now is the source
of all value; therefore he affirms everything in the world.
History is dethroned; nature deified. And in this godless world
the burden lies solely on man to define his values and himself. In The Rebel, Camus refers to Nietzsche's concept of
responsibility, saying that

> From the moment that man believes neither in God
> nor in immortal life, he becomes 'responsible for
> everything alive, for everything that, born of suf-
> fering, is condemned to suffer from life.' It is he,
> and he alone, who must discover law and order. [71]

Or as Kirilov says to Peter Verkhovensky, "'If God exists,
then the whole will is His and I can do nothing. If He doesn't
exist, then all will is mine and I must exercise my own will,
my free will.'"[72] Man as God must create law, since in total freedom chaos reigns and no man is free. Nietzsche replaces Ivan Karamazov's "'everything is permitted'" with the

alternative, "'if nothing is true, nothing is permitted.'"[73]
The individual submerges himself in the "destiny of the species and the eternal movement of the spheres."[74] Nature--
the world itself--becomes God. One thus says "yes" to
everything in the world:

> In a certain sense, rebellion, with Nietzsche, ends
> again in the exaltation of evil.... It is accepted
> as one of the possible aspects of good and, with
> rather more conviction, as part of destiny.[75]

Total approbation thus allows the possibility of murder.

Either way metaphysical rebellion turns, it destroys,
according to Camus:

> Each time that it deifies the total rejection, the
> absolute negation, of what exists, it destroys.
> Each time that it blindly accepts what exists and
> gives voice to absolute assent, it destroys again.
> Hatred of the creator can turn to hatred of creation
> or to exclusive and defiant love of what exists.
> But in both cases it ends in murder and loses the
> right to be called rebellion. One can be nihilist
> in two ways, in both by having an intemperate re-
> course to absolutes.[76]

Whether the rebel desires death for himself or for others,
he is nonetheless striving for order and value. Preferring as a consequence "generalized injustice to mutilated
justice,"

> The victims have found in their own innocence the
> justification for the final crime. Convinced of their
> condemnation and without hope of immortality, they
> decided to murder God.... From this moment,
> man decides to exclude himself from grace and to
> live by his own means.[77]

In The Outsider Hilton expresses this attitude when he
tries to argue Cross out of killing him, "'What the hell is
there so important about men dying?'" (275). Cross counters
with an attack on the communists' method: that of inflicting
suffering rather than outright merciful killing. His inability
to accept meaningless suffering mirrors Ivan Karamazov's;
so he swears, like Ivan, to keep fighting against the unfair-
ness of the world:

> [Eva:] "'But I thought you were against brutality
> ... I thought you hated suffering--'"

> [Cross:] "'I do!' he shouted.   'That's why I did
> it!   I couldn't stand the thought of it, the
> sight of it.... !'" (369).

Although he claims to be a reluctant victim of his compulsions
to set the world straight, he can't quit. He can't stop the one
thing that keeps him trapped: his continual killing:

> 'I won't stop; I can't stop as long as men like
> you keep playing your dirty games,' Cross said;
> and there was a genuine despair in his voice.   'I
> won't ever feel free as long as you exist, even if
> you aren't hunting me down.   You and men like you
> are my enemies' (274).

Rebellion, having become a revolution, looks to replace the
reign of grace with that of justice.

> To rebuild an empire from the rubble of ruined reli-
> gion, rebellion must annex the world, encompass all men,
> carry freedom to the corners of the universe.   Rebellion be-
> comes a crusade:

> Henceforth, with the introduction of moral nihilism, it
> will retain, of all its acquisitions, only the will to
> power.   In principle, the rebel only wanted to con-
> quer his own existence and to maintain it in the
> face of God.   But he forgets his origins and, by
> the law of spiritual imperialism, he sets out in
> search of world conquest by way of an infinitely
> multiplied series of murders. [78]

Cross ruminates on the will to power and its implications
after observing the communists in action: "Suppose Gil was
right in assuming that the Party was justified in coercing
obedience from others purely on the basis of its strength?
What was there, then, to keep an individual from adopting the
same policy?   Apparently nothing save cunning and ruthless-
ness ... " (175).   He has come a long way since the epiphany
he had when he murdered Joe Thomas, his friend.   Up until
that point his running had had little reality to it.   But once
he learns that he can murder, he destroys the possibility of
turning back.   He commits himself to a new life by taking
another's.

Feeling essentially free of guilt, Cross admits to being lonely--an aloneness he felt even while he had been with Gladys and Dot. A new breed of man, he is conscious of his difference and fears his own absolute dedication to self-preservation. This fear is compounded by other emotions: the anxiety of having no identity and the alarm of a hunted animal.

His attitude toward the priest whom he meets on the train to New York clarifies his feelings about religion. He considers him a savage. Cross is the new man, the rebel who must create his own values without religious guidance. He

> had to discover what was good or evil through his own actions, which were more exacting than the edicts of any God because it was he alone who had to bear the brunt of their consequences with a sense of absoluteness made intolerable by knowing that this life of his was all he had and would ever have (114).

This passage lies in the shadow of a more famous one by Sartre, found in his lecture, L'existentialisme est un humanisme (1946), where he states,

> Everything is indeed permitted if God does not exist, and man is in consequence forlorn, for he cannot find anything to depend upon either within or outside himself. He discovers forthwith, that he is without excuse. For if indeed existence precedes essence, one will never be able to explain one's actions by reference to a given and specific human nature; in other words, there is no determinism-- man is free, man is freedom. Nor, on the other hand, if God does not exist, are we provided with any values or command that could legitimize our behavior. Thus we have neither behind us, nor before us in a luminous realm of values, any means of justification or excuse. We are left alone, without excuse. That is what I mean when I say that man is condemned to be free. Condemned, because he did not create himself, yet is nevertheless at liberty, and from the moment that he is thrown into this world he is responsible for everything he does. [79]

Cross' first action after coming to this same conclusion,

that he is responsible for everything he does, is to defend a
black waiter against the hysterical accusations of a white woman. But later he betrays this same impulse by giving the
man a false name and address, thus destroying the man's
hopes for a fair hearing before his union and the railroad.

Cross' constant denial of the demands of others on him
illustrates his basic deviation from the true metaphysical rebel, who, we remember, protests in the name of all men.
At Bob Hunter's apartment, for example, he realizes that his
feeling of alienation stems from his disregard of other men.
He had had the

> illusion of feeling at home with these outsiders,
> but now he felt himself being pushed more than
> ever into that position where he looked at others
> as though they weren't human. He could have
> waved his hand and blotted them from existence
> with no more regret than if he were swatting a
> couple of insects.... In his eyes their value as
> human beings had gone ... (157).

It isn't until he is near death that Cross finally realizes the
inalienable bond that men have with one another. His only
emotional tie had been with Eva Blount, wife of one of the
communists he killed. But Cross also kills Eva--indirectly
but decidedly, when she leaps from a window to her death
upon discovering the monster that he is.

Cross simply will not allow himself to be manipulated
by other people. He is totally free--too free, as he observes.
But his situation is metaphoric of Everyman who, as Sartre
says, is condemned to be free. This absolute freedom is a
grave responsibility, as Nietzsche knew. And at one time
Cross recognized the societal implications of this freedom to
act and create, realizing that "he alone had been responsible
for what he had done to Gladys and Dot" (131). But as he
exercises his new-found freedom--gazing with despair at its
limitless depths--he progressively becomes more and more
god-like, removed from humanity. He forgets to affirm life.
He breaks all promises:

> It was not because he was a Negro that he had
> found his obligations intolerable; it was because
> there resided in his heart a sharp sense of free-
> dom that had somehow escaped being dulled by
> intimidating conditions. Cross had never really
> been tamed ... (347).

Fascinated by the will to power of the communists, Cross is lured into a deadly combat of the will with these gods. He begins to live; his trance-like state evaporates. He struggles valiantly, but he loses. And he loses because the communists work from such a limited perspective that they cannot grasp the motives of a "psychological" man. They cannot believe that his battle is not a personal vendetta but an intellectual detached struggle--a cool game of chess. Because of their near-sightedness, their failure to admit any subjectivity in men, they misjudge Cross, eventually shooting him as a counter-revolutionary.

Although they will ultimately destroy him, Cross' initial response toward the communists is ambivalent, comprised of disgust and admiration. What they preach totally opposes his philosophy, since they require him to release his will to them, to negate himself, to blot out his life and only listen to the Party (168). Yet he understands them. He admires their power, the fact that they have found an answer to live by--to rule by. They are the new Grand Inquisitors, the mutant offspring of Nietzsche--the spoiled fruit of nihilism.

In another epiphany Cross grasps the key to Communism: power. It is, he recognizes, deeper than religious intensity, more sensual than sexual passion. It is a strategy of life, of binding man to man:

> They had reached far back into history and had dredged up from its black waters the most ancient of all realities: man's desire to be a god.... What these men wanted was ... power, not just the exercise of bureaucratic control, but personal power to be wielded directly upon the lives and bodies of others (183-184).

Determined to recruit Cross for the Party, Gil Blount demonstrates the potential of this power that leaves men sniveling and mewling. Cross again is simultaneously fascinated and repelled; the psychological truths stun him and the abject cowering of the victims disgusts him. He obviously sides emotionally with the masters and scorns the slaves (an unusual position for a metaphysical rebel). And like Tillich, Cross sees that such systems can tolerate no rivals--especially the subjective voice of the arts:

> The violent reactions against modern art in collec-tivist (Nazi, Communist) as well as conformist (American democratic) groups show that they feel

seriously threatened by it.

> The creators of modern art have been able to see
> the meaninglessness of our existence; they partici-
> pated in its despair. At the same time they have
> had the courage to face it and express it in their
> pictures and sculptures. They had the courage to
> be as themselves. [80]

This courage to be appears in Eva Blount, a young ex-
pressionist painter who exhibited before her marriage to Gil
Blount, a communist. At that point she was forbidden to display her works publicly, since the communists feared her
message of independent thinking. Cross perspicaciously identifies this same jealousy of power in fascism, capitalism,
and religion. "Cross ... marveled at the astuteness of both
Communist and Fascist politicians who had banned the demonic contagions of jazz" (185). Any organization that wants
man's minds cannot allow freedom of artistic expression in
painting, drama, or novels.

Unfortunately, although Cross is determined to fight
the enemy, he falls prey to its tactics. In a flame and darkness scene straight out of Hawthorne, Damon murders Blount,
the communist, and Herndon, the fascist. Soon afterwards,
Cross mulls over his deed. It suddenly seems terribly complicated to him. He has killed two little gods without regret,
but he himself "had acted like a little god ... ":

> he had assumed the role of policeman, judge, su-
> preme court, and executioner--all in one swift and
> terrible moment. But if he resented their being
> little gods, how could he do the same? His self-
> assurance ebbed, his pride waned.... He had been
> subverted by the contagion of the lawless; he had
> been defeated by that which he had sought to des-
> troy ... had taken on the guise of the monster he
> had slain (212).

To destroy the little gods he must himself become a god.
And to become god is to murder. Cross is torn by the rebel's eternal dilemma: that of having to fight evil with evil:

> To fight Hilton meant fighting Hilton on Hilton's own
> ground, just as he had had to kill Gil and Herndon
> on their own ground, and that in itself was a defeat,
> a travesty of the impulse that had first moved him....

Perhaps he was staring right now at the focal point
of history: if you fought men who tried to conquer
you in terms of total power you too had to use total power and in the end you became what you tried
to defeat ... (225).

In fulfilling the prophecy of the section's epigraph from St.
Paul, "what I hate, that I do," Cross has taken his place in
the line up of other American heroes who are confounded by
that which they attempt to conquer; for example, Young Goodman Brown, who insists on avoiding sin to such an extent that
he breaks "the magnetic chain of humanity," like Ethan Brand
whose heart could not keep pace with his head ("The sin of
an intellect that triumphed over the sense of brotherhood ... ";
both quotes from "Ethan Brand"); and Captain Ahab, who
sailed in league with the devil to slay his personal symbol of
evil, the white whale.

The next section of The Outsider, "Despair," records
the philosophical conversations between Cross and Houston and
Cross and Blimin; the first a dialogue of psychologically akin
outsiders, the second more a monologue from an independent
god to a totalitarian one. Here also Cross struggles to maintain meaning and falls in love with Eva who becomes his goal
for life. But she is an unblemished innocent, a victim by
chance; he is culpable, a victim by choice. Eva is the only
person he feels guilty about: he feels uncomfortable in the
knowledge of her submission to him, in the fact that while he
loves her he betrays her trust. His despair increases.

And his only true psychological equal, Ely Houston,
D. A. and hunchback, terrifies him. He is the one man who
can admit the possibility of Cross' crime. He too is an outsider, a criminal himself who holds himself in check by track-
ing other aberrants. His basic impulse also centers in the
demonic. But he is dedicated to the control of crime--he is,
after all, Cross' most dangerous enemy.

It is to Houston that Cross had stated, "'Man is nothing
in particular'" (125). And it is this clue, coupled with the
myriads appearing in their later conversations, that convinces
Houston of Cross' guilt. Although the action is slow, the dialogue reveals the heart of Wright's thesis: that twentieth-century man, a lawless outsider, considers himself a god. The
result is pure terror.

What Wright envisions on an individual level, Camus

had witnessed on the state level: the pogroms and concentration camps of German Nazism. Both men struggle to find meaning in this world gone mad. Both come essentially to the same conclusion that men must refuse to become gods; that they must continually balance the yes and the no, reaffirming always their basic responsibility to one another--murdering only to destroy evil and then willingly relinquishing their own lives to reestablish the community of man. Man is metaphysically alone but morally bound to others in a mutual sense of responsibility to life.

Since these modern men feel no need for outside ideas to justify their acts, Houston says, "'A lawless man has to rein himself in. A man of lawless impulses living in a society which seeks to restrain instincts for the common good must be in a kind of subjective prison'" (259). When these men, for whom all ethical laws are suspended, see a wrong they set out to correct it. Ironically, according to Houston, they are conceivably the real lawgivers. Horrified by the inequities of justice as it now exists, these rebels ignore its laws and create their own. Religious morality is also junked. Houston calls these men pre-Christian, men without the succor of myths (290 et passim). And when the myths disappear, man returns.[81] Again, this is a Nietzschean idea that Christianity is at fault for nihilism's existence, having created false values; man is compelled to reject them and create a new set that affirms life as it is. History is rejected; nature glorified.[82]

This is the basic difference between the rebels and the totalitarians; for the latter, history is the justification of all acts. Their plans, programs, and actions all look to the future for approval; the now has no importance. In contrast, the rebels regard the present as the only period of value. They do not prepare for future justification; they seek it immediately.

Given the opportunity to reveal his rather Nietzschean philosophy during a grilling by Blimin, Cross lashes out at Communism, Fascism, and capitalism. Finding in all three systems the drive to total power, Cross condemns them and their industrial sources. As far as he is concerned, the dominant factor in human existence is fear:

'The degree and quality of man's fears can be gauged by the scope and density of his myths; that is, by the ingenious manner in which he disguised

the world about him.... Until today almost all of
man's worlds have been either preworlds or back-
worlds, never the real world.... That real world
man did not want ... ' (328).

Science and industry have together destroyed these illusive
myths. Religion is dead. All men are atheists. In Cross'
opinion,

> 'They live, dream, and plan on the assumption that
> there is no God ... [S]ince religion is dead, religion
> is everywhere.... Religion was once an affair of
> the church; it is now in the streets in each man's
> heart. Once there were priests; now every man's
> a priest' (330-331).

For Cross, the implications of this situation lead directly to
Ivan Karamazov's "everything is permitted":

> 'Now, what does this mean--that I don't believe
> in God? It means that I, and you too, can do what
> we damn well please on this earth' (331).

As a consequence, according to Cross, today's govern-
ments--both totalitarian and democratic--prefer their citizens
to be ignorant of their moral freedom, since a man who recognizes his absolute freedom is not to be coerced or controlled. And because history to these governments is of ultimate value, they rewrite events to suit the needs of this
new god. They are the Grand Inquisitors who control men's
minds by feeding them false myths that require no thinking
and allow no fear or dread.

At the top of the hierarchy are the truly modern men,
the men in power, the Jealous Rebels. Of all men, they alone
have had the courage to recognize the essential meaninglessness of the world. They face the real world and admit it is
nothing beyond their own dreams. They understand that the
key to power is a psychological one. Cross explains that

> 'Their programs are but the crude translations of
> the daydreams of the man in the street, daydreams
> in which the Jealous Rebels do not believe!
>
> 'In order to catch their prey, they deliberately
> spin vast spiderwebs of ideology, the glittering
> strands of which are designed to appeal to the hopes

of hopeful men....

'Their aims? Direct and naked power! ...
They are out to grab the entire body of mankind and
they will replace faith and belief with organization
and discipline' (335-336).

And they have a good chance of succeeding (here Cross sounds
like a Marxist): industrialism's assembly lines help by de-
grading the meaning of work and men's lives (unions should
not bargain for more money but for freer men whose work is
not alienating). Better communication allows for stronger or-
ganizations. Commercial advertising cheapens and devalues
the individual personality. The future leads inexorably to totalitarian systems. Wars are futile since war cannot destroy
men's beliefs.

With this bleak outlook as his source of action, Cross
Damon takes the only way out. He steps out of society, creates his own world and values. He becomes his own god;
therefore he murders and continues to do so until he himself
is murdered by the Jealous Rebels he sought not to fight but
to understand. His engagement with the members of the Communist Party has been an intellectual war game. Thus he did
not set out to destroy them, knowing full well the futility of
such a plan. Instead, he used them as a foil to test his ideas.
Bouncing off their philosophy, he was able to synthesize his
own. But it proved a dangerous game that he lost: the stake
being his life.

Like the other Wright heroes we have studied, Cross
Damon is a neurotic. Although much of what he does is psychologically inexplicable, some aspects of his behavior are
definitely the result of his neurosis. The solution that Cross
unconsciously has stumbled upon to relieve his inner conflicts
is that which Horney labels "the pattern of streamlining ...
the attempt to suppress permanently and rigidly one self and
be exclusively the other."[83] Thus Cross attempts to be exclusively his expansive self. As Horney characterizes this
solution,

It chiefly entails his determinism, conscious or
unconscious, to overcome every obstacle--in or
outside himself--and the belief that he should be
able, and in fact is able, to do so. He should
be able to master the adversities of fate, the
difficulties of a situation, the intricacies of in-

tellectual problems, the resistances of other people,
conflicts in himself. The reverse side of the necessity for mastery is his dread of anything connot-
ing helplessness; this is the most poignant dread he
has. [84]

Of the three subdivisions of this expansive type, Cross best
fits the category of "arrogant-vindictiveness."

Cross' need for revenge shows itself very nicely in his
scenes with his wife when he attempts to prove to her that he
is crazy so she will drive him out of the house. When Gladys
finally reaches a nervous frenzy and sends him away, Cross
feels good. This need also manifests itself in his murder of
Jack Hilton; as he admits to himself, "it had been to rid himself of that sense of outrage that Hilton's attitude had evoked
in him, Hilton's assumption that he could have made a slave
of him" (280). He has no intention of letting anyone control
his life--neither his wife, his mistress, the postal officials,
nor the communists.

As Horney describes this type, "he is openly arrogant,
often rude and offensive, although sometimes this is covered
up by a thin veneer of civil politeness. "[85] Thus Cross inter-
nally scorns the stupidity and weakness of his acquaintances
but is careful to maintain an air of shallow friendliness. He
joins in the barroom conversation, for example, but does not
really involve himself with his postal buddies, remaining always a tolerant outsider, bemused by their human failings.
He acts the same way when he is with Bob and Sarah Hunter.

Although the sources of Cross' neurosis could undoubtedly be found in the experiences of his childhood, we are
given very little evidence to support this. We do learn, however, that Cross' father was a victim of a race riot--so Cross
must have learned early how whites felt about blacks. He also must have begun at this time to deny his positive feelings,
his impulse toward love, because of the whites' hostility. [86]
This "hardening of feelings, originally a necessity for survival," however, according to Horney, "allows for an unhampered growth of the drive for a triumphant mastery of life. "[87]
By the time we begin our study of Cross he is in his late
twenties, well-established in his compulsion to be the master
of his fate.

Because he feels like an outsider, "he must prove his
own worth to himself. "[88] Horney's further descriptions of

the arrogant-vindictive type fit Cross perfectly:

> For a person as isolated and as hostile as he, it
> is of course important not to need others. Hence
> he develops a pronounced pride in a godlike self-
> sufficiency.... Having smothered positive feelings,
> he can rely upon only his intellect for the mastery
> of life. Hence his pride in his intellectual powers
> reaches unusual dimensions.... [89]

If it is because of his insistence on being free that he originally decides to take advantage of the accident, it is because
of his faith in his intelligence that he finally takes on the
dreadful task of creating a personality from scratch. Com-
peting with the communists in a game for his soul is also an
intellectual challenge to him, as are his conversations with
Ely Houston. In these talks Cross intentionally posits obvious
analogies to his own condition, just to see if Houston is up to
recognizing their application to him.

But as Cross' intellectual pride increases so does his
vulnerability. Horney says:

> Actually, as his pride becomes all consuming, his
> vulnerability also assumes unbearable dimensions.
> But he never allows himself to feel any hurt because
> his pride prohibits it. Thus the hardening process
> ... must gather momentum for the sake of protect-
> ing his pride. His pride then lies in being above
> hurts and suffering. [90]

Above being hurt, Cross can stand unemotionally by when
Houston brings in his wife and three small sons to test his
character:

> Cross vowed that Houston would never see him hum-
> bled, unnerved, or weeping.... He would make a
> supreme effort and remain cold, hard. Sentiment
> must not subvert him now. He was lost ... but,
> he must not let human claims drag him into a posi-
> tion where Houston could crow over him (258-259).

Houston is outraged with Cross' unconcern: "'You are the
lowest sonofabitch I've ever seen in all of my life'" (301).

As part of his feelings of impunity, Cross feels he
can do with others what he pleases. And so he abuses Gladys,

deserts Dot, fools Eva, and murders four men--all seemingly
without guilt. He also breaks all promises with other people.
"His own experience had shown him that he was cold-blooded-
ly brutal when trapped in situations involving his self-respect"
(26).

Another manifestation of Cross' extreme neurosis is
the extraordinary depth of his self-hate. All through the book
he despises himself, often becoming overwhelmed with feelings of self-loathing. As Horney has observed,

> Such self-hate calls for rigorous self-protective
> measures. Its externalization seems a matter of
> sheer self-preservation. As in all expansive solu-
> tions, it is primarily an active one. He hates and
> despises in others all he suppresses and hates in
> himself: their spontaneity, their joy of living, their
> appeasing trends, their compliance ... their 'stu-
> pidity.'[91]

Cross, therefore, externalizes his own self-hate when he sees
Bob Hunter groveling in front of Gil Blount for his life. Like
other arrogant types Cross "has very little, if any, sympathy
for others."[92] He is lacking in human compassion basically
because he envies others their place in life, feeling himself
to be outside it.

Finally, because of his need to deny his positive impulses, Cross' self-hate convinces him that he is unlovable.[93]
Therefore, the one person he tries to love must be sheltered
from his true nature.

It isn't until he is on his death bed that Cross realizes
the futility of what he has tried to do. Motivated by unconscious psychological factors and conscious philosophical premises, Cross has attempted to live alone, in complete control
of his life. Given the unique opportunity of being able to
create a new personality for himself, Cross can do no better
the second time around. Whether Wright was suggesting that
Cross' psychological makeup was irreversible or whether he
was suggesting that modern man left to his own devices would
naturally end up in the depths of nihilism is not clear; it is
conceivable, of course, that he was suggesting both. Whatever
ever the argument behind Wright's theme, his book is a bitter
one. And the deathbed conversion fails to leave the reader
with either a sense of relief or hope.

Perhaps Robert Bone is not too far afield when he
reads The Outsider as a "recapitulation of the author's spiritual journey":

> Books I and II are concerned with Wright's identity
> as Negro; Books III and IV with his identity as
> Communist; Book V with his identity as lonely in-
> tellectual, disillusioned outsider, marginal man. [94]

Certainly the ultimate fate of the alienated man, the rebel-
victim, is total estrangement from society and then from himself. And Cross Damon dies a stricken man, frightened by
his attempt to live as a free agent.

The initiate has come a long way by the closing scene
in The Outsider. He has been victimized, estranged, outraged. And finally he has rebelled--at first timidly and then
arrogantly. Cross' story begins with his unhappiness and un-
rest, and moves rapidly after the accident into the abyss of
nihilism; an educated man and reader of existential philosophy,
Cross is usually aware of what he does--that is one reason
that his actions are so terrifying. Wright also strongly suggests that Cross' color is not necessarily the primary cause
of his rebellion, although it is always a potential factor in his
behavior, especially in regards to his determination to be his
own master: it takes someone whose control was severely
threatened to be so jealous of it.

The next story not only reveals the Negro as representative of all men but also illustrates the inherent guilt of
all mankind. "The Man Who Lived Underground" is a modern
allegory that depicts the black man as the symbol of man's
isolation, loneliness, and despair. In its call for brotherhood, moreover, the story is an expansion of the theme expressed in the last scene of The Outsider.

Although "The Man Who Lived Underground" was published in 1944, its hero illustrates what I believe to be the
definitive stance of Richard Wright; that is, a plea for brotherhood coupled with a dire warning of what can happen if men
are not given the full freedom to control their own lives. It
is a good story, a well-written, tense piece which illustrates
the major influences on Wright's thinking, combining as it
does elements of Freudianism, Marxism, and existentialism--

and continuing as a result the eternal debate as to whether
Wright's heroes are individuals in their own right or simply
mouthpieces of protest literature. Furthermore, "The Man
Who Lived Underground" is just enough the story of a black
man to raise the question of whether Wright is protesting
against the racial situation or the human condition.

But strangely enough, although it is one of Wright's
best and most provocative pieces, "The Man Who Lived Underground" has received very little critical attention. Moreover, as we might expect from the divergence of critical
opinion surrounding Wright's other works, the critics vary
radically in their evaluation and interpretation of this story.
Some examples: Gloria Bramwell in a review of Eight Men
is displeased with what she calls Wright's "inverse paternalism"; she also contends that the "protagonist is merely presented as an instrument for the author's ideas.... "[95] Irving
Howe, on the other hand, admires Wright's style, stating that
he "shows a sense of narrative rhythm, a gift for shaping the
links between sentences so as to create a chain of expectation,
which is superior to anything in his full-length novels.... "[96]
Ronald Ridenour calls it "a magnificent short story";[97] and Edward Margolies says that "Wright is at his storytelling best. "[98]
Robert Bone regards the story as an extension of Wright's
protest against racism, calling "Wright's subterranean world
... a symbol of the Negro's social marginality. "[99] Conversely, Edward Margolies argues that the hero "is not merely a
victim of a racist society but a symbol of all men in that society.... "[100]

Most critics do agree, however, on the existential content of the story. Stanley Edgar Hyman, for example, calls
it "pre-existentialist" (i.e., Wright naturally came to existential conclusions in his writing--he did not attempt to create
an existential story: existence of the story precedes its essence).[101] Again, Ronald Ridenour says that here "Wright
expounds existential themes.... There is an appreciable lack
of the immediate, of the ephemeral, and of the well-worn
white-black conflicts. "[102] And Shirley Meyer remarks that
the story "is a work which is motivated by the existential
vision. "[103]

Besides being one of the best examples of Wright's existential thinking, "The Man Who Lived Underground" is also
without question Wright's most surrealistic story. Although
it is presented as actually happening--not as a subjective
nightmare, but as objective reality--its surrealistic overtones

and descriptions argue for a symbolic interpretation:

> The reader may grant that the events of the short
> story could possibly occur (improbability does not
> give rise to the story's surrealistic quality), but
> at the same time it seems that the events are in
> large part a projection of unconscious forces lying
> dormant within the psyche of the central character.
> The lack of clear delineation in the story of inter-
> nal from external, of subjective from objective, is
> the source of its surrealism. [104]

Because the story is told entirely through the eyes of Fred
Daniels without any authorial intrustion, we see only what Fred
sees, and see it only as he sees it. [105] His viewpoint controls ours completely; therein lies the difficulty of trying to
separate subjective from objective reality.   The story therefore has at least two levels.   Superficially, this is the story
of an innocent man who has been framed by the police and so
is hiding in the sewers where he gains a new perspective on
life.   Symbolically, this is the allegory of the hero as Everyman who journeys into the mouth of leviathan and tries upon
returning from the dead to save the rest of the world.   Because the story is tragic irony, the hero fails in his quest:
he dies and the land continues to be laid waste by evil and
corruption.

Although the critics are quick to point out the existential nature of the hero's experiences, they seem unaware of
these archetypal patterns exemplified by his adventures.   After looking at Native Son from this same archetypal
perspective, it seems fairly reasonable to suggest that "The
Man Who Lived Underground" also fits into Northrup Frye's
mythos of winter, more specifically in the sixth or late phase
of tragic irony which "presents human life in terms of large-
ly unrelieved bondage." [106]   The symbols appearing in this
phase are, according to Frye, generally parodies of those in
romance, corresponding to the demonic world.   'In this low
mimetic area we enter a world that we may call the analogy
of experience ... [therefore] the images are the ordinary images of experience.... "[107]   These images, however, take
on unpleasant and even sinister overtones because of their
context. [108]   "Cities take of course the shape of the labyrinthine modern metropolis, where the main emotional stress is
on loneliness and lack of communication. "   As another example, water takes on negative connotations, becoming destructive instead of life-giving.   Frye calls this reversal of

"customary moral associations of archetypes" the phenomenon of "demonic modulation."[109]

Thus, the setting for "The Man Who Lived Underground" is appropriately the labyrinthine sewers of a modern metropolis. As the controlling image of the story, this symbol represents the decadence, aimlessness, loneliness, and despair of the lives of the city-dwellers--and by extension, all men. The story's other images--the floating debris, the dead baby, the corpse, the movie theater, the church, the bloody cleaver, the suicide--support the major symbol by contributing to the general impression of isolation, futility, and cruelty. The fact that no one will listen to Fred illustrates the lack of communication among people. Furthermore, in a typical demonic modulation, the normally beneficent symbol of water has taken on sinister aspects; not only does the water threaten to drown the hero as it has apparently drowned the baby, but the very fact that it is the city's sewage instils it with malevolence. As one critic has pointed out, because we are so intimately involved in the mind of the hero we do not immediately regard these images as symbols, accepting them instead simply as the conceivable experiences of a desperate man.[110] It isn't until we begin to study the story that we realize the significance of these "images of experience."

Besides inverting the symbols of romance, as its parody, tragic irony also exhibits certain characteristic patterns of romance. For example, the three-fold structure of romance appears in tragic irony, specifically in "The Man Who Lived Underground" "in the three-day rhythm of death, disappearance and revival which is found in the myth of Attis and other dying gods, and has been incorporated in our Easter."[111] Furthermore, Frye notes that tragic irony in its latest phase often uses what he calls "parody-religious symbols."[112] This observation is important to Wright's story since Fred is underground for three days and nights and seems to rise again from the dead in a parody of Christ's resurrection.

It is also pertinent to our study to look at some of the manifestations of the symbolic displacement of the dragon-slaying (which is the primary objective of the quest-romance in its non-displaced form), since they appear as parodies in a low mimetic fiction such as "The Man Who Lived Underground." Frye notes that the leviathan (the biblical dragon), who is the enemy of Christ, becomes by extension "the whole fallen world of sin and death and tyranny into which Adam fell. "[113] Therefore the hero, Christ, comes into the leviathan to save us. A more displaced version has the hero travel in underground labyrinths in place of the monster's belly. This pattern also appears in solar myths "where the hero travels perilously through a dark labyrinthine underworld full of monsters between sunset and sunrise. "[114] Moreover, as Frye observes, the "leviathan is usually a sea-monster, which means metaphorically that he is the sea.... As denizens of his belly, therefore, we are also metaphorically under water. "[115] "Lastly," says Frye, "if the leviathan is death, and the hero has to enter the body of death, and if his quest is completed, the final stage of it is, cyclically, rebirth, and, dialectically, resurrection. "[116]

The watery labyrinth that Fred wanders in can be seen, therefore, as the leviathan, symbol of death, sin, and destruction--which works well in conjunction with the fact that the leviathan is a sea-monster. In the belly of the monster, Fred as Everyman is also in the heart of the fallen world. Furthermore, although Fred does not literally die on his first trip to the sewers, he does lose his earthly identity by forgetting his name. Ultimately, of course, Fred does find the leviathan the body of death, for he is shot and left to die when he returns to the sewers after his initial rebirth from them. But here the cycle ends. There is no rebirth from death--no resurrection. For the hero in the low mimetic mode, death is final--the displacement from the romance is complete: the inverted Christ-figure is only too human.

According to Frye, the "quest-romance has analogies to both rituals and dreams." Ritualistically, it is related to the "victory of fertility over the waste land"; and in dream terms, it corresponds to the wish-fulfillment dream. [117] In tragic irony, however, the patterns are reversed; i.e., the quest is foiled, the desert remains eternal and the dream has become a nightmare. [118] This is Wright's vision of life not only in "The Man Who Lived Underground," but also in The Long Dream, Lawd Today, Native Son, and The Outsider-- and it is an apt metaphor. As part of their nightmare Wright's heroes are continually thwarted in their quest for love and acceptance; they exist in a world that rejects them. It is truly a waste land more than ready for the gentle rains from heaven. But the land needs a hero to save it, and these heroes--Fred and Bigger--are inarticulate, unable to communicate with the world that so desperately needs their message. The nightmare continues.

To describe his heroes' sense of unreality Wright often uses the phrase "waking dreams" in addition to "nightmare."[119] In this surrealistic world where time and space are twisted and warped, all logical cause and effect relationships are lost. As a consequence, Wright's heroes experience a curious alienation not only from other men but from themselves and the world of reality. Constants like right and wrong, that we have grown accustomed to, have no validity for Cross, Bigger, or Big Boy. For theirs is a sick world where innocent men are stalked like animals and lynched, where criminals roam free tortured only by their own conscience. It is a world where those in power interpret the laws to suit themselves and let the rest be damned. Truly, for Cross, Bigger, and Big Boy as for Hamlet, another outsider by a quirk of fate and birth, "The time is out of joint." Adrift on the periphery of life, these men struggle to find some sort of meaning to cling to. Stumbling through their waking dreams they remind one of the persona in Roethke's poem who explains paradoxically,

> I wake to sleep, and take my waking slow.
> I learn by going where I have to go. [120]

Wright begins his parable of Everyman with descriptions of a nightmare world. [121] This is a land of dark shadows and corners, whose blackness is pierced by the wail of a siren seeking an innocent man. This man, so overcome with terror that he thinks he must be dreaming, leaps into an open manhole, where the nightmare is continued and intensified. Once in the sewers he completely loses contact with the world above. Wright's impressionistic descriptions heighten the sense of terror and foreboding:

> From the perforations of the manhole cover, delicate lances of hazy violet sifted down and wove a mottled pattern upon the surface of the streaking current. His lips parted as a car swept past along the wet pavement overhead, its heavy rumble soon dying out, like the hum of a plane speeding through a dense cloud. He had never thought that cars could sound like that; everything seemed strange and unreal under here. He stood in darkness for a long time, knee-deep in rustling water, musing. [122]

Although he wants to leave this hell, he cannot, bound as he is by an "irrational impulse" to stay (30). And so the dream images flit by him, inviting his participation. Wright's effective use of color contributes to the impression that Fred is in hell:

> He went back to the basement and stood in the red darkness, watching the glowing embers in the furnace. He went to the sink and turned the faucet and the water flowed in a smooth silent stream that looked like a spout of blood. He brushed the mad image from his mind and began to wash his hands leisurely, looking about for the usual bar of soap. He found one and rubbed it in his palms until a rich lather bloomed in his cupped fingers, like a scarlet sponge (39).

While he is underground, frightened and terribly alone, trapped by the "lure of darkness and silence" (his desire for safety attracts him fatally to this moist, dark womb of the world), he witnesses a montage of horrors. He sees a "huge rat, wet with slime, blinking beady eyes and baring tiny fangs" (30). He sees a baby "snagged by debris and half-submerged in water" (34). Wright's imagery is again superb:

> Water blossomed about the tiny legs, the tiny arms, the tiny head, and rushed onwards. The eyes were closed, as though in sleep; the fists were clenched, as though in protest; and the mouth gaped black in a soundless cry (34).

He sees his own people in church "groveling and begging for something they could never get" (33). He sees the waking dead watching a movie, reminding one of Plato's cave: "They were shouting and yelling at the animated shadows of themselves" (38). He sees an employee steal money from a safe, another kill himself.

Fred's reaction to these nightmare scenes is one compounded of pain, despair, and disgust. He identifies with the blacks in church and wants to tell them to be proud and unrepentant. He longs to warn the movie-goers that they laugh at their own images on the screen. He steals but considers his own thievery and the employee's as two different things, since he has no intention of spending the money he stole. He regards the innocent man who kills himself as really guilty--of something just by virtue of being a man--and so deserving to die.

Although innocent of murder, Fred himself feels guilty, condemned (49). Guilty of stealing, he feels innocent:

> He did not feel that he was stealing, for the cleaver, the radio, the money, and the typewriter were all on the same level of value, all meant the same thing to him. They were the serious toys of the men who lived in the dead world of sunshine and rain he had left, the world that had condemned him, branded him guilty (55).

Dread and anxiety torment him, yet he feels powerful, indulgently refusing to kill the guard asleep at his feet. He feels so distant from the rest of the world that its values mean nothing to him, as though he were from a different planet. He knows that he cannot awaken these people for they are "children, sleeping in their living, awake in their dying" (38). He has seen the world as it really is--meaningless.

Finally, as part of the general meaninglessness of things, "freddaniels" forgets his own name. Experimenting with a new identity, he imitates a couple of white businessmen. Irrationally he rushes to paper his mud walls with stolen money and lay his floors with diamonds. Recklessly he winds all his stolen watches, not bothering to set them since time has lost its meaning too. It has become just another gimmick that man uses to hide life's meaninglessness from himself.

Then, the man with no name begins to think. And what he discovers about himself frightens him:

> Maybe anything's right, he mumbled. Yes, if the world as men had made it was right, then anything else was right, any act a man took to satisfy himself, murder, theft, torture (64).

If the way Fred has been treated is right--as the world assures him it is--then it follows that nothing is wrong. [123] Horrified by these thoughts, the man tries to shove them out of his mind, but he is drawn to them inexorably. Fear, dread, anxiety--the hallmarks of existentialism--plague him as he tries to reason out his life. And like Cross Damon his greatest source of dismay is himself,

> He did not know how much fear he felt, for

> fear claimed him completely; yet it was not a fear
> of the police or of people, but a cold dread at the
> thought of the actions he knew he would perform if
> he went out into that cruel sunshine (73).

By the third day Fred begins to probe the cause of man's essential guilt, discovering what Peter Verkovensky asserts in
The Possessed: "We're all villains. '"[124] Fred asks himself

> Why was this sense of guilt so seemingly innate,
> so easy to come by, to think, so verily physical?
> It seemed that when one felt this guilt one was re-
> tracing in one's feelings a faint pattern designed
> long before; it seemed that one was always trying
> to remember a gigantic shock that had left a haunt-
> ing impression upon one's body which one could not
> forget or shake off, but which had been forgotten
> by the conscious mind, creating in one's life a state
> of eternal anxiety (68).

Fred recognizes that what he finds in himself is the
same underground man that he has witnessed at work in church,
the funeral parlor, the jewelry store, the theater. What he
has discovered in the depths of the earth is the message of
nihilism: all values are destroyed; nothing has meaning.
Everything is permitted. According to Margolies, he learns
that

> the nether world in which he dwells is the real
> world of the human heart--and that the surface
> world which hums above him in the streets of the
> city is senseless and meaningless--a kind of un-
> reality which men project to hide from themselves
> the awful blackness of their souls. He is invested
> suddenly with a sense of pity for all mankind.[125]

Like a visionary, this low mimetic hero burns to communicate
his newly discovered truths to all people; overcome with a
feeling of goodwill, he feels he can no longer remain in the
sewers while people in the streets continue in their ignorance.
He surfaces from the belly of leviathan to save his people.

Out of the sewers after three days, the man runs into the church he had seen from below to give the singers his
message. But he is thrown out as a drunk. Thus are the
true prophets scorned. And like Jeremiah, Isaiah, and Hab-

bakuk, his own life is emblematic of what he preaches. "He
was the statement, and since it was all so clear to him,
surely he would be able to make it clear to others" (77). He
is the underground man realized in full, symbolic of all men,
as Margolies has observed: "The underground man is the essential nature of all men--and is composed of dread, terror,
and guilt. "126 But the rest of the world chooses to ignore
this inner core of corruption and nausea, pretending it doesn't
exist--frantically buzzing from one activity to the next to keep
from thinking.

As a parody of them, Fred Daniels is very much like
the Old Testament prophets in many ways (perhaps Wright
was remembering the stories of his old granny who was on
fire with evangelical religion). Scorned and rejected, as they
were, Fred Daniels is forced to live as an outcast. And
while in the sewers he undergoes a transformation that could
be called a religious conversion. Alone, hungry, with time
at last to think, Fred has a vision. It is a vision of a cor-
rupt and meaningless world. Like the true prophets before
him, Fred sees gloom and despairs. 127 Furthermore, like
these prophets, Fred is mocked by the men who need saving
the most, here the police who have framed him:

'All the people I saw was guilty, ' he began slowly.

'Aw, nuts, ' a policeman muttered (80).

What he hopes to do is instil these men with pity for the sad
condition of mankind by showing them what he has seen. But,
inarticulate, he cannot make his vision clear to these men.
And, like Daniel whose message displeased Darius, who there-
upon cast him into the lions' den, Fred Daniels, doomed prophet of a new order, is shot in the head and cast into the
sewers. "'You've got to shoot his kind. They'd wreck
things'" (92). 128

Having seen man's guilt before himself (instead of before God as Jeremiah did), Fred tries desperately to save
him. But his cries fall on deaf ears. Like the white men
in Native Son and The Outsider, these people are blind. Not
only don't they see blacks, they don't hear them. Fred
Daniels, man with no name, doesn't exist for them--nor does
Ralph Ellison's Invisible Man, who remains entirely nameless
throughout his story.

Ely Houston predicts in The Outsider that Negroes

blessed (or cursed) with a double vision will become the prophets of a new age. Edward Margolies has found the same message in Wright, suggesting that what he really is saying is that

> All of men's strivings, activities, and ideals are simply a means of keeping from themselves the knowledge of their underground nature ... [129]

Historically, forced by the special nature of their isolation to measure the white man's world objectively, these judges in black skin will inevitably become the nemeses of white society. Like the furies who haunted the conscience of a blood-murderer, the black man of America will goad his white brother into repentance. The first of these new men, Fred Daniels, the man who lived underground, fails. But others will follow who, seeing the truth, will seek to warn man. And failing that, will seek to destroy him.

In this story, Wright himself must be given credit for prophesying certain aspects of the black power movement of the sixties. For as early as 1944 he could see the effect on a man's soul of a three hundred year old national program of rejection and alienation. Having brought the black man to America to be his slave, the white man could not accept him as a brother once he had emancipated him. Thus, although the black was free of his shackles, the white ironically was not. He was trapped by his own imperfect vision of life that had him master and the other slave. What greater cruelty could man perpetrate against his own kind than the refusal to admit an entire people's existence? Driven to an underground mentality by this relentless treatment, the blacks, as Wright envisions them, will find their own values existentially and rise up to confront the whites with their truths.

Notes

1. Saunders Redding, "The Alien Land of Richard Wright," Soon, One Morning: New Writing by American Negroes, 1940-1962, ed. by Herbert Hill (New York: Alfred A. Knopf, 1963), p. 59. See also Redding's comment in his review of The Long Dream, where he states in part that "Wright has been away too long.... Come back, Dick Wright, to life again. " ("The Way It Was," New York Times Book Review Oct. 26, 1958, p. 38).

2. Webb, Biography, p. 279.

3. That is, Wright as implied author does not step into the narrative and comment directly, but he has his characters do this for him--as he does in Max's speech in Native Son. As Wayne Booth points out, this is not bad a priori but only in terms of whether it works in context or not. I suggest it does not in this instance. (See Chapter V for a more complete discussion of Wright's rhetoric.)

4. See Chapter V, pp. 179-181.

5. Charles I. Glicksberg, "Existentialism in The Outsider," Four Quarters, VII (Jan., 1958), 23.

6. R. W. B. Lewis, The American Adam: Innocence, Tragedy, and Tradition in the Nineteenth Century (Chicago: The University of Chicago Press, 1971), pp. 50, 51.

7. Richard Wright, The Outsider (New York: Harper & Row, 1953), p. 78. (All subsequent page references to this work will appear in parentheses in the text.)

8. Lewis, The American Adam: Innocence, Tragedy, and Tradition in the Nineteenth Century, p. 55.

9. See Chapter II, p. 16.

10. Hassan, Radical Innocence: The Contemporary American Novel, p. 33.

11. Lewis, The American Adam: Innocence, Tragedy, and Tradition in the Nineteenth Century, p. 89.

12. Hassan, Radical Innocence: The Contemporary American Novel, p. 39.

13. Lewis, The American Adam: Innocence, Tragedy, and Tradition in the Nineteenth Century, p. 128.

14. Darwin Turner, "The Outsider: Revision of an Idea," CLA Journal, XII (June, 1969), 310-321.

15. Hassan, Radical Innocence: The Contemporary American Novel, pp. 26-27.

16. <u>Ibid</u>., p. 27.

17. Cf. Robert Penn Warren, <u>All the King's Men</u> (New York: Bantam, 1970): (Jack Burden thinking) "Then I thought how all knowledge that is worth anything is maybe paid for by blood. Maybe that is the only way you can tell that a certain piece of knowledge is worth anything: it has cost some blood" (p. 429).
    John A. Williams, <u>The Man Who Cried I Am</u> (New York: The New American Library, 1967): (Max Reddick thinking) "He had come to know, <u>really</u> know that to be oppressed was not enough to win ultimately; that to be in the right was not enough. You had to win the way they had won--with blood" (p. 174).

18. Jean-Paul Sartre, <u>Nausea</u>, trans. Lloyd Alexander (New York: New Directions, 1964), p. 100.

19. Camus, <u>Rebel</u>, pp. 22, 297.

20. Jean-Paul Sartre, <u>Being and Nothingness: An Essay on Phenomenological Ontology</u>, trans. Hazel E. Barnes (New York: Washington Square Press, 1971), pp. ii, iii.

21. Turner, "<u>The Outsider</u>: Revision of an Idea," 320-321.

22. See Chapter V, pp. 179-181.

23. Glicksberg, "Existentialism in <u>The Outsider</u>," 23. See also Nick Aaron Ford, "The Ordeal of Richard Wright," <u>College English</u>, XV (Oct., 1953): "the motivation for the four murders committed by Cross is neither natural nor compelling. It lies outside the normal pattern of human psychology" (94).

24. Galloway, <u>The Absurd Hero in American Fiction</u>, pp. xix-xx.

25. Glicksberg, "Existentialism in <u>The Outsider</u>," 17.

26. Richard Wright, "Big Boy Leaves Home," <u>Uncle Tom's Children</u>, pp. 17-53.

27. Wright's "pastoral impulse" is evident here, as it is in <u>Black Boy</u> and <u>Lawd Today</u>. See: Keneth Kinnamon, "The Pastoral Impulse in Richard Wright," <u>Midcon-</u>

tinent American Studies Journal, X (Spring, 1969), 41-47.

28. Albert Camus, Caligula and Three Other Plays, trans. Stuart Gilbert (New York: Vintage Books, 1958), p. vi.

29. See: James Baldwin, "Alas, Poor Richard," Nobody Knows My Name (New York: Dell, 1961), p. 151.

30. Kent, "Adventure of Western Culture," 324.

31. Baldwin, "Alas," Nobody Knows My Name: "In most of the novels written by Negroes until today ... there is a great space where sex ought to be; and what usually fills this space is violence. This violence, as in so much of Wright's work, is gratuitous and compulsive ... because the root of the violence is never examined. The root is ... the rage, almost literally the howl of a man who is being castrated" (p. 151).

32. "In his review of Native Son in March, 1940, Malcolm Cowley, having in mind the consistency with which Mr. Wright's executive design ... had been a design of violence, suggested that his 'sense of the indignities heaped on his race' might well go so deep as to make it his unconscious tendency in his fiction to revenge himself 'by a whole series of symbolic murders.' And though Mr. Cowley may at this point have been somewhat overstating things, the propensity for violence cannot, it is true, be gainsaid: Mr. Wright may not have been bent on symbolic murder, but at least it can be asserted that he was eager to sound a hue and a cry and had something of a penchant for 'holding a loaded pistol at the head of the white world while he muttered between clenched teeth: "Either you grant us equal rights as human beings or else this is what will happen."'" (Nathan Scott, "The Dark and Haunted Tower of Richard Wright," Graduate Comment, VII [July, 1964], 96. Quoted Charles I. Glicksberg, "Negro Fiction in America," The South Atlantic Quarterly, 45 [October, 1946], 482.)

33. In 1959 Richard Lehan called it "the most express treatment of the existential theme in American fiction" (Lehan, "Existentialism in Recent American Fiction: The Demonic Quest," p. 74).

34. Sartre, Age, p. 64.

35. Ibid. , p. 38.

36. Paul Tillich, The Courage to Be (New Haven: Yale University Press, 1967), p. 36.

37. Kierkegaard's The Concept of Dread, trans. Walter Lowrie (Princeton: Princeton University Press, 1944), p. 37.

38. Martin Heidegger, Being and Time, trans. John Macquarrie and Edward Robinson (London: SCM Press Ltd. , 1962), pp. 179, 227, 232, 233.

39. See: Lewis Lawson, "Cross Damon: Kierkegaardian Man of Dread," CLA Journal, XIV, 3 (March, 1971), 298-316.

40. Kierkegaard's The Concept of Dread, p. 38.

41. Ibid. , p. 40.

42. Ibid. , p. 55.

43. Sartre, Being, p. 68.

44. Ibid. , pp. 71, 72.

45. Ibid. , p. 186.

46. See also pp. 347, 375, 397.

47. Tillich, The Courage to Be, p. 35.

48. Ibid. , p. 41.

49. Ibid. , p. 56.

50. Ibid. , p. 56.

51. Ibid. , p. 44.

52. Ibid. , p. 47.

53. Ibid. , pp. 49-50.

54. Ibid., p. 52.

55. See Chapter III, pp. 73-75, 84-85, 98 for similarities between Bigger and Camus' rebel.

56. Camus, Rebel, pp. 3, 4.

57. Ibid., p. 6.

58. Ibid., p. 7-8.

59. Ibid., p. 10.

60. See Chapter III, pp. 84-85.

61. Nathan Scott, "The Dark and Haunted Tower of Richard Wright," Graduate Comment, VII (July, 1964), 93.

62. Camus, Rebel, p. 20.

63. Ibid., p. 13.

64. Ibid., p. 14-15.

65. Fyodor Dostoyevsky, The Brothers Karamazov, trans. Constance Garnett (New York: The Modern Library, 1950), p. 289.

66. Camus, Rebel, p. 25.

67. Ibid., p. 57.

68. Dostoyevsky, Brothers, p. 289.

69. Camus, Rebel, p. 59.

70. Friedrich Nietzsche, The Will to Power, trans. Walter Kaufmann and R. J. Hollingdale (New York: Random House, 1967), pp. 10-11, 13.

71. Camus, Rebel, p. 70.

72. Fyodor Dostoyevsky, The Possessed, trans. Andrew R. MacAndrew (New York: Signet Classic, 1969), p. 635.

73. Camus, Rebel, p. 71.

74. Ibid., p. 73.

75. Ibid., p. 74.

76. Ibid., pp. 101-102.

77. Ibid., p. 102.

78. Ibid., p. 103.

79. Sartre, "Existentialism Is a Humanism," Existentalism From Dostoevsky to Sartre, ed. by Kaufmann, p. 295.

80. Tillich, The Courage to Be, pp. 141, 147-148.

81. Cf. Kirilov's ideas in The Possessed when he declares that "'Man kept inventing God in order to live'" (636), and with God dead, man will become a god.

82. See Chapter IV, pp. 139-141.

83. Horney, Neurosis and Human Growth: The Struggle Toward Self-Realization, p. 190.

84. Ibid., p. 192.

85. Ibid., p. 199.

86. Although there is little empirical evidence to support this in The Outsider, it does seem to be the pattern of Wright's other heroes as we have seen in The Long Dream and Native Son.

87. Horney, Neurosis and Human Growth: The Struggle Toward Self-Realization, p. 203.

88. Ibid., p. 204.

89. Ibid., p. 204.

90. Ibid., pp. 204-205.

91. Ibid., p. 208.

92. Ibid., p. 211.

93. Ibid., p. 210.

94. Bone, Pamphlet, p. 39.

95. Gloria Bramwell, "Articulated Nightmare," Midstream, VII (Spring, 1961), 112.

96. Irving Howe, "Richard Wright: A Word of Farewell," New Republic, CXLIV (Feb., 1961), 17.

97. Ronald Ridenour, "The Man Who Lived Underground," Phylon, XXXI (Spring, 1970), 54.

98. Margolies, Art of Richard Wright, p. 78.

99. Bone, Pamphlet, p. 26.

100. Margolies, Art of Richard Wright, p. 78.

101. Stanley Edgar Hyman, "Some Trends in the Novel," College English, XX (Oct., 1958), 6.

102. Ridenour, "The Man Who Lived Underground," 54.

103. Shirley Meyer, "The Identity of 'The Man Who Lived Underground,'" Negro American Literature Forum, VI (July, 1970), 52.

104. Gibson, "Tyranny of Convention," 352.

105. See Chapter V, pp. 183-185.

106. Frye, Anatomy of Criticism, p. 238. Native Son, we discovered, fits into the fourth phase of this mythos.

107. Ibid., p. 154.

108. Ibid., "Any symbol at all takes its meaning primarily from its context ... " (p. 156).

109. Ibid., pp. 155, 156.

110. McCall, The Example of Richard Wright: "It is not entirely accurate to speak of the story's symbols.' We are forced to participate in the central character's mind so utterly that the objects looming up before our eyes rarely seem symbolic" (p. 170).

111. Frye, Anatomy of Criticism, p. 187.

112. Ibid., p. 238.

113. Ibid., p. 190.

114. Ibid., p. 190.

115. Ibid., p. 191.

116. Ibid., p. 192.

117. Ibid., p. 193.

118. Thus we approach the story's Freudian content--since it is being told in dream images. The manifest content of these dreams is undesirable, but the latent content reveals them to be disguised wish-fulfillment dreams: Fred desperately wants to be able to communicate, to end his isolation.

119. See Chapter IV, pp. 128-129.

120. Theodore Roethke, "The Waking," The Collected Verse of Theodore Roethke: Words for the Wind (Bloomington: Indiana University Press, 1970), p. 124.

121. McCall, The Example of Richard Wright: "The energy of the story so successfully fuses naturalistic detail and Gothic allegory that it becomes almost hallucinatory in its effect" (p. 170).

122. Richard Wright, "The Man Who Lived Underground," Eight Men (Cleveland: The World Publishing Company, 1961), p. 29. (All subsequent page references to this work will appear in parentheses in the text.)

123. Cf. Wright's statement in "The Literature of the Negro in the United States": "These Negroes seemed to have said to themselves: 'Well, if what is happening to me is right then, dammit, anything is right'" (White Man, Listen!, p. 90).

124. Dostoyevsky, Possessed, p. 633. Compare this to what the officer in Kafka's "In the Penal Colony" states: "'Guilt is never to be doubted'" (Selected Stories of Franz Kafka, trans. Willa and Edwin Muir (New York: The Modern Library, 1952, p. 97).

125. Margolies, Art of Richard Wright, p. 77.

126. Ibid. , p. 78.

127. "The prophets that have been before me and before thee of old prophesied both against many countries, and against great kingdoms, of war, and of evil, and of pestilence" (Jeremiah 28: 8). " ... for spoiling and violence are before me: and there are that raise up strife and contention. Therefore the law is slacked, and judgment doth never go forth: for the wicked doth compass about the righteous ... " (Habbakuk 1: 3,4).

128. The policemen's fear stems from two causes: one, the seemingly irrational ravings of a man who would ruin their system; and, two, the fact that Fred could press charges against them for brutality and for forcing him to sign a confession (they are so blind to Fred's reality that they are unable to realize not only that Fred wouldn't think of such an action but that [given the idea] he wouldn't dare to carry it out).

129. Margolies, Art of Richard Wright, p. 79.

CHAPTER V

CONCLUSION

One of the most difficult critical activities involved in a study of Wright's fiction is to determine just where Wright the man stood on the ethical questions his books raise. Although it seems fairly clear that in general terms Wright sympathized with all his characters to a greater or lesser extent, it is also conceivable that he disapproved of many of their individual deeds. Because he was writing in protest of the American system and in support of its victims, it is obvious that his heroes would have values contrary to those of his audience. And what is so remarkable about Wright's literary endeavors is that he was able to create a sympathetic bond between his readers and men who are liars, thieves, and killers. Seeing these men on the streets or reading about them in terse newspaper accounts, the reader would no doubt have serious reservations about identifying with them; but yielding to the skillful craft of an artist, the reader (to his own surprise perhaps) can fully sympathize and empathize with these disoriented men. A brief look at Wright's rhetoric, therefore, should not only reveal how Wright allows readers to identify with his anti-heroes, but it should also suggest where Wright stands morally in regard to these men's behavior.

All of Wright's major fictional works are written from the same viewpoint. That is, Wright consistently employs a dramatized narrator who is unaware that he is telling the story and who acts as a narrator-agent rather than a passive observer--he is, in fact, in each case the novel's protagonist. Although this narrator is often referred to in the third person, our knowledge of the action and other characters is totally and consistently confined to what this person knows, feels, intuits, or sees. As narrator he has the option of showing us what happens (scene) or telling us (summary or commentary). [1]

174

But standing behind this narrator and continually manipulating him is what Wayne Booth calls the "implied author"--the "implied version of 'himself'" that a reader must distinguish from the "real author":

> Even the novel in which no narrator is dramatized creates an implicit picture of an author who stands behind the scenes.... This implied author is always distinct from the 'real man'--whatever we may take him to be--who creates a superior version of himself, a 'second self' as he creates his work. [2]

Thus it is possible--even probable--that the implied authors of a single man's writings will all differ not only from other authors' "implied authors" but from each other. It is necessary therefore to determine two things: 1) how the values (expressed or covert) of the implied author affect our reaction to the book, and 2) how or even whether the implied author reflects the values of his creator. It seems rather dangerous to assume, for example, that Richard Wright condoned the actions of either Bigger Thomas or Cross Damon (or even Fish Tucker and his father) and yet the implied authors of these novels certainly strive to gain our sympathy for their heroes (narrators, centers of consciousness). As Booth says,

> It is clear that the picture the reader gets of this presence is one of the author's most important effects. However impersonal he may try to be, his reader will inevitably construct a picture of the official scribe who writes in this manner--and of course that official scribe will never be neutral toward all values. Our reactions to his various commitments, secret or overt, will help to determine our response to his work. [3]

Because the implied author affects our response to the work ("The 'implied author' chooses, consciously or unconsciously, what we read.... "[4]) it is important to discover his relationship to all parties concerned:

> In any reading experience there is an implied dialogue among author, narrator, the other characters, and the reader. Each of the four can range, in relation to each of the others, from identification to complete opposition, on any axis of value, moral, intellectual, aesthetic, and even physical. [5]

In The Long Dream there is considerable intellectual
distance between the implied author and his narrator, the
narrator being the hero who at the beginning of the book is
a young child and at the end a high school dropout. Although
it is true that as Fish matures the intellectual distance les-
sens, because he is so desperately uneducated, the intellectual difference is generally maintained. One result of this
intellectual distance is an awareness on Fish's part that does
not ring true. Apparently Wright (as implied author) was unwilling to intrude on his story with direct commentary about
the development of Fish's psyche; instead he elected to give
the illusion of letting the story tell itself. And because he
had limited himself to the viewpoint of Fish, only Fish himself could reveal his inner thoughts. But Fish is not always
intellectually capable of understanding the full implications of 3
what he experiences; he is certainly not able to articulate or
summarize the universality of his initiation--and yet he is
asked to. Therefore we have here a narrator who cannot do
more than have vague unexpressed intuitions about the events
of his life burdened with the responsibility of reporting the
special significance of these events to the reader.

The result, unfortunately, can be quite confusing to
the reader who is attempting to establish the nature of this
character's personality. On the one hand, we are asked to
believe that Fish is arrogant, ignorant, and interested only
in power, money, and sex--willing to live on the surface of
things; on the other, we are shown that he is introspective,
sensitive, and conscious of his maturation. While it is true
that Fish is neurotic and consequently daily confronted with
the war between his expansive and self-effacing selves, it is
not true that he is aware of this battle within. In fact, Fish
suppresses the conflict, preferring to believe that he is only
his expansive self, denying the self-effacing qualities that conflict with his idealized image of himself as strong and powerful and the master of his fate. 6 He tries to be hard, tries
to forget his weakness in the face of the white world, tries
not to realize what is happening to himself as he slowly but
inexorably turns into a second Tyree.

Therefore, because we cannot attribute much psychological awareness to Fish, those scenes in which the implied
author tries to make us believe that Fish is pondering the
meaning of his life seem contrived to us. As a result, the
implied author interferes with our bond with Fish, whereas
what should or could be happening in these intimate scenes
is a reaffirmation of our sympathy for the narrator; as Booth

says, "the sustained inside view leads the reader to hope for
good fortune for the character with whom he travels, quite independently of the qualities revealed."[7]   Because Fish is isolated and the story is told entirely through his eyes (he has
no companion--not even an intrusive author), the reader for
the most part does identify emotionally with him; but in these
scenes where Fish manifests qualities we feel are not his own
but the implied author's, we lose our feeling of rapport and
tend to look down on Fish, lessening our pity for him;[8] for
example:

> Fishbelly felt a creepy sensation grip his skull.
> This was a ceremony. He did not think it; he felt
> it, knew it. He was being baptized, initiated; he
> was moving along the steep, dangerous precipice
> leading from childhood to manhood (64).

> As he knelt, the dog's dying associatively linked
> itself with another vivid dying and another far-off
> death: the lynched body of Chris that had lain that
> awful night upon the wooden table in his father's
> undertaking establishment ... (134-135).

> . . . .

> Then he bent forward and, before he realized it,
> he was acting out the role that Dr. Bruce had played
> that night ... (135).

> . . . .

> 'That's what they did to Chris,' he spoke aloud,
> announcing an emotional discovery (135).

Although there is nothing inherently wrong with summarizing
statements such as those contained in the above passages,
somehow we just cannot attribute them to Fish.

A more controlled rendering of a black adolescent, and
thus a more successful novel, is Native Son.   In this book
Wright uses the same technique as he does in The Long
Dream, a center of consciousness who is the hero and through
whose limited vision we receive the entire account of the story.
But here Wright more fully admits the limitations of his narrator and does not try to imbue him with intellectual powers
of ratiocination he does not possess.   To compensate for Bigger's inability to assign meaning to events, Wright employs

two techniques: ironical juxtaposition (a technique, as we have seen, used frequently by proletarian authors) and a long speech by another (smarter) character intended to summarize[9] one of the book's themes. Although there is a vast intellectual distance between the implied author and narrator--and even an extreme moral distance--the emotional distance is so minute as to be practically undetectable. Consequently, the reader is continually encouraged to sympathize with Bigger Thomas, even when he murders Mary and brutally chops up her body. Wright is able to portray so convincingly the ter-tor of Bigger's situation that the reader sides emotionally with him, hoping against hope that he won't get caught, for suddenly Bigger's getting caught means the reader's arrest too:

> Frenzy dominated him.... Frantically, he caught a corner of the pillow and brought it to her lips. He had to stop her from mumbling, or he would be caught (73).

. . . .

> He clenched his teeth and held his breath, intimi-dated to the core by the awesome white blur float-ing toward him (74).

. . . .

> The reality of the room fell from him; the vast city of white people that sprawled outside took its place. She was dead and he had killed her. He was a murderer, a Negro murderer, a black murderer. He had killed a white woman (75).

These flat, staccato phrases pile up in our minds the horror of what it means to be black and guilty in a white world--where to be black means to be guilty. Wright carries his readers with him skillfully, even through the terrible ordeal of burning her body:

> Ought he to put her in head or feet first? Because he was tired and scared, and because her feet were nearer, he pushed her in, feet first. The heat blasted his hands (78).

"Because he was tired and scared." This is no master crim-inal; this is a confused, very unhappy boy who is frightened to death, of what he has done and is doing. How easy Wright makes it for us to sympathize with him:

> He got his knife from his pocket and opened it
> and stood by the furnace, looking at Mary's white
> throat. Could he do it? He had to. Would there
> be blood? Oh, Lord! He looked round with a
> haunted and pleading look in his eyes. ... He touched
> the sharp blade to the throat, just touched it, as if
> expecting the knife to cut the white flesh of itself,
> as if he did not have to put pressure behind it.
> Wistfully, he gazed at the edge of the blade resting
> on the white skin. ... Yes; he had to. Gently, he
> sawed the blade into the flesh and struck a bone.
> He gritted his teeth and cut harder (79).

Although intellectually and morally we think we ought to be
outraged at what Bigger is doing, we cannot help but identify
with his own dismay at what he must do. And amazingly
enough we too feel that it must be done[10] (much as we hate
to witness the gory deed).

Later, however, we recoil with Max when Bigger jubi-
lantly announces his satisfaction with being a murderer. Although the implied author does not betray Bigger at this crucial moment, it is just too much to expect the reader to be
entirely happy for Bigger. At the same time that we are
glad he feels whole, we are horrified at his solution. Here
we reverse our distances: feeling intellectually satisfied with
Bigger's discovery but emotionally repelled.

We are further emotionally antagonized by the narrator
in The Outsider. In this book, unlike the other two, the implied author is very close to his narrator intellectually (neither
the implied author nor the narrator seems to express Wright's
philosophy, however). The implied author also expects the
reader to sympathize with Cross, although he continually fails
to give us any real emotional reason for doing so. Unlike
Bigger, who is afraid and an unwilling murderer, Cross just
seems to enjoy the idea of being able to kill too much to allow us to side with him. As a consequence, in one respect,
the book fails because the implied author fails to carry the
reader with him.

> From the author's viewpoint, a successful reading
> of his book must eliminate all distance between the
> essential norms of his implied author and the norms
> of the postulated reader.... A bad book, on the

other hand, is often most clearly recognizable because the implied author asks that we judge according to norms that we cannot accept. [11]

It isn't until the very end of the book that we begin to identify with Cross through the efforts of the implied author, for it
is there that Cross realizes that a man cannot expect to live
at the expense of others. Although there are a few isolated
instances where the implied author tries overtly to win our
sympathy (for example, by having Cross vow to dedicate his
life to Eva), his hero is just too hard to be embraced. A
thoroughgoing nihilist for most of the book, Cross seems in-
sincere when he attempts to live for love--especially because
he and we know that what Eva loves when she sees him is
pure fabrication, a falsehood he has created out of his need
for her. She does not love him; she loves what he has made
her, in her innocence and trust, see in him. Instead of
helping us to sympathize with Cross, these avowed good intentions toward Eva further alienate us from him. As a result, we wish only that he would leave her alone.

At the same time as the implied author is trying un-
successfully to win our emotional sympathy, he is showing us
that he himself isn't really committed morally to what Cross
does. Although Cross' intellectual arguments have a certain
logical appeal, they are based on a system of amorality that
even the implied author cannot accept. It is almost as if he
is experimenting with a philosophical premise here--" what
would happen if all men were nihilists ... " --and working it
out to satisfy his own curiosity. His hero is certainly his
philosophical and intellectual equal, but they are miles apart
morally--and that is precisely why we cannot identify with
Cross.

Our relationship to the other characters in The Outsider is also determined by the implied author's as filtered
through the eyes of his narrator. None of the characters is
truly admirable, but Cross and his implied author do differ
in their response to them. For example, Cross is thoroughly disgusted by Bob Hunter (and his wife, too, although not
in exactly the same way). In Cross' eyes

their value as human beings had gone; if they existed, all right; if they did not exist, that was all
right too ... (157).

He wanted to rise and place his foot on Bob's neck

and cut off the flow of whining words (203).

. . . .

He hated Bob for his weakness (203).

Although Cross despises Bob's cravenness, the implied author pleads for a little sympathy. [12] Cross fails to realize that Bob is fighting the only way he knows how against a stronger foe. Even though Cross cannot accept Bob's behavior, the reader can. And the reader accepts it because the implied author presents Bob sympathetically, as a mistreated earnest man, trying to help his race by organizing unions--and trying to save himself from certain death in the tropics (not unworthy objectives). Another weak creature who cannot fight for her rights is Eva Blount, with whom Cross falls in love instead of condemning (one can forgive weakness in someone one must protect). Except for Sarah, whose fight ends in her returning to religion, the other characters are in the camp of the arrogant and strong. [13] Although Cross does not like any of them, he admires their power and brains, feeling intellectually akin to them. Moreover, because both the D. A. and the communists would like nothing more than to tame him, he is wary of them, enjoying what they stand for--absolute power-- just so long as they don't try to curtail his freedom.

In contrast, the implied author does not admire either the communists or the fascists, presenting them as calculating, power-hungry demagogues; and because he never presents the story from their viewpoint, he more or less guarantees an emotional distance between them and the reader. On the other hand, the implied author does seem to be attracted to Ely Houston, the D. A. --we assume this is because of a psychological kinship based on the fact that Houston is a potential rebel who has managed to keep his violence in check. In conversation with Cross he sounds like a sympathizer but when he sees Cross' nihilism in action he is repelled. Ultimately, Houston is the only character that the reader can respect (the reader pities Eva and Bob and so has trouble identifying with or respecting them since they are below him).

The implied authors of The Long Dream and Native Son do not give their readers any great number of characters to admire either. Although the implied author is sympathetic to Tyree Tucker, drawing the reader into a grudging respect for him, because the social and moral norms of Tyree do not coincide with the reader's it is difficult for the latter to be

182 / Richard Wright's Hero

wholly involved in Tyree's welfare (again the reader feels superior). None of the whites receives or deserves either the
respect of the implied author or the reader. Tyree's wife,
Emma, is another weak character whom we pity rather than
sympathize with.

In Native Son heavy irony is used by the implied author to separate the reader from the characters other than
the narrator. This is not the type of irony arising in Huckleberry Finn, for example, where the reader knows the innocent narrator is not evil ("'All right, then, I'll go to hell. '")[14]
--where the implied author and the reader are in collusion,
both knowing Huck's real worth even though Huck himself is
oblivious to it. Instead, Native Son's irony emanates from
the conversation and actions of the other characters, related
without comment by the narrator (like the scenes in Huck
Finn with the Duke and King)--authorial silence is maintained
through juxtaposition. Thus, a conflict appears between a
character's spoken intentions and the actual result of his actions. For example, Mr. Dalton regards himself as a philanthropist, dedicated to the improvement of black youth; but he
owns the building that Bigger lives in and refuses to rent to
blacks outside the ghetto area. As another example, his
daughter, Mary, speaking of blacks, gushingly tells Bigger
that she would like to see how "they" live but is incapable of
being sensitive to the black man sitting beside her.[15] Thus
the implied author disposes of the Daltons.

The communists are another matter. Although they
are loyal and sympathetic to Bigger they cannot really understand him emotionally as a single individual, seeing him as
a representative of his class and race. They have a certain
intellectual grasp of his situation but are really quite repelled
when he begins to accept himself as a killer (a far cry from
the hardened communists of The Outsider) because, we can
safely assume, in placing himself above the community Bigger
is asserting his individuality to men who would have him sub-
merge it in the group. In Native Son, therefore, it is Max
and Jan who attract the reader the most after Bigger himself.
But because we are never given clues from inside these people as to what their true motivation for helping Bigger is, we
hesitate to embrace them completely, preferring instead to
travel with the isolated narrator--just as we stick with Fish
for all his faults, because we follow the story completely
through his eyes. To quote Booth:

Perhaps the most important effect of traveling with

a narrator who is unaccompanied by a helpful author is that of decreasing emotional distance.

In reducing the emotional distance, the natural tendency is to reduce--willy-nilly--moral and intellectual distance as well. [16]

Wright successfully narrows the emotional distance between
narrator and reader in The Long Dream and Native Son but
fails to do so in The Outsider. As a result, we can identify fairly well with Fish and Bigger but quite inadequately with
Cross.

Because the values of the implied author conflict with
those of his narrator in The Outsider, we have trouble locating the theme of the book--and the authorial silence contributes to our confusion. Just where does Wright the man
stand? Although we cannot state for certain, his implied author strongly suggests that the real author is highly critical
of Cross' philosophy and actions. But because the effect of
traveling with an otherwise unaccompanied narrator tends to
lessen the emotional distance between narrator and reader,
we are torn in our response to him. We want to be able to
identify with him, but we absolutely cannot bring ourselves
to, since the implied author himself cannot identify with him.
Where Wright himself stands remains an enigma unless we
look outside the book to his own life.

"The Man Who Lived Underground" is told more successfully from the viewpoint of its narrator-hero. Although
the intellectual distance between the implied author and his
narrator is extreme, there is a strong bond of sympathetic
understanding between them, helpful in establishing a rapport
between reader and narrator. On the other hand, the story
presents an interesting problem in the area of the moral relationship between implied author and narrator. Because it
takes place outside the world (although paradoxically literally
inside it), life's normal values are reversed. Therefore, the
implied author presents the reader with some ironic paradoxes,
asking always that we side with his hero. To wit: topside,
Fred Daniels is an innocent man framed for a murder by the
police who are desperate for a victim. It is certainly not
difficult for the reader to realize that the implied author is
sympathetic to Fred in this situation; it is also, so far, not
difficult for the reader to be sympathetic to Fred. Standard
reactions to a standard situation are evoked: it is eminently
unfair to unjustly accuse and trap an innocent man. The

184 / Richard Wright's Hero

reader can easily identify with Fred's feelings of bewilderment
and fear (Wright very effectively sets the tone in his opening
scene).

But once Fred goes underground things change. The
surface morality no longer applies. Whereas Fred was innocent and felt guilty on the streets, in the sewers he is guilty
of many little crimes but feels innocent, since he has come
to the conclusion that all men are guilty by virtue of being
human. Because all men are guilty anyway, it doesn't matter
that another man is accused of a crime that he, Fred Daniels,
commits underground. And when he sees an employee of the
jewelry store pilfer from the safe, Fred distinguishes between
his own theft and the man's. To him they are acts origina-
ting from two different value systems. Thus the man is wrong
because he intends to use the money for what it was intended
--to buy things; the man is working from the surface code of
ethics that maintains it is wrong to steal because money has
value. But Fred is acting from the underground code that
declares money and jewels worthless; therefore, because he
does not take the money to spend it, because it is just so
much green paper according to his system, he is not a thief
--not guilty of stealing, just guilty of being a man. Fred has
reached the same conclusion that the heroes of Dostoyevsky's
The Possessed reach, that all men are guilty.

Whether or not the reader can accept this metaphysical
assertion of all men's inherent guilt, and thus Fred's innocence in stealing thousands of dollars in diamonds and cash,
depends upon how he reacts to the attitude of the implied author toward the hero and his values. I believe that Wright
successfully presents the surrealistic world of the underground
as the true condition of mankind. And so I yield to his skillful portrayal of Fred as innocent of crime because life is a
crime itself. If all men are guilty, all men are also innocent.
If God is dead, says Ivan Karamazov, then everything is permitted; but if everything is permitted, just as surely nothing
is permitted, according to Nietzsche. These moral entangle-
ments intrigued Wright who himself was a black living in a
subculture outside the mainstream of American life. Thus,
as Tyree Tucker points out in The Long Dream, the blacks
are forced to work from their own moral code that best suits
their chances for survival in a hostile environment. Moreover, as Ely Houston observes in The Outsider, blacks have
the advantage of an outsider's mentality which gives them a
unique perspective on the world. Blacks are at once inside
and outside the world, living in its streets and under them.

They are the world's latest prophets. They know the heart of darkness.

Although Lawd Today is told from the same viewpoint as the other four works just discussed, its narrator-agent is generally unreliable, [17] and thus presents certain problems not encountered in the other stories (with the possible exception of The Outsider, which, as we have seen, presents its own problem of locating the moral stance of the implied author). Initially, therefore, we must establish why we consider the narrator fallible (i.e., how the implied author lets us know we are dealing with a narrator whom we cannot trust); then we can consider our own response as readers to this situation. The distances which we will examine, therefore, are primarily those between implied author and narrator and between implied author and reader.

The most direct route to establishing the fact that a narrator is unreliable, of course, would be for the implied author to step in and tell us he is--or at least to use other narrators whose different perspectives could strongly suggest an element of fallibility in the main narrator. But Wright has chosen neither method. By his complete reticence[18] and by confining himself to Jake's viewpoint he has forced us to look for other textual clues to support our belief in his narrator's unreliability, such as the implied author's choice of words, the actions he chooses to relate, and his use of irony --this latter, the clearest indication in Lawd Today of the narrator's fallibility.

Through the use of irony in selected passages, Wright as implied author invites the reader to share in his judgment of the narrator, Jake Jackson. As Booth points out,

> Whenever an author conveys to his reader an un-
> spoken point, he creates a sense of collusion against
> all those, whether in the story or out of it, who do
> not get that point. Irony is thus in part a device
> for excluding as well as for including, and those
> who are included, those who happen to have the
> necessary information to grasp the irony, cannot
> but derive at least part of their pleasure from a
> sense that others are excluded. In the irony with
> which we are concerned, the speaker is himself
> the butt of the ironic point. The author and reader
> are secretly in collusion, behind the speaker's back,
> agreeing upon the standard by which he is found
> wanting. [19]

Although it is true, as we shall see, that the implied author is often sympathetic to Jake, he is more frequently critical of him. Between the two exist extreme intellectual, aesthetic, and moral distances. The emotional distance fluctuates from scene to scene, depending on the amount of irony employed.

Wright's most telling disapproval appears in the book's early scenes between Jake and his wife. Although the implied author never directly tells us his attitudes, we learn that, as far as he is concerned, Jake is: lazy, selfish, spoiled, ill-tempered, mean, ignorant, and vain. Annoyed with having his erotic dream interrupted and with having to get up, Jake blames his wife for disturbing him: "That bitch!" he says to himself, "How come she leave that door open and wake me up?" (10). But mostly he vents his anger over her innocent conversation with the milkman (which takes on more ironical overtones when we see Jake later partying in a whorehouse):

> He heard Lil talking to somebody in the kitchen.
> He bent lower, listening. What in hell can she
> find to talk about all the time? I certainly would
> like to know. And bawling her out don't seem to
> do a bit of good, neither. Yeah, she's going to
> keep on with her foolishness till I teach her a damn
> good lesson one of these days. And furthermore,
> it ain't right for a decent woman to stand talking
> common that way to strangers. And she knows
> that! Jake ... hurried to the bathroom door, and
> listened with his ear to the keyhole. Still talking!
> And laughing, too! What to hell? What she think
> this is, a picnic? (13).

Jake proceeds to verbally abuse his wife, cowing her with his violent shouting. Finally he beats her.

> A hot sense of elation bubbled in him. He felt
> the muscles of his back stiffening. Just a few more
> words from her, just a few more, and, by God, he
> would slap her into the middle of next Christmas.
> His right hand itched. His voice dropped to a low
> growl.
>
> . . . .
>
> She dodged but too late. Jake's open palm
> caught her square on the cheek, sounding like a
> pistol shot. She spun around from the force of

the blow, falling weakly against the wall, screaming.

. . . .

He kicked her in her side with his foot (19).

This last, simple declarative sentence speaks volumes.

The implied author has made no comment whatsoever about either Jake's action or his thoughts, but he has pretty well established how he feels about Jake. He has seemingly allowed the narrator to try to win the reader's sympathy by letting him reveal his inner thoughts--and Jake obviously thinks he's in the right. But these self-righteous complaints serve only to alienate us from him. And, as Booth has remarked of reading Jason's section of The Sound and the Fury,

> What all this amounts to is that on the moral level we discover a kind of collaboration which can be one of the most rewarding of all reading experiences. To collaborate with the author by providing the source of an allusion or by deciphering a pun is one thing. But to collaborate with him by providing mature moral judgment is a far more exhilarating sport. [20]

In reading these scenes in Lawd Today, there is something especially gratifying in the fact that the author remains silent; to quote Booth again: "we find our ironic pleasure heightened as we travel with less sympathetic protagonists whose faults are never described directly."[21]

Although this dramatic irony permeates most of the book, it is significantly absent throughout much of Part II, "Squirrel Cage," in which we see Jake in relation to the white power structure. In the scene where Jake is before the postal Board of Review, Jake's character is still unsavory: he lies outrageously and exudes self-pity; but here the reader can sympathize with a man placed in the untenable position of having his wife tattle on him to his superiors--of having a wife who is in collusion with the white paternalism that destroys his manhood. The scene, pitiful as it is however, is actually funny as Jake attempts to con his white bosses when they accuse him of beating his wife:

> 'She says you kicked her in her side with your foot.'

> 'Kicked her!' Jake stepped back with amaze-
> ment. 'Kicked her? Do I look like a man what
> would kick a sick woman?' (109).

Then, to himself on the way out he says:

> I'm going to break that bitch's neck if it's the last
> thing I ever do! I'm going to stomp her guts out
> as sure as my name's Jake Jackson ... (111).

Later, during the mail sorting, the author gives us
other opportunities to sympathize with Jake. We learn that
Jake's feelings were hurt when the black sitting on the Review
Board had called Jake a "Negro" in front of the whites: "He
could've called me colored at least" (120). We also learn,
partially anyway, why Jake is forced to act so hard:

> Anything which smacked of farms, chain gangs,
> lynchings, hunger, or the South in general was re-
> pugnant to him. These things had so hurt him once
> that he wanted to forget them forever; to see them
> again merely served to bring back the deep pain for
> which he knew no salve (120).

Soon we again witness his helplessness towards whites when
he is disciplined for shirking his job: "if only there was
something he could do to pay the white folks back for all they
had ever done!" (125). Finally, we learn that Jake and his
buddies, much as they hated and feared living in the South,
are homesick for it: "there was some good times in the
South ... '" (154). [22]

In the last section, "Rats' Alley," the implied author
gives the reader one more reason to grudgingly admire his
unreliable narrator: Jake's ability to have a rousing good
time. But, significantly, the author ends Jake's story with
another fight between him and his wife. Our final judgment,
then, must be that, though there are valid reasons for Jake's
behavior (his past, his emasculation, his frustrations), there
is no real reason for us to respect or identify with him. We
have occasionally been able to sympathize with him, but the
implied author seems more concerned with our being repelled
by him. His intention seems to be to shock and horrify us,
to egg us on to protest the conditions he was protesting, those
that dehumanize an individual, that make him mean-spirited
and even dangerous. For Jake is no humble nigger--he is a
boiling potential murderer.

Another potential murderer who escaped the clutches of the South is the author himself. His personal story is told in his fictionalized autobiography,[23] Black Boy, whose implied author is totally identified with its narrator. The book as an autobiography is told, predictably, through a first person center of consciousness, the narrator-agent being Wright himself as a child. Of interest here is the relationship between the implied author and narrator, that between the implied author and other characters, and that between the narrator and other characters.

Although there is a great age difference between the implied author and the narrator (the story begins when Wright is four and ends when he is 17), there is total emotional correspondence between the two. Where a touch of irony might have shown the author a bit bemused by his own stubborn self-righteousness, there is nothing but straight sympathy. Everything, it seems, was justified since it led to Wright's absolute rejection of his upbringing. As implied author, Wright nods empathic approval of his young narrator's recalcitrant behavior.

Furthermore, the moral distance is practically non-existent; Wright the elder sympathizes completely with Wright the child as he defends himself against his uncles, aunts, and grandmother, and even as he steals. As he recounts his stealing, it is obvious that he never identified himself as a thief. It was simply something he had to do to survive, and something he would never do again once he escaped the South. As he remembers,

> If I stole, I would have a chance to head northward quickly... (177).

> He was white, and I could never do to him what he and his kind had done to me. Therefore, I reasoned, stealing was not a violation of my ethics, but of his; I felt that things were rigged in his favor and any action I took to circumvent his scheme of life was justified. Yet I had not convinced myself (178).

> I never stole again; and what kept me from it was the knowledge that, for me, crime carried its own punishment (181).

Throughout the book the implied author intrudes on his

narrator's story, mostly to comment on the impact his environment has had on him.   The most famous passage appears
parenthetically in Chapter II and brought much wrath upon
Wright from other blacks.   Wright also comments bitterly
about the effect of religion on his family:

> There were more violent quarrels in our deep-
> ly religious home than in the home of a gangster,
> a burglar, or a prostitute....   Wherever I found
> religion in my life I found strife, the attempt of
> one individual or group to rule another in the name
> of God.   The naked will to power seemed always to
> walk in the wake of a hymn (119).

Most of the time, however, the implied author allows
the harshness of his hero's life to speak for itself through
stunning dialogue.   For example, after Wright's dog (which
he couldn't bear to sell even though he was literally starving)
is crushed by a coal wagon, his mother's comment is, "'You
could have had a dollar.   But you can't eat a dead dog, can
you?'" (62).   Or the scene when Wright looks for work:

> 'Now, boy, I want to ask you one question and
> I want you to tell me the truth,' she said.
> 'Yes, ma'am,' I said, all attention.
> 'Do you steal?' she asked me seriously.
> I burst into a laugh, then checked myself.
> 'What's so damn funny about that?' she asked.
> 'Lady, if I was a thief, I'd never tell anybody.'
> 'What do you mean?' she blazed with a red
> face.
> I had made a mistake during my first five mi-
> nutes in the white world (127).

Or his granny's response to Wright's publishing a story:

> 'Richard, what is this you're putting in the
> papers?' she asked....
> 'It's just a story I made up,' I said.
> 'Then it's a lie,' she said.
> 'Oh, Christ,' I said.
> 'You must get out of this house if you take the
> name of the Lord in vain,' she said (146-147).

The book is replete with such instances of cruelty and callous
indifference.

Because of the implied author's complete identification with his narrator, there is less distance than perhaps there should be for him to give us a more balanced picture of his life. The young Wright always appears to advantage, as Edward Margolies has noted:

> Nowhere in the book are Wright's actions and thoughts reprehensible. The characteristics he attributes to himself are in marked contrast to those of other characters in the book. He is 'realistic,' 'creative,' 'passionate,' 'courageous,' and maladjusted because he refuses to conform. [24]

Every misdeed of the young Wright is either rationalized or justified by the implied author.

By supporting the actions of his narrator at all times, the implied author is asking the reader to join in the condemnation of the other characters in the story. The whites emerge as little less than monsters, although a few make feeble attempts to help Wright--some out of sincere motives, some out of guilt--but these men either cannot fight the solid Southern bigotry or they bungle their overtures to Wright by unwittingly shaming or scaring him (see pages 201-204, for example). The blacks fare no better at the hand of the implied author; both he and his narrator despise most of the other blacks, not only because they allow themselves to be victimized but also because they attempt to make Wright one of them. Wright the man, the implied author, and the narrator, balks at this, refusing to have a fixed personality. He goes north to discover himself:

> ... as I had lived in the South I had not had the chance to learn who I was. The pressure of Southern living kept me from being the kind of person that I might have been. I had been what my surroundings had demanded, what my family--conforming to the dictates of the whites above them--had exacted of me, and what the whites had said that I must be (227).

And yet, as he leaves, he realizes that he takes the South with him. He might have despised the Uncle Toms, but in his heart he cannot reject them. He must speak out for them.

It is fairly obvious that Wright intended to present the

bleakest possible picture of the South in Black Boy, since he selectively left out details of his life that would show his basically middle-class background.[25] He wished to identify himself with the poor blacks, to function as a symbol of their lives--only because he rebelled could he escape the strictures of the South. The book, therefore, protests both against bigotry and against men who accept its teachings--black and white. It is also, like Wright's fiction, the story of a black man who must fight--and fight hard--to discover who he is.

Reading Richard Wright, then, is an adventure in black perspectives. Although the white reader might predict that he was going to have certain difficulty in accepting some of the actions of Wright's black heroes because their social mores differ, Wright has been able to create sympathetic characters so well that there is virtually no emotional distance between the reader and Fishbelly, Bigger, Fred Daniels, and the young Wright himself. There is, however, as I have pointed out, a problem with Cross Damon because of the attitude of the implied author; and there is, of course, a problem with Jake Jackson for the same reason. But in the other stories no real problem exists because there is constant rapport between implied author and narrator-hero. The reader travels willingly with these sad, troubled men, accepting the norms postulated by the implied author.

It is evident by now that one of the outstanding characteristics of Wright's fiction is the ease with which the reader can identify with his anti-heroes. Wright has been able to establish this relationship primarily through a controlled point of view whereby the reader is privy only to the thoughts and experiences of his narrator. As a consequence, although many secondary characters are developed incompletely, each major hero emerges as a fully conceived personality: each man's motivations are explored and his background sketched in. Each book, therefore, can stand on its own merits and reward the textual critic, who, as he studies Wright, discovers his extraordinary originality within traditional literary forms. One finds, for example, an autobiography that is constructed as a piece of fiction.[26] One finds a novel, which the reviewers have condemned outright, to be, in fact, a skillful symbiosis of form and content--where the plot (ritual) amplifies the thought (dream). One finds a naturalistic novel with an existential ending. And, most surprisingly, one finds outcasts and criminals with whom one willingly sympathizes.

But having looked in detail at the heroes in Wright's

major fiction, it is also clear from such a study that a heroic model emerges--that, although the books can unquestionably
be read as separate entities, they can also be read as parts
of a whole.   Therefore, instead of narrowing in on a particular book's individual hero, we can, by reversing the process,
expand our perspective and discover a sort of mega-hero, a
paradigm of all Wright's heroes.   This archetypal figure is
best described as Hassan's rebel-victim, the innocent whose
radical vision forces him to reject his slavery.   Marked from
birth as an outcast, this anti-hero continues to be alienated
from society until he dies; if he is stubborn he can create his
own identity by refusing first of all to accept the one society
brands him with, and then by actively seeking experiences
that will help form his character.   In his stories, Wright
chose the Negro not only to be emblematic of all oppressed
peoples but also to be the metaphor for modern man.   Isolated, alienated, and haunted by a sense of dread, modern
man and the black man have much in common.

     In Black Boy and The Long Dream Wright suggests the
causes for the black man's alienation.   Victims of a national
program of racial oppression, the youths in these two books
learn early the fear and danger of being black in America.
Treated as less than human by the whites, taught to conceal
their true feelings and deny their positive feelings, Wright
the persona and Fish soon lose their sense of self-respect.
Alienated from their real selves, they become bitter, frightened men.   The outcome of their initiation is truly victimization and renunciation.   Instead of being welcomed into society, they are turned away.   Ordinary men, even at times
pitiful, they fail to attain tragic stature.   Thus their story
is tragic irony.   They are the archetypal scapegoats who are
punished for no justifiable reason--who are innocent victims
of a guilty society.

     The consequences of such treatment are discoverable
in Lawd Today and Native Son.   In both of these books the
hero has reached maturity through the same violent initiation
rituals that we witnessed in the two preceding works.   Rather
than concentrating on the process of victimization as he did
in Black Boy and The Long Dream, however, Wright explores
the effects of victimization.   Lawd Today illustrates the plight
of the oppressed black worker.   A slave to white capitalism,
Jake Jackson is a disgruntled, unsavory character who is incapable of improving his situation.   He is under the thumb of
the U.S. Government and controlled by his environment.   Bigger Thomas, coming from the same background as the other

three heroes, is initially a victim also. But he, like the metaphysical rebels before him refuses to participate in his own bondage. Using an accidental murder to free himself, this hero makes the existential decision to accept himself for what he is. The victim has finally rebelled.

The continuation of the metaphysical rebellion occurs in The Outsider. Here, the black victim begins to blend into a more obvious identification with all men. An outsider by virtue of his race, like the other heroes, Cross Damon is also an outsider by choice--by virtue of being a man. Convinced that all men are totally free, that God is dead and that everything is permitted, Cross is the existential hero par excellence. A nihilist, he hungrily explores the farthest edges of freedom, in the process breaking all bonds with humanity, forgetting his responsibility to others, murdering wantonly--in short, regarding himself as above the laws of men and thus a god in his own right. As he dies, Cross recognizes the existential truth that men, having no god, must stick together.

The rebel-victim has come full circle. He is now Fred Daniels. He is Everyman who learns, by living in the sewers of a large city (the symbol of the fallen world), that all men are alike, that all men are guilty. And the world has no meaning. Man must therefore not only invent his own meaning but must also be responsible for his own actions and for other people. The black rebel-victim has become symbolic of all men and his vision prophetic.

In summary, although Wright sympathized with the blacks he created, he did not necessarily condone their behavior. "Understood" would be a better word. A victim himself of prejudice and coercion, he felt a strong bond with these dispossessed men he created. As a result, all his life, in and outside of his fiction, Richard Wright struggled to improve the black man's condition by protesting against the dreadful injustices he witnessed and experienced. For he felt that the community of man could only be strengthened by admitting all men as equals into it. Moreover, because he was attempting to present a realistic picture of the depths of despair and degeneracy so prevalent in black lives, he was forced to attribute certain undesirable characteristics to his heroes. Therefore, although he could not help but disapprove of their violent crimes, he recognized the need to have his heroes reveal their desperation through asocial means in order to shock society into an awareness of what it had done. His autobio-

graphy and last novel present the disgraceful initiation of
black youth, his other fiction reveals the extremes to which
the disinherited can go to claim their rights as men. Wright
was too aware of how close he had come to being a Bigger
Thomas to ever let society forget it. The final impression
of his hero that one takes from reading his fiction, therefore,
is that of a man beaten to the ground but determined to rise
from his subjugation to join his fellow men in perhaps a godless world, but one where mutual respect gives life some
dignity.

Notes

1. Although some critics would disagree, there seems to be
   no valid reason for automatically condemning the technique of summary; instead it seems much more reasonable (and critically sound) to judge an individual
   scene on its own merits, deciding on the basis of intention and success whether or not telling was the
   better technique to use (see Wayne C. Booth, The
   Rhetoric of Fiction [Chicago: The University of Chicago Press, 1967] for a strong argument supporting
   this position).

2. Wayne C. Booth, The Rhetoric of Fiction (Chicago: The
   University of Chicago Press, 1967), p. 151.

3. Ibid., p. 71.

4. Ibid., p. 74.

5. Ibid., p. 155.

6. See Horney, p. 192, for a discussion of this trend in
   neurotics. Also, see Chapter II, pp. 30-32.

7. Booth, The Rhetoric of Fiction, p. 246.

8. See Booth, p. 277.

9. Not a particularly effective technique in this instance
   since the story itself has been powerful enough to
   establish the theme without contrived assistance.

10. See Booth, The Rhetoric of Fiction, p. 249, where he
    discusses the effects of maintaining a single inside

view using Austen's Emma as his example. See
also Walcutt, American Literary Naturalism: A
Divided Stream, p. 22, for a discussion of the fact
that the goriest scenes in naturalistic fiction are
usually the most understated.

11. Booth, The Rhetoric of Fiction, p. 157.

12. As I have pointed out (Chapter IV, p. 153), it is conceivable that Cross is actively externalizing his
self-hate when he scorns Bob's behavior, since,
according to Karen Horney, the neurotic "hates and
despises in others all he suppresses and hates in
himself ... " (p. 208). Bob's desire to please conflicts with Cross' idealized image of himself as
emotionally uninvolved and in command of his life.

13. Even Cross' wife and mistress have a certain strength
that allows them to control Cross early in the book.

14. Mark Twain, Adventures of Huckleberry Finn, ed. by
Henry Nash Smith (Boston: Houghton Mifflin Co. ,
Riverside Edition, 1958), p. 180.

15. See Chapter III, pp. 68-69.

16. Booth, The Rhetoric of Fiction, pp. 274, 249.

17. I accept Wayne Booth's definition of "unreliable narrator": "For lack of better terms, I have called a
narrator reliable when he speaks for or acts in ac-
cordance with the norms of the work (which is to
say, the implied author's norms), unreliable when
he does not" (Ibid. , pp. 158-159).

18. Except for the two instances already mentioned in Chapter III, occurring on pages 48 and 133 of the novel,
which are strictly informational--not involved with
character development or theme at all.

19. Booth, The Rhetoric of Fiction, p. 304.

20. Ibid. , p. 307.

21. Ibid. , p. 306.

22. See Kinnamon, "Pastoral Impulse, " Midcontinent Am.

Stds. Journal, 41-47. See also William Attaway's novel of black migrants, Blood on the Forge: "We have been tricked away from our poor, good-as-bad-ground-and-bad-white-men-will-let-'em-be hills. What men in their right minds would leave off tending green growing things to tend iron monsters?" (New York: Collier Books, 1970, p. 44; See also pp. 43, 45, 46, 170 et passim).

23. See Webb, Biography, p. 205 et passim; and Brignano, pp. 4-7, where he calls it "ostensibly an autobiography" (p. 4), saying that "the story of one Negro and his family is projected into a tale of all Negroes of the South" (p. 6).

24. Margolies, Art of Richard Wright, p. 19.

25. See Webb, Biography, pp. 205ff.

26. See: John M. Reilly, "Self-Portraits by Richard Wright," The Colorado Quarterly, XX (Summer, 1971), 31-45: 'It is easy to receive Black Boy as fiction rather than autobiography, since, apart from chronology, it does not possess the conventional autobiographical form. There is no neat summary of forebears and no continuous narrator. Objective details are hard to order as one reads" (33).

BIBLIOGRAPHY

Primary Sources

Books

Wright, Richard. Black Boy: A Record of Childhood and Youth. New York: Harper & Brothers Publishers, 1945.

_____. Black Power: A Record of Reactions in a Land of Pathos. New York: Harper & Brothers Publishers, 1954.

_____. Bright and Morning Star. New York: International Publishers, 1938.

_____. The Color Curtain: Report on the Bandung Conference. Cleveland: The World Publishing Co., 1956.

_____. Eight Men. Cleveland: The World Publishing Company, 1961.

_____. "Five Episodes from An Unfinished Novel." Soon, One Morning. Edited by Herbert Hill. New York: Alfred A. Knopf, 1963.

_____. Lawd Today. New York: Walker and Company, 1963.

_____. The Long Dream. Chatham, N.J.: The Chatham Bookseller, 1958, 1969.

_____. Native Son. New York: Harper & Brothers Publishers, 1940.

_____. The Outsider. New York: Harper & Brothers Publishers, 1953.

198

_____. Pagan Spain. New York: Harper Brothers, 1957.

_____. Savage Holiday. New York: Award Books, 1969.

_____. Twelve Million Black Voices. New York: The Viking Press, 1941.

_____. Uncle Tom's Children. New York: Harper & Row, Publishers (Perennial Library edition), 1965.

_____. White Man, Listen! Garden City, N.Y.: Doubleday & Co., Inc. (Anchor Books), 1964.

Articles, Interviews, Letters, Poems

Delpech, Jeanne. "An Interview with Native Son." Crisis, XVII (November, 1950), 625-626, 678.

Fleurent, Maurice. "Richard Wright à Paris." Paru (France), No. 25 (December, 1946), 7-8.

"Une Interview de Richard Wright: Les Etats-Unis sont-ils une nation, une loi, un peuple?" [Anon. interview.] La Nef, II (November, 1957), 57-60.

Smith, William Gardner. "Black Boy in France." Ebony, VIII (July, 1953), 32-36, 39-42.

Wright, Richard. "The American Problem--Its Negro Phase." New Letters (Special Issue on Richard Wright), XXXVIII (Winter, 1971), 9-16.

_____. "Blueprint for Negro Writing." New Challenge, II (Fall, 1937), 53-65.

_____. "Fourteen Haikus." Studies in Black Literature (Special Issue on Richard Wright), I, 3 (Autumn, 1970), 1.

_____. "Haiku." New Letters (Special Issue on Richard Wright), XXXVIII (Winter, 1971), 100-101.

_____. "How 'Bigger' Was Born." Black Voices: An Anthology of Afro-American Literature. Edited by Abraham Chapman. New York: A Mentor Book, 1968.

_____. "I Tried to Be A Communist." The God that Failed. Edited by Richard Crossman. New York: Harper & Row, Publishers, 1963.

_____. "King Joe." New Letters (Special Issue on Richard Wright), XXXVIII (Winter, 1971), 42-45.

_____. "Letter to Owen Dodson." New Letters (Special Issue on Richard Wright), XXXVIII (Winter, 1971), 125-127.

_____. Letters to Joe C. Brown. Edited by Thomas Knipp. Kent, Ohio: Kent State University Libraries, 1968.

Secondary Sources

Books

Addison, Gayle, Jr., ed. Black Expression: Essays by and About Black Americans in the Creative Arts. New York: Weybright and Talley, 1970.

Attaway, William. Blood on the Forge. New York: Collier Books, 1970.

Baker, Houstan A., Jr. Long Black Song: Essays in Black American Literature and Culture. Charlottesville: University Press of Virginia, 1972.

Baldwin, James. Nobody Knows My Name. New York: Dell, 1967.

_____. Notes of a Native Son. New York: Bantam, 1968.

Barton, Rebecca Chalmers. Witnesses for Freedom: Negro Americans in Autobiography. New York: Harper & Brothers, 1948.

Bell, Daniel. The End of Ideology. New York: The Free Press, 1962.

Blackmur, R. P. Language as Gesture. New York: Harcourt, Brace, 1952.

Bluefarb, Sam. The Escape Motif in the American Novel: Mark Twain to Richard Wright. Columbus: Ohio State University Press, 1972.

Bone, Robert A. The Negro Novel in America. New Haven: Yale University Press, 1958.

_____. Richard Wright. Minneapolis: The University of Minnesota Pamphlets on American Writers (no. 74), 1969.

Booth, Wayne C. The Rhetoric of Fiction. Chicago: The University of Chicago Press, 1961.

Bowles, Paul. Let It Come Down. New York: Random House, Inc., 1952.

Brignano, Russell Carl. Richard Wright: An Introduction to the Man and His Works. Pittsburgh: University of Pittsburgh Press, 1970.

Brown, Claude. Manchild in the Promised Land. New York: New American Library, 1965.

Brown, Deming Bronson. Soviet Attitudes Toward American Writing. Princeton: Princeton University Press, 1965.

Brown, John. Panorama de la Littérature Contemporaine aux Etats Unis. Paris: Gallimard, 1954.

Camus, Albert. Caligula and Three Other Plays. Translated by Stuart Gilbert. New York: Vintage Books, 1958.

_____. The Fall. Translated by Justin O'Brien. New York: Vintage Books, 1956.

_____. The Myth of Sisyphus and Other Essays. Translated by Justin O'Brien. New York: Vintage Books, 1955.

_____. The Rebel. Translated by Anthony Bower. New York: Alfred A. Knopf, 1961.

Chapman, Abraham, ed. Black Voices: An Anthology of Afro-American Literature. New York: A Mentor Book, 1968.

Cleaver, Eldridge. Soul on Ice. New York: Dell Publishing
Co., Inc., 1968.

Crossman, Richard, ed. The God that Failed. New York:
Harper & Row, Publishers, 1963.

Cruse, Harold. The Crisis of the Negro Intellectual. New
York: William Morrow & Co., 1967.

Dostoyevsky, Fyodor. The Brothers Karamazov. Translated
by Constance Garnett. New York: The Modern Library, 1950.

_____. Crime and Punishment. Translated by Michael
Scammell. New York: Washington Square Press, Inc.,
1968.

_____. The Possessed. Translated by Andrew R. Mac-
Andrew. New York: Signet Classic, 1969.

Douglass, Frederick. Narrative of the Life of Frederick
Douglass, An American Slave: Written by Himself.
Garden City, N.Y.: Dolphin Books, 1963.

✓ Ellison, Ralph. Invisible Man. New York: New American
Library, 1952.

_____. Shadow and Act. New York: New American Li-
brary (A Signet Book), 1966.

Embree, Edwin R. Thirteen Against the Odds. New York:
Viking, 1944.

Fabre, Michel. Les Noirs Americains. Paris: Librairie
Armand Colin, 1970.

Finkelstein, Sidney. Existentialism and Alienation in American Literature. New York: International Publishers,
1965.

Fisher, Dorothy Canfield. "Introduction," Native Son. New
York: Harper & Row, Publishers, 1940.

French, Warren. The Social Novel at the End of an Era.
Carbondale: Southern Illinois University Press, 1966.

Freud, Sigmund. The Interpretation of Dreams. Translation

by James Strachey. New York: Avon Books, 1972.

Frye, Northrop. Anatomy of Criticism. Princeton: Princeton University Press, 1957.

Galloway, David. The Absurd Hero in American Fiction. Austin: The University of Texas Press, 1970.

Genet, Jean. Our Lady of the Flowers. Translated by Bernard Irechtman, intro. by Jean-Paul Sartre. New York: Grove Press, 1963.

Gibson, Donald B. Five Black Writers: Essays on Wright, Ellison, Baldwin, Hughes and LeRoi Jones. New York: New York University Press, 1972.

Gloster, Hugh Morris. Negro Voices in American Fiction. Chapel Hill: University of North Carolina Press, 1948.

Gray, Yohma. "An American Metaphor: The Novels of Richard Wright. " Unpublished Ph. D. dissertation, Department of English, Yale University, 1967.

Hand, Clifford. "The Struggle to Create Life in the Fiction of Richard Wright. " The Thirties: Fiction, Poetry, Drama. Edited by Warren French. DeLand, Fla. : Everett Edwards, 1967.

Hassan, Ihab. Radical Innocence: The Contemporary American Novel. New York: Harper & Row, Publishers, 1961.

Heidegger, Martin. Being and Time. Translated by John Macquarrie and Edward Robinson. London: SCM Press, Ltd. , 1962.

Hill, Herbert, ed. Anger, and Beyond: The Negro Writer in the United States. New York: Harper & Row, Publishers (Perennial Library), 1968.

_____. Soon, One Morning: New Writing by American Negroes, 1940-1962. New York: Alfred A. Knopf, 1963.

Horney, Karen. Neurosis and Human Growth: the Struggle Toward Self-Realization. New York: W. W. Norton & Co. , Inc. , 1950.

Hughes, Carl Milton (Pseud. of John Milton Charles Hughes).
    The Negro Novelist. New York: Citadel Press, 1953.

Hughes, Langston. "Harlem." Black Voices: An Anthology
    of Afro-American Literature. Edited by Abraham
    Chapman. New York: A Mentor Book, 1968.

Isaacs, Harold R. The New World of Negro Americans.
    New York: John Day, 1963.

Kafka, Franz. Selected Short Stories of Franz Kafka. Trans-
    lated by Willa & Edwin Muir. New York: The Modern
    Library, 1952.

Kaufmann, Walter, ed. Existentialism From Dostoevsky to
    Sartre. New York: World Publishing, 1972.

Kazin, Alfred. On Native Grounds. Garden City, N.Y.:
    Doubleday Anchor Books, 1956.

Kinnamon, Keneth. The Emergence of Richard Wright: A
    Study in Literature and Society. Urbana: University
    of Illinois Press, 1972.

Klein, Marcus. After Alienation: American Novels in Mid-
    Century. New York: The World Publishing Co., 1965.

Lehan, Richard. "Existentialism in Recent American Fiction:
    The Demonic Quest." Recent American Fiction: Some
    Critical Views. Edited by Joseph Waldmeir. Boston:
    Houghton Mifflin Co., 1963.

Lewis, R. W. B. The American Adam: Innocence, Tragedy,
    and Tradition in the Nineteenth Century. Chicago:
    The University of Chicago Press, 1971.

Littlejohn, David. Black on White: A Critical Survey of
    Writing by American Negroes. New York: The Viking
    Press (A Viking Compass Book), 1969.

Lowrie, Walter, trans. & ed. Kierkegaard's The Concept of
    Dread. Princeton: Princeton University Press, 1944.

McCall, Dan. The Example of Richard Wright. New York:
    Harcourt, Brace & World, 1969.

Malamud, Bernard. The Fixer. New York: Dell Publishing
    Co., Inc., 1971.

Mannoni, O. Prospero and Caliban: The Psychology of Colonization. Translated by Pamela Powesland. New York: Frederick A. Praeger, Publishers, 1964.

Margolies, Edward. The Art of Richard Wright. Carbondale: Southern Illinois University Press, 1969.

_____. Native Sons: A Critical Study of Twentieth-Century Negro American Authors. New York: J. B. Lippincott Co., 1969.

Maslow, Abraham H. Toward a Psychology of Being. 2nd ed. New York: Van Nostrand Reinhold Co., 1968.

Mendelson, Moris Osipovich. Soviet Interpretation of Contemporary American Literature. Translated by Deming B. Brown and Rufus W. Mathewson. Washington: Public Affairs Press, 1948.

Miller, James E. Quests Surd and Absurd. Chicago: University of Chicago Press, 1967.

Molina, Fernando R., ed. The Sources of Existentialism as Philosophy. Englewood Cliffs, N. J.: Prentice-Hall, Inc., 1969.

Myrdal, Gunnar. "Preface." Color Curtain. London: Dobson, 1956.

Nietzsche, Friedrich. The Will to Power. Translated by Walter Kaufmann and R. J. Hollingdale. New York: Random House, 1967.

Owens, William A. "Introduction." Native Son. New York: Harper & Row, Publishers, 1957.

Pavese, Cesare. La Letteratura Americana e Altri Saggi. Torino: Einaudi, 1953.

Pipes, William. Death of an "Uncle Tom." New York: Carlton Press, Inc., 1967.

Prescott, Orville. In My Opinion. New York: Bobbs-Merrill, 1952.

Record, Wilson. The Negro and the Communist Party. Chapel Hill: University of North Carolina Press, 1951.

Redding, Saunders. "The Alien Land of Richard Wright."
Soon, One Morning. Edited by Herbert Hill. New
York: Knopf, 1963.

Reilly, John. "Afterward." Native Son. New York: Harper
& Row, Publishers (A Perennial Classic), 1966.

Rideout, Walter B. The Radical Novel in the United States,
1900-1954: Some Interrelations of Literature and Society. Cambridge, Mass.: Harvard University Press,
1956.

Roethke, Theodore. The Collected Verse of Theodore Roethke: Words for the Wind. Bloomington: Indiana
University Press, 1970.

Roth, Henry. Call It Sleep. New York: Avon Books, 1970.

Sartre, Jean-Paul. The Age of Reason. Translated by Eric
Sutton. New York: Alfred A. Knopf, 1966.

_____. Being and Nothingness: An Essay on Phenomeno-
logical Ontology. Translated by Hazel E. Barnes.
New York: Washington Square Press, 1971.

_____. Nausea. Translated by Lloyd Alexander. New
York: New Directions, 1964.

Scott, Nathan A., Jr. "Judgment Marked by a Cellar: The
American Negro Writer and the Dialectic of Despair."
The Shapeless God: Essays on Modern Fiction. Edi-
ted by Harry J. Mooney, Jr., and Thomas F. Staley.
Pittsburgh: University of Pittsburgh Press, 1968.

_____. Modern Literature and the Religious
Frontier. New York: Harper & Row, Publishers,
1958.

Silberman, Charles E. Crisis in Black and White. New
York: Random House, 1964.

Slochower, Harry. No Voice Is Wholly Lost. New York:
Creative Age, 1945.

Sullivan, Richard. "Afterword." Native Son. New York:
New American Library of World Literature, 1961.

Tillich, Paul. The Courage To Be. New Haven: Yale University Press, 1967.

Tischler, Nancy M. Black Masks: Negro Characters in Modern Southern Fiction. University Park: Pennsylvania State University Press, 1969.

Trimmer, Joseph F. Black American Literature: Notes on the Problem of Definition. Muncie, Indiana: Ball State Monograph Number Twenty-Two, 1971.

Twain, Mark. Adventures of Huckleberry Finn. Edited by Henry Nash Smith. Boston: Houghton Mifflin Co., Riverside Edition, 1958.

Walcutt, Charles Child. American Literary Naturalism: A Divided Stream. Minneapolis: University of Minnesota Press, 1956.

Waldmeir, Joseph J., ed. Recent American Fiction: Some Critical Views. Boston: Houghton Mifflin Co., 1963.

Warren, Robert Penn. All the King's Men. New York: Bantam, 1970.

Webb, Constance. Richard Wright: A Biography. New York: G. P. Putnam's Sons, 1968.

Weitz, Morris. A Philosophy of the Arts. Cambridge, Mass.: Harvard University Press, 1950.

Wheelis, Allen. The Quest for Identity. New York: W. W. Norton and Co., Inc., 1958.

Williams, John A. "Introduction." White Man Listen! Garden City, N.Y.: Doubleday & Co., 1964.

_____. The Man Who Cried I Am. New York: Signet Books, 1968.

_____. The Most Native of Sons: A Biography of Richard Wright. Garden City, N.Y.: Doubleday & Co., Inc., 1970.

_____. Sissie. Garden City: Doubleday Anchor Books, 1969.

Articles, Poems, Reviews

Aaron, Daniel. "Richard Wright and the Communist Party. " New Letters (Special Issue on Richard Wright), XXXVIII (Winter, 1971), 170-181.

Adams, Phoebe. "The Wrong Road. " (Rev. of The Outsider), Atlantic Monthly, CLXLI (May, 1953), 77-78.

Alexander, Margaret Walker. "Richard Wright. " New Letters (Special Issue on Richard Wright), XXXVIII (Winter, 1971), 182-202.

Algren, Nelson. "Remembering Richard Wright. " Nation, CXCII (January 28, 1961), 85.

Arden, Eugene. "The Early Harlem Novel. " Phylon, XX (Spring, 1959), 25-31.

Bakish, David. "Underground in an Ambiguous Dreamworld. " Studies in Black Literature, II, 3 (Autumn, 1971), 18-23.

Baldwin, James. "Ce qui Survivra de Richard Wright. " Prevues, no. 146 (April, 1963), 76-79.

_____. "Everybody's Protest Novel. " Zero (France), 1 (Spring, 1949), 54-58.

_____. "Richard Wright. " Encounter, XVI, 4 (April, 1961), 58-60.

_____. "Richard Wright tel que je l'ai connu. " Prevues, no. 120 (February, 1961), 42-45.

_____. "The Survival of Richard Wright. " Reporter, XXIV (March 16, 1961), 52-55.

Barksdale, Richard K. "Alienation and the Anti-Hero in Recent American Fiction. " CLA Journal, X, 1 (Sept. , 1966), 1-10.

Bayliss, John F. "Native Son: Protest or Psychological Study?" Negro American Literature Forum, I, 1 (Fall, 1967), n. p.

Beja, Morris. "It Must Be Important: Negroes in Contemporary American Fiction. " Antioch Review, XXIV (Fall, 1964), 323-336.

Bosschère, Guy de. "Fishbelly de Richard Wright. " Synthèses, no. 174 (November, 1960), 63-66.

Bramwell, Gloria. "Articulated Nightmare. " Midstream, VII (Spring, 1961), 110-112.

Brignano, Russell C. "Richard Wright: A Bibliography of Secondary Sources. " Studies in Black Literature, II, 2 (Summer, 1971), 19-25.

Britt, David. "Native Son: Watershed of Negro Protest Literature. " Negro American Literature Forum, I, 1 (Fall, 1967), n. p.

Bryer, Jackson. "Richard Wright: A Selected Check List of Criticism. " Wisconsin Studies in Contemporary Literature, 1 (Fall, 1960), 22-33.

Burgum, Edwin Berry. "The Art of Richard Wright's Short Stories. " Quarterly Review of Literature, I (Spring, 1933), 198-211.

_____. "The Promise of Democracy in the Fiction of Richard Wright. " Science and Society, VII (September, 1943), 338-353.

Burns, Ben. "Return of the Native Son. " Ebony, VII (Dec., 1951), 100.

_____. "They're Not Uncle Tom's Children. " Reporter, XIV (March 8, 1956), 21-23.

Cayton, Horace. "Frightened Children of Frightened Parents. " Twice a Year, XII-XIII (Spring-Summer, Fall-Winter, 1945), 262-269.

Charney, Maurice. "James Baldwin's Quarrel with Richard Wright. " American Quarterly, XV (Spring, 1963), 65-75.

Clark, Edward. "Images of the Negro in the American Novel. " Jahrbuch für Amerikastudien, V (1960), 175-184.

Cohn, David L. "The Negro Novel: Richard Wright." Atlantic Monthly, CLXV (May, 1940), 659-661.

Creekmore, Hubert. "Social Factors in Native Son." University of Kansas City Review, VII (1941), 136-143.

Cripps, Thomas. "Native Son in the Movies." New Letters
(Special Issue on Richard Wright), XXXVIII (Winter,
1971), 49-63.

Davis, Arthur P. "'The Outsider' as a Novel of Race."
Midwest Journal, VII (Winter, 1955-1956), 320-326.

Dean, Dwight G. "Alienation: Its Meaning and Measurement."
American Sociological Review, XXVI, 5 (Oct., 1961),
753-8.

Dickstein, Morris. "Wright, Baldwin, Cleaver." New Letters (Special Issue on Richard Wright), XXXVIII (Winter, 1971), 117-124.

Ellison, Ralph. "Richard Wright's Blues." Antioch Review,
V (June, 1945), 198-211.

_____. and James Alan McPherson. "Indivisible Man."
The Atlantic, CCXXVI, 6 (December, 1970), 45-60.

Emanuel, James A. "Lines for Richard Wright." Poem,
Studies on Black Literature, I, 3 (Autumn, 1970), 2.

Fabre, Michel. "An Interview with Simone De Beauvoir."
Studies in Black Literature (Special Issue on Richard
Wright), I, 3 (Autumn, 1970), 3-5.

_____. "The Poetry of Richard Wright." Studies in Black
Literature (Special Issue on Richard Wright), I, 3 (Autumn, 1970), 10-22.

_____. "Wright's Exile." New Letters (Special Issue on
Richard Wright), XXXVIII (Winter, 1971), 136-154.

_____. and Edward Margolies. "A Bibliography of Richard
Wright's Works." New Letters (Special Issue on Richard Wright), XXXVIII (Winter, 1971), 155-169.

_____. _____. "Richard Wright (1908-1960): A Biblio-
graphy." Bulletin of Bibliography, XXIV (January-April,
1965), 131-133, 137.

Ford, J. W. "The Case of Richard Wright. " Daily Worker. XXI (September 5, 1944), 6.

Ford, Nick A. "Battle of the Books: A Critical Survey of Significant Books by and About Negroes Published in 1960. " Phylon, XXII (Summer, 1961), 119-134.

_____. "Four Popular Negro Novelists. " Phylon, XV (1st Quarter, 1954), 29-39.

_____. "The Ordeal of Richard Wright. " College English, XV (October, 1953), 87-94.

_____. "Rev. of Lawd Today, by Richard Wright. " CLA Journal, VII (March, 1964), 269-270.

_____. "Richard Wright: A Profile. " Chicago Jewish Forum, XXI (Fall, 1962), 26-30.

Fuller, H. W. "Contemporary Negro Fiction. " Southwest Review, L (Autumn, 1965), 321-335.

Fuller, Hoyt. "On the Death of Richard Wright. " Southwest Review, XLVI (Autumn, 1961), vi-vii, 334-337.

Galen Last, Henk van. "Richard Wright. " Vrij Nederland (Netherlands), No. 22 (January 25, 1947), 16.

Gérard, Albert. "Négritude et humanité chez Richard Wright. " La Revue Nouvelle, XXX (October 15, 1960), 337-343.

_____. "Vie et vocation de Richard Wright. " Revue Générale Belge, XCVIII (No. 1, 1961), 65-78.

Gibson, Donald B. "Richard Wright: A Bibliographical Essay. " CLA Journal, XII (June, 1969), 360-365.

_____. "Richard Wright and the Tyranny of Convention. " CLA Journal, XII (June, 1969), 344-357.

_____. "Wright's Invisible Native Son. " American Quarterly, XXI (Winter, 1969), 728-738.

Glicksberg, Charles I. "The Alienation of Negro Literature. " Phylon, XI (1st Quarter, 1950), 49-58.

_____. "Existentialism in The Outsider." Four Quarters, VII (January, 1958), 17-26.

_____. "The Furies in Negro Fiction." Western Review, XIII (Winter, 1949), 107-114.

_____. "The God of Fiction." Colorado Quarterly, VII (Autumn, 1958), 207-220.

_____. "Negro Fiction in America." South Atlantic Quarterly, XLV (October, 1946), 477-488.

Grana, Gianni. "Oltre L'Estetica della Violenza." La Fiera Letteraria (Italy), X (October 30, 1955), 4.

Green, Gerald. "Black to Bigger." Kenyon Review, XXVIII (September, 1966), 521-539.

Harper, Michael S. "Poems for Richard Wright: A Sequence." New Letters (Special Issue on Richard Wright), XXXVIII (Winter, 1971), 83-87.

Harrington, Ollie. "The Last Days of Richard Wright." Ebony, XVII (February, 1961), 83-86, 88, 90, 92-94.

Hermans, W. F. "Korte bes Prekingen." Litterair Paspoort (Netherlands), No. 11 (September, 1947), 12-13.

Hicks, Granville. "The Power of Richard Wright." (Rev. of The Long Dream by Richard Wright), Saturday Review, XLI (Oct. 18, 1958), 13, 65.

Hill, Herbert. "Uncle Tom, an Enduring American Myth." The Crisis, LXXII, 5 (May, 1965), 289-295, 325.

Houseman, John. "Native Son on Stage." New Letters (Special Issue on Richard Wright), XXXVIII (Winter, 1971), 71-82.

Howe, Irving. "Black Boys and Native Sons." Dissent, X (Autumn, 1963), 353-368.

_____. "Richard Wright: A Word of Farewell." New Republic, CXLIV (February 13, 1961), 17-18.

Hughes, Langston. "Richard Wright's Last Guest at Home." Ebony, XVII (February, 1961), 94.

Hyman, Stanley Edgar. "Some Trends in the Novel." College English, XX (October, 1958), 1-9.

Isaacs, Harold R. "Five Writers and Their Ancestors." Phylon, XXI (Fall, 1960, Winter, 1960), 243-265, 317-336.

Jackson, Blyden. "The Negro's Image of the Universe as Reflected in His Fiction." CLA Journal, IV (Sept., 1960), 22-31.

_____. "The Negro's Negro in Negro Literature." Michigan Quarterly Review, IV (Fall, 1965), 290-295.

_____. "Richard Wright: Black Boy from America's Black Belt and Urban Ghetto." CLA Journal, XII (June, 1969), 287-309.

_____. "Richard Wright in a Moment of Truth." Southern Literary Journal, III (Spring, 1971), 3-17.

Jackson, Esther Merle. "The American Negro and the Image of the Absurd." Phylon, XXIII (1962), 359-71.

James, Charles L. "Bigger Thomas in the Seventies: A Twentieth-Century Search for Significance." English Record, XXII (Fall, 1971), 6-14.

Jarrett, Thomas D. "Recent Fiction by Negroes." College English, XVI (November, 1954), 85-91.

Kaempffert, Waldemar. "Science in Review--An Author's Mind Plumbed for the Unconscious Factor in the Creation of a Novel." New York Times, September 24, 1944, Sec. IV, p. 11.

Kearns, Edward. "The 'Fate' Section of Native Son." Contemporary Literature, XII, 2 (Spring, 1971), 146-155.

Keniston, Kenneth. "Alienation and the Decline of Utopia." American Scholar, XXXIX (1960), 161-200.

Kennedy, James G. "The Content and Form of Native Son." College English, XXXIV, 2 (Nov., 1972), 269-288. Followed by Comment by Annette Conn, pp. 284-286.

Kent, George E. "On the Future Study of Richard Wright."

CLA Journal, XII (June, 1969), 366-370.

_____. "Richard Wright: Blackness and the Adventure of
Western Culture." CLA Journal, XII (June, 1969),
322-343.

Kim, Jean-Jacques. "La Culpabilité Multiple des Noirs
Américains." Critique (France), XIII (January, 1957),
80-88.

Kinnamon, Keneth. "Lawd Today: Richard Wright's Appren-
tice Novel." Studies in Black Literature, II, 2 (Summer, 1971), 16-18.

_____. "Native Son: The Personal, Social, and Political
Background." Phylon, XXX (Spring, 1969), 66-72.

_____. "The Pastoral Impulse in Richard Wright." Mid-
continent American Studies Journal, X (Spring, 1969),
41-47.

_____. "Richard Wright's Use of 'Othello' in Native Son."
CLA Journal, XII (June, 1969), 358-359.

Klotman, Phyllis R., and Melville Yancy. "Gift of Double
Vision: Possible Political Implications of Richard
Wright's 'Self-Consciousness' Thesis." CLA Journal,
XVI, 1 (Sept., 1972), 106-116.

Knox, George. "The Negro Novelist's Sensibility and the Outsider Theme." Western Humanities Review, XI
(Spring, 1957), 137-148.

Kostelanetz, Richard. "The Politics of Unresolved Quests
in the Novels of Richard Wright." Xavier University
Studies, VIII (May, 1969), 31-63.

Las Vergas, Raymond. "Richard Wright." Revue de Paris
(France), No. 65 (August, 1958), 121-131.

Lawson, Lewis. "Cross Damon: Kierkegaardian Man of
Dread." CLA Journal, XIV, 3 (March, 1971), 298-316.

Leary, Lewis. "Lawd Today: Notes on Richard Wright's
First/Last Novel." CLA Journal, XV, 4 (June, 1971),
411-420.

Lehan, Richard. "Existentialism in Recent American Fiction: the Demonic Quest. " Texas Studies in Literature and Language, 1 (Summer, 1959), 181-202.

Lemaire, Marcel. "Fiction in the USA from the South ... " Revue des Langues Vivantes, XXVII (No. 3, 1961), 244-253.

"Letters to Richard Wright. " New Letters (Special Issue on Richard Wright), XXXVIII (Winter, 1971), 128-135.

Lewis, Theophilus. "The Saga of Bigger Thomas. " Catholic World, CLIII (May, 1941), 201-206.

Marcus, Steven. "The American Negro in Search of Identity." Commentary, XVI (November, 1953), 456-463.

Maund, Alfred. "The Negro Novelist and the Contemporary Scene. " Chicago Jewish Forum, XIII (Fall, 1954), 28-34.

Meyer, Shirley. "The Identity of 'The Man Who Lived Underground. '" Negro American Literature Forum, IV, 2 (July, 1970), 52-55.

Miller, Eugene E. "Voodoo Parallels in Native Son. " CLA Journal, XVI, 1 (September, 1972), 81-95.

"'Native Son' Filmed in Argentina. " Ebony, VI (January, 1951), 82-86.

Padmore, Dorothy. "A Letter from Dorothy Padmore. " Studies in Black Literature (Special Issue on Richard Wright), I, 3 (Autumn, 1970), 5-9.

Radine, Serge. "Ecrivains Américains Non-Conformists. " Suisse Contemporaine (Switzerland), IX (June, 1949), 287-295.

Rascoe, Burton. "Negro Novel and White Reviewers. " American Mercury, L (May, 1940), 113-117.

Record, C. Wilson. "The Negro as Creative Artist. " Crisis, LXXII (March, 1965), 153-158.

Redding, J. Saunders. "American Negro Literature. " American Scholar, XVIII (Spring, 1949), 137-148.

_____. "The Problems of the Negro Writer." Massachu-
setts Review, VI (Winter, 1965), 57-70.

_____. "Richard Wright's Posthumous Stories." (Rev. of
Eight Men, by Richard Wright), New York Herald Tri-
bune Book Review, January 22, 1961, p. 33.

_____. "The Way It Was." (Rev. of The Long Dream,
by Richard Wright), New York Times Book Review,
October 26, 1958, p. 4, 38.

Reilly, John M. "Lawd Today: Richard Wright's Experiment
in Naturalism." Studies in Black Literature, II, 3,
(Autumn, 1971), 14-17.

_____. "Self-Portraits by Richard Wright." Colorado
Quarterly, XX (Summer, 1971), 31-45.

Ridenour, Ronald. "'The Man Who Lived Underground': A
Critique." Phylon, XXXI, 1 (Spring, 1970), 54-57.

Riesman, David. "Marginality, Conformity and Insight."
Phylon, XIV (September, 1953), 245-253.

Rogge, Heinz. "Die Amerikanische Negerfrage in Lichte der
Literatur von Richard Wright und Ralph Ellison." Die
Neueren Sprachen (Germany), VII (Heft 2, 1958), 56-69.

_____. "Die Amerikanische Negerfrage in Lichte der Lit-
eratur von Richard Wright und Ralph Ellison." Die
Neueren Sprachen (Germany), VII (Heft 3, 1958), 103-
115.

Sablonière, Margrit de. "Afrekening van ein Buitenstaander."
Litterair Paspoort (Netherlands), VIII (July-August,
1953), 164-165.

Scott, Nathan A., Jr. "The Dark and Haunted Tower of
Richard Wright." Graduate Comment VII (July, 1964),
93-99.

_____. "Search for Beliefs: Fiction of Richard Wright."
University of Kansas City Review, XXIII (Autumn,
1956), 19-24.

_____. "Search for Beliefs: Richard Wright." Univer-
sity of Kansas City Review, XXIII (Winter, 1956), 131-
138.

Seeman, Melvin. "On the Meaning of Alienation. " American Sociological Review, XXIV, 6 (December, 1959), 783-791.

Sillen, Samuel. "The Meaning of Bigger Thomas. " New Masses, XXXV (April 30, 1940), 26-28.

_____. "Native Son: Pros and Con. " New Masses, XXX (May 21, 1940), 23-26.

_____. "The Response to Native Son. " New Masses, XXXV (April 23, 1940), 25-27.

Singh, Raman K. "The Black Novel and Its Tradition. " The Colorado Quarterly, XX, 1 (Summer, 1971), 23-29.

_____. "Wright's Tragic Vision in The Outsider. " Studies in Black Literature (Special Issue on Richard Wright), I, 3 (Autumn, 1970), 23-27.

Smith, William G. "Richard Wright, 1908-1960: The Compensation for the Wound. " Two Cities (Paris), No. 6 (Summer, 1961), 67-69.

S[ordo], E[nrique]. "Richard Wright y la Epopeya Negra. " Cuadernos Hispanoamericanos (Spain), No. 49 (January, 1954), 110-114.

Sprague, M. D. "Richard Wright: A Bibliography. " Bulletin of Bibliography, XXI (September-December, 1953), 39.

Sprandel, Katherine. "The Long Dream. " New Letters (Special Issue on Richard Wright), XXXVIII (Winter, 1971), 88-96.

Timmerman, John. "Symbolism as a Syndetic Device in Richard Wright's 'Long Black Song. '" CLA Journal, XIV (March, 1971), 291-297.

Turner, Darwin T. "The Outsider: Revision of an Idea. " CLA Journal, XII (June, 1969), 310-321.

Vaal, Hans de. "Interview mid Richard Wright. " Litterair Paspoort (Netherlands), VIII (July-August, 1953), 161-163.

Watson, Edward A. "Bessie's Blues. " New Letters (Special

Issue on Richard Wright), XXXVIII (Winter, 1971), 64-70.

Webb, Constance. "What Next for Richard Wright?" Phylon, X (Summer, 1949), 161-166.

Weigel, Henrietta; Benjamin Appel; Harry Budoff; Winburn T. Thomas; Owen Dodson; Frank K. Stafford; Jack Conroy; Horace Cayton and Sidney Williams. "Personal Impressions." New Letters (Special Issue on Richard Wright), XXXVIII (Winter, 1971), 17-40.

Wertham, Frederic. "An Unconscious Determinant in Native Son." Journal of Clinical Psychopathology and Psychotherapy, VI, 1 (July, 1944), pp. 111-115.

White, Grace McSpadden. "Wright's Memphis." New Letters (Special Issue on Richard Wright), XXXVIII (Winter, 1971), 107-116.

White, Ralph K. "Black Boy: A Value Analysis." Journal of Abnormal and Social Psychology, XLII (October, 1947), 440-461.

Widmer, Kingsley. "The Existential Darkness: Richard Wright's The Outsider." Wisconsin Studies in Contemporary Literature, 1 (Fall, 1960), 13-21.

Winslow, Henry F. "Richard Nathaniel Wright: Destroyer and Preserver (1908-1960)." Crisis, LXIX (March, 1962), 149-163, 187.

INDEX
(Works are under author's name)

DATE			